AQA GCSE (9–1)
Biology

for Combined Science: Trilogy

Student Book

John Beeby
Anne Pilling
Series editor: Ed Walsh

William Collins' dream of knowledge for all began with the publication of his first book in 1819.

A self-educated mill worker, he not only enriched millions of lives, but also founded a flourishing publishing house. Today, staying true to this spirit, Collins books are packed with inspiration, innovation and practical expertise. They place you at the centre of a world of possibility and give you exactly what you need to explore it.

Collins. Freedom to teach

HarperCollins Publishers
1 London Bridge Street
London SE1 9GF

Browse the complete Collins catalogue at
www.collins.co.uk

First edition 2016

10 9 8 7 6 5

© HarperCollins*Publishers* 2016

ISBN 978-0-00-817504-7

Collins® is a registered trademark of
HarperCollins*Publishers* Limited

www.collins.co.uk

A catalogue record for this book is available from the British Library

Commissioned by Lucy Rowland and Lizzie Catford
Edited by Hamish Baxter
Project managed by Elektra Media Ltd
Development edited by Joan Miller and Nik Prowse
Copy edited by Sophia Ktori and Anna Clark
Proofread by Judith Shaw, Laurice Seuss and Jo Kemp
Typeset by Jouve India and Ken Vail Graphic Design
Cover design by We are Laura
Printed by Grafica Veneta, S.p.A., Italy
Cover images © Shutterstock/Komsan Loonprom, Shutterstock/Everett Historical

MIX
Paper from responsible sources
FSC™ C007454

FSC™ is a non-profit international organisation established to promote the responsible management of the world's forests. Products carrying the FSC label are independently certified to assure consumers that they come from forests that are managed to meet the social, economic and ecological needs of present and future generations, and other controlled sources.

Find out more about HarperCollins and the environment at
www.harpercollins.co.uk/green

Approval message from AQA

This textbook has been approved by AQA for use with our qualification. This means that we have checked that it broadly covers the specification and we are satisfied with the overall quality. Full details of our approval process can be found on our website.

We approve textbooks because we know how important it is for teachers and students to have the right resources to support their teaching and learning. However, the publisher is ultimately responsible for the editorial control and quality of this book.

Please note that when teaching the GCSE Combined Biology course, you must refer to AQA's specification as your definitive source of information. While this book has been written to match the specification, it cannot provide complete coverage of every aspect of the course.

A wide range of other useful resources can be found on the relevant subject pages of our website: aqa.org.uk

ACKNOWLEDGEMENTS

The publishers gratefully acknowledge the permissions granted to reproduce copyright material in this book. Every effort has been made to contact the holders of copyright material, but if any have been inadvertently overlooked, the Publisher will be pleased to make the necessary arrangements at the first opportunity.

Chapter 1
p. 12 Claudio Divizia/Shutterstock, Valeriy Velikov/Shutterstock; p. 13 royaltystockphoto.com/Shutterstock, royaltystockphoto.com/Shutterstock, Digieva/Shutterstock; p. 14 Jose Luis Calvo/Shutterstock Dimarion/Shutterstock, Alexander Raths/Shutterstock; p. 16 Milkovasa/Shutterstock, Science Photo Library; p. 17 Jubal Harshaw/Shutterstock; p. 18 Pan Xunbin/Shutterstock, royaltystockphoto.com/Shutterstock; p. 19 toeytoey/Shutterstock, Dlumen/Shutterstock, CNRI/SCIENCE PHOTO LIBRARY, Dr Jeremy Burgess/Science Photo Library, AMMRF, UNIVERSITY OF SYDNEY/SCIENCE PHOTO LIBRARY; p. 20 Beeby Education Limited, anyaivanova/Shutterstock, Ed Reschke/Getty, Visuals Unlimited, Inc./Dr. Gladden Willis/Getty; p. 21 Lebendkulturen.de/Shutterstock, D. Kucharski K. Kucharska/Shutterstock, Power_J/Shutterstock, toeytoey/Shutterstock, Lebendkulturen.de/Shutterstock; p. 22 DR. MARLI MILLER/VISUALS UNLIMITED, INC. /SCIENCE PHOTO LIBRARY; p. 23 Zack Frank/Shutterstock; p. 25 Power_J/Shutterstock; p. 26 Leptospira/Shutterstock; p. 28 EPSTOCK/Shutterstock; p. 30 Lisa S./Shutterstock; p. 31 royaltystockphoto/Shutterstock; p. 32 Elena Pavlovich/Shutterstock; p. 33 memorisz/Shutterstock; p. 36 Ralf Herschbach/Shutterstock; p. 37 BMJ/Shutterstock, Dave Massey/Shutterstock; p. 38 wavebreakmedia/Shutterstock, Knorre/Shutterstock; p. 39 Africa Studio/Shutterstock; p. 40 StudyBlue inc.; p. 41 StudyBlue inc.;

Chapter 2
p.48 Heiti Paves/Shutterstock, Ethan Daniels/Shutterstock; p. 49 Jubal Harshaw/Shutterstock, MARCELODLT/Shutterstock, Brian Maudsley/Shutterstock; p. 55 Claudio Divizia/Shutterstock; p. 58 Andreas Altenburger/Shutterstock, bjul/Shutterstock, Anton_Ivanov/Shutterstock; p. 60 Lizard/Shutterstock; p. 61 Gemenacom/Shutterstock; p. 65 Jubal Harshaw/Shutterstock; p. 67 Stephen VanHorn/Shutterstock; p. 71 Brian Maudsley/Shutterstock; p. 78 Marketa Mark/Shutterstock, YuG/Shutterstock, PearlNecklace/Shutterstock, Jubal Harshaw/Shutterstock;

Chapter 3
p. 80 Jubal Harshaw/Shutterstock; p. 81 eAlisa/Shutterstock, SUSUMU NISHINAGA/SCIENCE PHOTO LIBRARY, Jubal Harshaw/Shutterstock; p. 87 Mopic/Shutterstock; p. 88 SCIENCE SOURCE/SCIENCE PHOTO LIBRARY, Sakarin Sawasdinaka/Shutterstock; p. 95 dreamerb/Shutterstock, Lebendkulturen.de/Shutterstock, Abel Tumik/Shutterstock, Monika Vosahlova/Shutterstock, Yann hubert/Shutterstock; p. 96 Collins Separate Sciences B OCR Gateway ISBN-13-978 0 00 741534-2, p28; p. 108 PROFESSORS P.M. MOTTA & S. CORRER/SCIENCE PHOTO LIBRARY; p. 119 Steve Boice/Shutterstock, Bildagentur Zoonar GmbH;

Chapter 4
p. 120 Stefano Carnevali/Shutterstock, royaltystockphoto.com/Shutterstock, fusebulb/Shutterstock, Maxim Tupikov/Shutterstock; p. 121 WitthayaP/Shutterstock, JPC-PROD/Shutterstock; p. 123 Antonio Guillem/Shutterstock; p. 124 WitthayaP/Shutterstock; p. 125 Edyta Pawlowska/Shutterstock; p. 126 Maksym Bondarchuk/Shutterstock, solkanar/Shutterstock, Australis Photography/Shutterstock; p. 127 Ehab Edward/Shutterstock; p. 130 IAN GOWLAND/SCIENCE PHOTO LIBRARY; p. 131 Chaikom/Shutterstock; muuraa/Shutterstock; p. 132 NORM THOMAS/SCIENCE PHOTO LIBRARY; p. 133 Jina K/Shutterstock; p. 134 MichaelTaylor3d/Shutterstock, royaltystockphoto.com/Shutterstock, Thailand Travel and Stock/Shutterstock; p. 136 Anne Pilling, Nigel Cattlin/Visuals Unlimited/Corbis; p. 137 gorillaimages/Shutterstock; p. 142 Roberto Piras/Shutterstock; p. 144 EM Karuna/Shutterstock, Zaharia Bogdan Rares/Shutterstock, P. FERGUSON, ISM/SCIENCE PHOTO LIBRARY; p. 146 JPC-PROD/Shutterstock; p. 148 Sarah Marchant/Shutterstock, Hellen Sergeyeva/Shutterstock, TwilightArtPictures/Shutterstock;

Chapter 5
p. 156 Alexilusmedical/Shutterstock, BlueRingMedia/Shutterstock, Pavel Chagochkin/Shutterstock; p. 158 lzf/Shutterstock; p. 159 Andrii Muzyka/Shutterstock; p. 160 3Dme Creative Studio/Shutterstock; p. 162 bikeriderlondon/Shutterstock; p. 166 NYTL/SCIENCE PHOTO LIBRARY, p. 170 Santibhavank P/Shutterstock; p. 172 Andrey_Popov/Shutterstock; p. 173 AnglianArt/Shutterstock; p. 174 ZEPHYR/SCIENCE PHOTO LIBRARY; p. 178 Keystone/getty, originalpunkt/Shutterstock; p. 179 nevodka/Shutterstock; p. 180 ALAIN POL, ISM/SCIENCE PHOTO LIBRARY, fotografixx/istock; p. 182 Pamela Moore/istock; p. 187 Roman Prishenko/Shutterstock, Ray Ellis/SCIENCE PHOTO LIBRARY, JPC-PROD/Shutterstock, Michael Kraus/Shutterstock, Image Point Fr/Shutterstock, areeya_ann/Shutterstock;

Chapter 6
p. 196 A. BARRINGTON BROWN, GONVILLE AND CAIUS COLLEGE/SCIENCE PHOTO LIBRARY, STEVE GSCHMEISSNER/SCIENCE PHOTO LIBRARY, itsmejust/Shutterstock; p. 197 hxdbzxy/Shutterstock, Julia Kuznetsova/Shutterstock; p. 198 PHILIPPE PSAILA/SCIENCE PHOTO LIBRARY, adike/Shutterstock; p. 199 alybaba/Shutterstock; p. 200 Gio.tto/Shutterstock; p. 201 isak55/Shutterstock; p. 202 Leah-Anne Thompson/Shutterstock, JEAN-FRANÇOIS PODEVIN/SCIENCE PHOTO LIBRARY; p. 206 khemporn tongphay/Shutterstock; p. 207 Anest/Shutterstock; p. 208 Levent Konuk/Shutterstock; p. 209 Africa Studio/Shutterstock; p. 210 Puwadol Jaturawutthichai/Shutterstock; p. 212 WILL & DENI MCINTYRE/SCIENCE PHOTO LIBRARY, SCIENCE PHOTO LIBRARY p. 215 Kazakov Maksim/Shutterstock, MARK THOMAS/SCIENCE PHOTO LIBRARY;

Chapter 7
p. 224 Sergey Novikov/Shutterstock, Kjersti Joergensen/Shutterstock, Esteban De Armas/Shutterstock; p. 225 Kenneth Keifer/Shutterstock, Everett Historical/Shutterstock, Surrphoto/Shutterstock; p. 226 Charlotte Purdy/Shutterstock; p. 227 BMJ/Shutterstock, outdoorsman/Shutterstock, photos2013/Shutterstock; p. 228 Tanor/Shutterstock; p. 231 Ryan M. Bolton/Shutterstock, Claude Huot/Shutterstock, Guido Vermeulen-Perdaen/Shutterstock, Ben Queenborough/Shutterstock, NATURAL HISTORY MUSEUM, LONDON/SCIENCE PHOTO LIBRARY, Joe Ravi/Shutterstock; p. 232 Olga Popova/Shutterstock; p. 234 PAUL TAFFOREAU/ESRF/PASCAL GOETGHELUCK/ SCIENCE PHOTO LIBRARY, Natursports/Shutterstock; p. 236 manfredxy/Shutterstock; p. 237 Martin Fowler/Shutterstock, Steve McWilliam/Shutterstock; p. 238 Everett Historical/Shutterstock; p. 242 dwphotos/Shutterstock, Nate Allred/Shutterstock; p. 243 Henk Vrieselaar/Shutterstock, Sergey Fatin/Shutterstock, Eric Isselee/Shutterstock; p. 244 Volodymyr Stakhiv/Shutterstock; p. 245 ur Zoonar GmbH/Shutterstock, Jorge Salcedo/Shutterstock, Gordana Sermek/Shutterstock, Texturis/Shutterstock; p. 246 VOLKER STEGER/SCIENCE PHOTO LIBRARY; p. 247 Denton Rumsey/Shutterstock; p. 248 sundetman/Shutterstock; p. 249 Lightspring/Shutterstock, Geoffrey Budesa/Shutterstock; p. 250 science photo/Shutterstock; p. 251 stocksolutions/Shutterstock, a katz/Shutterstock; p. 252 www.GloFish.com; p. 253 PETER MENZEL/SCIENCE PHOTO LIBRARY; p. 262 Kiselev Andrey Valerevich/Shutterstock;

Chapter 8
p. 266 apiguide/Shutterstock, patostudio/Shutterstock, Taiga/Shutterstock, Peshkova/Shutterstock; p. 267 Kirsanov Valeriy Vladimirovich/Shutterstock, Ethan Daniels/Shutterstock, Critterbiz/Shutterstock, FotoJoost/Shutterstock; p. 268 Tischenko Irina/Shutterstock; p. 269 Zack Frank/Shutterstock, Martin Fowler/Shutterstock, Ron Zmiri/Shutterstock; p. 270 so51hk/Shutterstock; p. 272 SJ Travel Photo and Video/Shutterstock, Joanne Weston/Shutterstock, Vaclav Volrab/Shutterstock; p. 274 Bjul/Shutterstock, Paula French/Shutterstock, Tom Roche/Shutterstock, LauraD/Shutterstock; p. 275 Polarpx/Shutterstock, Pichai Tunsuphon/Shutterstock, 7382489561/Shutterstock; p. 276 Yellowj/Shutterstock, richpav/Shutterstock; p. 277 Gajic Dragan/Shutterstock; p. 278 Darren Foard/Shutterstock, Pal Teravagimov/Shutterstock; p. 279 kamon_saejueng/Shutterstock, f9photos/Shutterstock; p. 280 Vladimir Melnik/Shutterstock, Joanna Zaleska/Shutterstock; p. 281 Straystone/Shutterstock, Tanor/Shutterstock; p. 282 topten22photo/Shutterstock; p. 283 Marek Velechovsky/Shutterstock; p. 284 Carlos Caetano/Shutterstock; p. 285 DrObjektiff/Shutterstock; p. 286 Richard Thornton/Shutterstock; p. 287 photoneye/Shutterstock, Lodimup/Shutterstock; p. 288 Gary Andrews/Shutterstock; p. 289 Bildagentur Zoonar GmbH/Shutterstock, Nathape/Shutterstock; p. 291 bikeriderlondon/Shutterstock, BOONCHUAY PROMJIAM/Shutterstock; p. 292 Huguette Roe/Shutterstock; p. 293 Anticiclo/Shutterstock; p. 294 Randimal/Shutterstock, gubernat/Shutterstock, Orla/Shutterstock; p. 296 Stephen Lavery/Shutterstock, sunsetman/Shutterstock; p. 297 Ilona Ignatova/Shutterstock, Vilainecrevette/Shutterstock; p. 301 Sarah Pettegree/Shutterstock;

Contents

How to use this book

Remember! to cover all the content of the AQA Biology Combined Science Specification you should study the text and attempt the End of chapter questions.

These tell you what you will be learning about in the lesson and are linked to the AQA specification.

This introduces the topic and puts the science into an interesting context.

Each topic is divided into three sections. The level of challenge gets harder with each section.

Each section has level-appropriate questions, so you can check and apply your knowledge.

Biology

Genetic engineering

KEY WORDS

genetic engineering
GM crops
vector

Learning objectives:

- give examples of how plant crops have been genetically engineered to improve products and describe how fungus cells are engineered to produce human insulin.
- describe the process of genetic engineering

Genetic engineering **involves taking specific genes from one organism and introducing them into the genome of another. Scientists can now, more or less, transfer genes from any organism, including plants, animals, bacteria or viruses.**

Producing human insulin

Patients with Type 1 diabetes need regular injections of the hormone insulin. Since the early 1920s, insulin was extracted from the pancreas of pigs or cattle. But these types of insulin differ *slightly* from human insulin in the amino acids they contain. They had some side effects.

With **genetic engineering** it became possible to genetically engineer the bacterium, *Escherichia coli*, and the fungus, yeast, to produce 'human' insulin. This is *identical* to the insulin produced by the human body.

Yeast produces a more complete version of the insulin molecule. Less processing is required, so this method is often preferred.

Figure 7.31 Human insulin production in India. This photograph shows the purification process.

① What is genetic engineering?

② Name two organisms that can be genetically engineered to produce insulin.

Genetically engineered plants

Genetic engineering has transformed crop production. Genes from many organisms, often not even plants, are cut out of their chromosomes and inserted into the cells of crop plants. Such crop plants and other organisms are called genetically modified, **GM crops** or GM organisms (GMOs).

Plants have been engineered to be resistant to disease, and to increase yields, such as producing bigger, better fruit. Several types of crop plant have been produced that are resistant to diseases caused by viruses.

In the wet summer of 2012, potato plants became exposed to the potato blight fungus. In 2014 British scientists produced a GM potato that is resistant to potato blight. Genes from two wild relatives of the potato were inserted into the Desiree potato variety.

246   AQA GCSE Biology for Combined Science: Trilogy: Student Book

---

Important scientific vocabulary is highlighted. You can check the meanings in the Glossary at the end of the book.

7.11

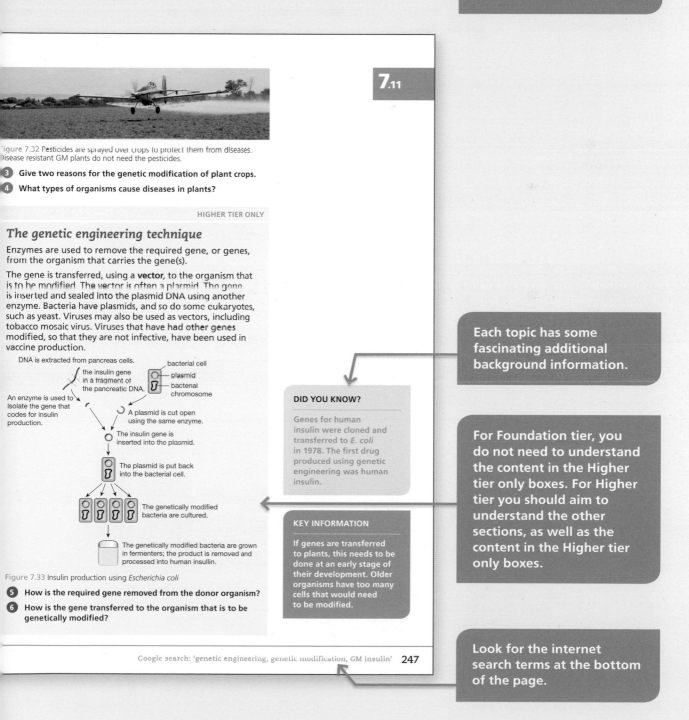

Figure 7.32 Pesticides are sprayed over crops to protect them from diseases. Disease resistant GM plants do not need the pesticides.

3 Give two reasons for the genetic modification of plant crops.

4 What types of organisms cause diseases in plants?

HIGHER TIER ONLY

The genetic engineering technique

Enzymes are used to remove the required gene, or genes, from the organism that carries the gene(s).

The gene is transferred, using a **vector**, to the organism that is to be modified. The vector is often a plasmid. The gene is inserted and sealed into the plasmid DNA using another enzyme. Bacteria have plasmids, and so do some eukaryotes, such as yeast. Viruses may also be used as vectors, including tobacco mosaic virus. Viruses that have had other genes modified, so that they are not infective, have been used in vaccine production.

DNA is extracted from pancreas cells.

the insulin gene in a fragment of the pancreatic DNA.

bacterial cell
plasmid
bacterial chromosome

An enzyme is used to isolate the gene that codes for insulin production.

A plasmid is cut open using the same enzyme.

The insulin gene is inserted into the plasmid.

The plasmid is put back into the bacterial cell.

The genetically modified bacteria are cultured.

The genetically modified bacteria are grown in fermenters; the product is removed and processed into human insulin.

Figure 7.33 Insulin production using *Escherichia coli*

5 How is the required gene removed from the donor organism?

6 How is the gene transferred to the organism that is to be genetically modified?

DID YOU KNOW?

Genes for human insulin were cloned and transferred to *E. coli* in 1978. The first drug produced using genetic engineering was human insulin.

KEY INFORMATION

If genes are transferred to plants, this needs to be done at an early stage of their development. Older organisms have too many cells that would need to be modified.

Each topic has some fascinating additional background information.

For Foundation tier, you do not need to understand the content in the Higher tier only boxes. For Higher tier you should aim to understand the other sections, as well as the content in the Higher tier only boxes.

Look for the internet search terms at the bottom of the page.

Google search: 'genetic engineering, genetic modification, GM insulin' **247**

The first page of a chapter has links to ideas you have met before, which you can now build on.

This page gives a summary of the exciting new ideas you will be learning about in the chapter.

CHAPTER OPENING

The Key Concept pages focus on core ideas. Once you have understood the key concept in a chapter, it should develop your understanding of the whole topic.

KEY CONCEPT

There is a dedicated page for every Required Practical in the AQA specification. They help you to analyse the practical and to answer questions about it.

The tasks – which get a bit more difficult as you go through – challenge you to apply your science skills and knowledge to the new context.

REQUIRED PRACTICAL

The Maths Skills pages focus on the maths requirements in the AQA specification, explaining concepts and providing opportunities to practise.

MATHS SKILLS

Biology

These lists at the end of a chapter act as a checklist of the key ideas of the chapter. In each row, the green box gives the ideas or skills that you should master first. Then you can aim to master the ideas and skills in the blue box. Once you have achieved those you can move on to those in the red box.

Use the comments to help you understand how to answer questions. Read each question and answer. Try to decide if, and how, the answer can be improved. Finally, read the comments and try to answer the questions yourself.

END OF CHAPTER

The End of chapter questions allow you and your teacher to check that you have understood the ideas in the chapter, can apply these to new situations, and can explain new science using the skills and knowledge you have gained. The questions start off easier and get harder. If you are taking Foundation tier, try to answer all the questions in the Getting started and Going further sections. If you are taking Higher tier, try to answer all the questions in the Going further, More challenging and Most demanding sections.

There are questions for each assessment object (AO) from the final exams. This will help you develop the thinking skills you need to answer each type of question:

AO1 – to answer these questions you should aim to **demonstrate** your knowledge and understanding of scientific ideas, techniques and procedures.

AO2 – to answer these questions you should aim to **apply** your knowledge and understanding of scientific ideas and scientific enquiry, techniques and procedures.

AO3 – to answer these questions you should aim to **analyse** information and ideas to: interpret and evaluate, make judgements and draw conclusions, develop and improve experimental procedures.

CELL BIOLOGY

IDEAS YOU HAVE MET BEFORE:

ALL LIVING ORGANISMS ARE MADE OF CELLS.

- Cells are the building blocks of life.
- Cells contain specialised structures.
- Organisms such as bacteria are unicellular.
- All plants and animals are multicellular.

IN MULTICELLULAR ORGANISMS CELLS BECOME SPECIALISED.

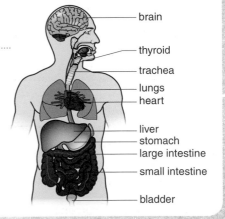

- Specialised cells have a particular job to do.
- Specialised cells are organised into tissues, tissues into organs, and organs into body systems.

ORGANISMS OBTAIN ENERGY BY THE PROCESS OF RESPIRATION.

- The energy that is released drives all the processes necessary for life.
- Most organisms respire by aerobic respiration, using oxygen.
- Some cells or organisms can survive without oxygen. They respire anaerobically.

IN THIS CHAPTER YOU WILL FIND OUT ABOUT:

HOW HAVE SCIENTISTS DEVELOPED THEIR UNDERSTANDING OF CELL STRUCTURE AND FUNCTION?

- The structures inside cells do different jobs within the cell.
- Cells can be studied using different types of microscopes.
- The cells of bacteria are different from the cells of plants and animals.

HOW DO WE DEVELOP INTO A COMPLEX ORGANISM FROM JUST A FERTILISED EGG CELL?

- The body's cells divide and the newly formed cells are identical to the existing cells.
- Cells differentiate to become specialised, and specialised cells are organised.
- When cell division accelerates out of control, cancer develops.
- Cells that are unspecialised in the embryo, and cells that remain unspecialised in us as adults, are called stem cells.
- Stem cells could be used to treat certain conditions and diseases that are currently untreatable.

HOW DO ORGANISMS OBTAIN THEIR ENERGY FROM FOOD?

- Anaerobic respiration: when some organisms run out of oxygen, they can respire without it.
- Many microorganisms can respire anaerobically, as can the muscles of mammals for short periods.

Looking at cells

Learning objectives:

- describe the structure of eukaryotic cells
- explain how the main sub-cellular structures are related to their functions.

KEY WORDS

chlorophyll
chloroplast
chromosome
DNA
eukaryotic
order of magnitude

Cell biology helps us to understand how parts of the cell function and interact with each other. It also helps us to learn how we develop, and about our relationships with other organisms.

Biomedical scientists use cells to look for signs of disease and in new drug development.

Plant and animal cells

Almost all organisms are made up of cells. Plant and animal cells have a basic structure.

The nucleus:
- controls the activities of the cell
- contains deoxyribonucleic acid (**DNA**)
- the DNA is organised into **chromosomes**.

The cell membrane:
- controls the passage of substances into and out of the cell.

The cytoplasm:
- is where most of the chemical reactions in the cell take place.

The vacuole:
- is surrounded by a membrane and fluid filled
- the fluid is called cell sap
- vacuoles are permanent structures in plants.

The **chloroplasts**:
- are found in plant cells above ground
- contain **chlorophyll** that absorbs the light the plant needs for photosynthesis.

The cell wall:
- is an additional layer outside the cell membrane
- is made from cellulose fibres
- contains fibres that provide strength
- unlike the cell membrane, does not regulate what enters or leaves the cell.

(a)   (b)

Figure 1.1 (a) A simple animal cell and (b) a plant leaf cell

This type of cell, containing a true nucleus in the cytoplasm, is called a **eukaryotic** cell.

1. List the sub-cellular structures found in both plant and animal cells.

2. Which sub-cellular structures are found only in plant cells?

   What is the function of:
   - the nucleus
   - the cell membrane?

3. What structure gives strength to a plant cell?

Figure 1.2 Growing cells in a laboratory

Cell size

The smallest thing we can see is about 0.04 mm, so you can see some of the largest cells with the naked eye. For all cells, however, we need a microscope to see them in any detail.

Most animal and plant cells are 0.01–0.10 mm in size. The unit we use to measure most cells is the micrometre, symbol µm. For some sub-cellular structures, or organisms such as viruses, it is best to use a smaller unit: the nanometre, symbol nm.

1 millimetre (mm) $= \dfrac{1}{1000}$ m   or 10^{-3} m

1 micrometre (µm) $= \dfrac{1}{1000}$ mm   or 10^{-3} mm   or 10^{-6} m

1 nanometre (nm) $= \dfrac{1}{1000}$ µm   or 10^{-3} µm   or 10^{-9} m

4 What size is the smallest thing our eye can see, in m?

5 What is the range in size of most animal and plant cells, in µm?

Order of magnitude

Figure 1.3 shows the size of plant and animal cells compared with some other structures.

| ant length 3 mm | hair diameter 100 µm | leaf cell length 70 µm | red blood cell diameter 7 µm | bacterium length 1 µm | virus 100 nm | DNA diameter 2.5 nm | carbon atom 0.34 nm |

Figure 1.3 Size and scale

When comparing the sizes of cells, scientists often refer to differences in **order of magnitude**. That's the difference calculated in factors of 10.

So, the difference in order of magnitude for the HIV and the plant cell:

The plant cell in Figure 1.1b is 100 µm = 0.1 mm = 10^{-4} m.

The human immunodeficiency virus (HIV) is 100 nm = 0.1 µm = 10^{-4} mm = 10^{-7} m.

The difference in order of magnitude is 10^3, expressed as 3.

6 A cell membrane measures 7 nm across. Convert this to micrometres.

7 A white blood cell measures 1.2×10^{-5} m. An egg cell measures 1.2×10^{-4} m. Calculate the difference in order of magnitude.

> **REMEMBER!**
>
> You'll notice that this system of units uses, and gives names to, multiples and sub-multiples of units at intervals of thousands (10^3) or thousandths (10^{-3}). A common exception is the centimetre, $\dfrac{1}{100}$ or 10^{-2} of a metre. But it is often convenient to use centimetres, particularly in everyday life.

The light microscope

Learning objectives:

- observe plant and animal cells with a light microscope
- understand the limitations of light microscopy.

KEY WORDS

magnification
micrographs
resolving power

The type of microscope you have used in the school laboratory is called a light microscope. Microscopes produce a magnified image of the specimen you are looking at, making them look bigger than they are.

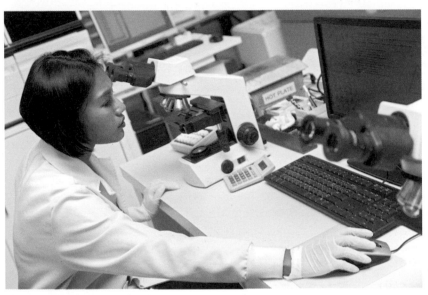

Figure 1.4 A compound microscope

Some early microscopes had just a single lens. The compound microscope has two.

As lens-making techniques improved, microscopes were developed with higher magnifications and resolutions.

Magnification

The magnified image is produced by two lenses, an eyepiece and an objective lens. There is usually a choice of objective lenses.

Total magnification = magnification of eyepiece × magnification of objective lens

For instance, if the eyepiece has a **magnification** of 10, which is written × 10, and the objective lens has a magnification of × 40, the total magnification is × 400.

1. Calculate the total magnification with an eyepiece magnification of × 15 and an objective lens magnification of × 40.

2. What magnification would the objective lens need to be to give a total magnification of × 300 with an eyepiece of × 15?

DID YOU KNOW?

British scientist Robert Hooke first used the term 'cell'. He recorded the first drawings of cells using a compound microscope in his book *Micrographia*, which was 350 years old in 2015.

You may also have heard of Hooke for his law of elasticity, Hooke's law, in physics.

Magnification of images

The magnification described on the previous page is the magnification used to *view* an image. Microscope images, or **micrographs**, books or scientific papers, must show the magnification in order to be meaningful.

$$\text{magnification of the image} = \frac{\text{size of the image}}{\text{size of real object}}$$

The cell in Figure 1.5 is 50 mm across on the page. In real life, it measures 40 µm.

To calculate the magnification, first convert the 50 mm into micrometres (or convert 40 µm to millimetres).

50 mm = 50 000 µm

The cell measures 40 µm

Therefore, the magnification of the image = $\frac{50\ 000}{40}$ = × 1250.

Figure 1.5 A drawing of a micrograph of a cell

3 A micrograph of a plant cell in a book is 150 mm long. The plant cell measures 120 µm long. Calculate the magnification.

4 Why is it essential to state the magnification of an image of a cell in a book but of little value on a website?

The limits of the light microscope

Very high magnifications are not possible with the light microscope. This is because of the light-gathering ability of the microscope and the short working distances of high-power lenses. The highest magnification possible is around × 1500.

Using higher magnification does not always mean that you can see greater detail in an image. This depends on the **resolving power**, or resolution. This is the ability to distinguish between two points. In other words, whether you see them as two points, or one.

The resolving power of a light microscope is around 0.2 µm, or 200 nm. This means that you could not separately pick out two points closer than 200 nm apart.

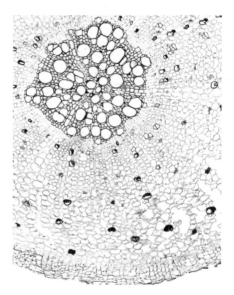

Figure 1.6 A micrograph of the cross section of a root. Magnification × 100

5 What is the maximum resolving power of the light microscope?

6 What is the maximum magnification possible with a light microscope?

7 Make a table to show the pros and cons of using a light microscope.

COMMON MISCONCEPTIONS

Do not confuse magnification, which is how much bigger we can make something appear, with resolving power, which is the level of detail we can see.

Think about a digital photo. You can make it as big as you like, but at a certain point you will not be able to see any more detail.

Looking at cells in more detail

KEY WORDS

scanning electron
microscope (SEM)
transmission
electron
microscope (TEM)

Learning objectives:

- identify the differences in the magnification and resolving power of light and electron microscopes
- explain how electron microscopy has increased our understanding of sub-cellular structures.

The *transmission electron microscope (TEM)* uses an electron beam instead of light rays.

Some of the electrons are scattered as they pass through the specimen. Those able to pass through it are focused in TEMs using electromagnetic coils instead of lenses.

Electron microscopes

TEMs are used for looking at extremely thin sections of cells. The highest magnification that can be obtained from a transmission electron microscope is around × 1 000 000, but images can also be enlarged photographically.

The limit of resolution of the transmission electron microscope is now less than 1 nm.

The **scanning electron microscope (SEM)** works by bouncing electrons off the surface of a specimen that has had an ultra-thin coating of a heavy metal, usually gold, applied. A narrow electron beam scans the specimen. Images are formed by these scattered electrons.

SEMs are used to reveal the surface shape of structures such as small organisms and cells. Because of this, resolution is lower and magnifications used are often lower than for a TEM.

Electrons do not have a colour spectrum like the visible light used to illuminate a light microscope. They can only be 'viewed' in black and white. Here, false colours have been added.

Figure 1.7 A transmission electron microscope. The electrons are displayed as an image on a fluorescent screen.

1. What is the maximum resolution of an electron microscope?

2. What types of samples would a TEM and an SEM be used to view?

3. How has electron microscopy improved our understanding of cells?

Figure 1.8 A scanning electron micrograph of a cancer cell

Cell ultrastructure

The TEM reveals tiny sub-cellular structures that are not visible with the light microscope. It also shows fine detail in those structures.

cell membrane

nucleus

cytoplasm

ribosomes

mitochondria

Figure 1.9 A white blood cell, as seen with a light microscope and a transmission electron microscope

We can see mitochondria and chloroplasts with the light microscope, but the electron microscope reveals their internal structure.

(a)

Mitochondria are where aerobic respiration takes place in the cell. A mitochondrion has a double membrane. The internal membrane is folded.

(b)

Chloroplasts are the structures in the plant cell where photosynthesis takes place. Like mitochondria, they also have a complex internal membrane structure.

(c)

Ribosomes are tiny structures where protein synthesis takes place. You can see them as dots in the micrograph. They can either lie free in the cytoplasm or be attached to an internal network of channels within the cytoplasm.

Figure 1.10 Viewing (a) mitochondria, (b) chloroplasts and (c) ribosomes by transmission electron microscopy

The size of sub-cellular structures is important. Mitochondria and chloroplasts vary in size and shape. The complexity of a mitochondrion indicates how active a cell is. Chloroplast size varies from one species to another. Scientists sometimes investigate the ratio of the area of the cytoplasm to that of the nucleus in micrographs. A high ratio of cytoplasmic:nuclear volume can indicate that the cell is about to divide. A low one can be characteristic of a cancer cell.

4 Name one structure visible using the electron microscope, but not the light microscope.

5 What process happens in ribosomes?

6 Which type of microscope would be best suited to viewing the 3D structure of a cell? Explain why.

COMMON MISCONCEPTIONS

Don't assume that we always use electron microscopes in preference to light microscopes, or that electron microscopes are always used at high magnifications. Confocal microscopy is used in a lot of biomedical research. It can give high resolution images of live cells. And SEM is often used at low magnifications.

DID YOU KNOW?

Three scientists won the Nobel Prize in 2014 for the development of super-resolved fluorescence microscopy. It allows a much higher resolution than normal light microscopy. And, unlike electron microscopy, it has the advantage of allowing scientists to look at living cells.

REQUIRED PRACTICAL

Using a light microscope to observe and record animal and plant cells

KEY WORDS

field of view
scale bar

Learning objectives:

- apply knowledge to select techniques, instruments, apparatus and materials to observe cells
- make and record observations and measurements
- present observations and other data using appropriate methods.

These pages are designed ❶ to help you think about aspects of the investigation rather than to guide you through it step by step.

Many scientists use electron microscopes to observe fine detail in cells. But much of the microscope work carried out – including in hospital and forensic science labs – is done with the light microscope.

Preparing cells for microscopy

Live cells can be mounted in a drop of water or dilute salt solution (saline) on a microscope slide.

Most cells are colourless. We must stain them to add colour and contrast. In the school laboratory, you may have used methylene blue to stain animal cells or iodine solution to stain plant cells.

Figure 1.11 A glass coverslip is carefully lowered onto the cells or tissue, taking care to avoid trapping air bubbles. The coverslip keeps the specimen flat, and retains the liquid under it.

① Write an equipment list for looking at cheek cells with a microscope. State why each piece of equipment is used.

② Suggest why it's better to mount the cells in saline than in water.

③ The micrograph of the frog's blood (Figure 1.12) shows red blood cells (the lower micrograph) and two types of white blood cell.

  a Label the different types of cell and the cell structures that are visible. Hint: use a photocopy or printout of the page.

  b How is the structure of the frog's red blood cells different from that of human red blood cells?

High and low power

The slide is first viewed with low power. This is because:

- The **field of view** with high power is small. It would be difficult to locate cells if starting with the high power objective
- It enables you to see the layout of cells within the tissue.

Figure 1.12 Cell biologists use other chemical stains. These are used to reveal or identify specific cell structures.

- It's useful when estimating the numbers of different types of cell on the slide or in a tissue (though here, high power may be needed).

A low power digital image (or drawing) can be used to show the arrangement of cells in a tissue. This includes regions of the tissue but not individual cells.

If required, the cells or tissue can then viewed with high power to produce a detailed image of a part of the slide.

A student's low power diagram

Figure 1.13 Low and high power micrographs, and a student diagram, of a plant root

4 Why is a slide viewed with low power first?

5 On a printout of a low power plan of the root (Figure 1.13), label the root cap, the meristem (the region of cell division) and the region of cell elongation.

Recording images

As you have seen in topic 1.3, a microscope drawing or micrograph is of little value if it gives no indication of size.

It's usual to add a magnification to the image. We can then envisage, or work out, the true size of a specimen.

Alternatively, we can use a **scale bar**. Any scale bar must be:

- drawn for an appropriate dimension
- a sensible size in relation to the image.

Look at Figure 1.14. For the top micrograph, the magnification of × 1000 means that a 10 *millimetre* scale bar can be drawn to represent 10 *micrometres*.

You will find out how scientists measure, or sometimes estimate, the size of cells in topic 1.14.

6 Complete the scale bar for the bottom micrograph.

7 Calculate the length of the protists in Figure 1.14.

10 µm

Figure 1.14 Light microscopy is also used to examine small organisms such as protists. The top image shows six blood cells infected with the malarial parasite. The bottom image shows two protists found in pond water - *Amoeba* on the left; *Paramecium* on the right (at × 200 magnification).

Primitive cells

Learning objectives:

- describe the differences between prokaryotic cells and eukaryotic cells
- explain how the main sub-cellular structures of prokaryotic and eukaryotic cells are related to their functions.

The oldest fossil evidence of life on Earth comes from Australia. It confirms that there were bacteria living around 3.5 billion years ago.

The bacteria probably formed thin purple and green mats on shorelines. The bacteria would have photosynthesised, but produced sulfur as waste instead of oxygen.

Figure 1.15 The organisms in this fossil are similar to purple bacteria that are living today.

Prokaryotic cells

The cells of most types of organisms – such as all animals and plants – are **eukaryotic**. These have a cell membrane, cytoplasm containing sub-cellular structures called organelles and a nucleus containing DNA.

Bacteria are among the simplest of organisms. Along with bacteria-like organisms called archaeans, they belong to a group of organisms called the **Prokaryota**. These are single cells with a **prokaryotic cell** structure.

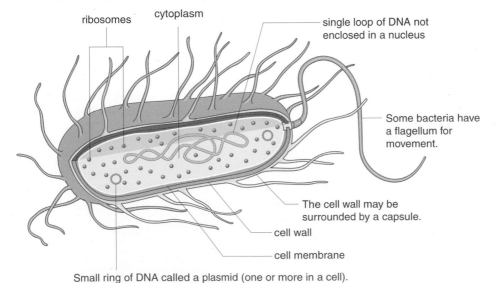

ribosomes

cytoplasm

single loop of DNA not enclosed in a nucleus

Some bacteria have a flagellum for movement.

The cell wall may be surrounded by a capsule.

cell wall

cell membrane

Small ring of DNA called a plasmid (one or more in a cell). Genes in the plasmids can give the bacterium advantages such as antibiotic resistance.

Figure 1.16 The structure of a prokaryotic cell

Prokaryotic cells are much smaller than eukaryotic cells, around 1 µm across. Their DNA is not enclosed in a nucleus. It is found as a single molecule in a loop. They may also have one or more small rings of DNA called **plasmids**.

1 List the differences between prokaryotic and eukaryotic cells.

2 Where is DNA found in prokaryotic cells?

A new classification system

By the 1970s, biologists had classified living organisms into five **kingdoms**.

Very small, microscopic organisms called archaeans were originally grouped in a kingdom with bacteria. But in 1977, American microbiologist Carl Woese suggested that certain types of organisms that lived in extreme environments or produced methane gas should be placed in a separate group.

Woese suggested that living things should be divided into three groups called **domains**: Bacteria, Archaea and Eukaryota.

3 What are the three domains of living things?

4 In which domain are plants and animals?

Chemical characteristics of archaeans

Acceptance of Woese's theory was a slow process. Even today, not everyone agrees with it, but chemical analyses have supported the idea that archaeans should be in a separate domain.

The ribosomes of archaeans are similar in size and structure to those of bacteria, but the **nucleic acid** in these structures is closer to that of eukaryotes.

When American biochemist Craig Ventner, one of the first scientists involved in the sequencing of the human **genome**, looked at the DNA of Archaea he was astounded to find that 'two-thirds of the genes [in Archaea] do not look like anything we've ever seen in biology before'.

5 Where do archaeans live?

6 What evidence suggests that archaeans should be placed in a separate domain from bacteria?

7 Suggest why scientists have only discovered Archaea quite recently.

DID YOU KNOW?

A 'superfood' called Spirulina is the dried cells of a blue-green bacterium. The cells contain high concentrations of protein, and are rich in essential fatty acids, vitamins and minerals.

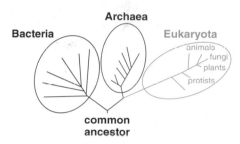

Figure 1.17 The three-domain classification system

Figure 1.18 Archaeans live in extreme environments, such as hot springs and salt lakes. Some produce methane and are important in the carbon cycle.

REMEMBER!

You should aim to be able to discuss how information on Archaea, Bacteria and Eukaryota allows them to be placed in separate domains.

Cell division

Learning objectives:

- describe the process of mitosis in growth, and mitosis as part of the cell cycle
- describe how the process of mitosis produces cells that are genetically identical to the parent cell.

KEY WORDS

daughter cell
mitosis
stem cells

As an adult, we are made up of 37 trillion (3.7×10^{13}) cells. To produce these cells, the fertilised egg needs to undergo many cell divisions.

Chromosomes

As we grow, the cells produced by cell division must all contain the same genetic information.

The genetic information of all organisms is contained in chromosomes, made of DNA. The DNA in resting cells is found in the nucleus as long, thin strands. For cell division, these strands form condensed chromosomes.

Human body cells have 46 chromosomes, or 23 pairs. Each chromosome in a pair has the same type of genes along its length.

1. **How many chromosomes are found in each human body cell?**

2. **How are the chromosomes arranged in a karyotype?**

Mitosis

New cells have to be produced for growth and development, and to replace worn out and damaged body cells.

When new cells are produced they must be identical to the parent cell. Cells divide to produce two new ones. This type of cell division is called **mitosis**. Two **daughter cells** are produced from the parent cell.

For some cell types, new cells are produced by the division of **stem cells** (discussed later in the chapter).

3. **When are new cells produced?**

4. **In this type of cell division:**
   - **how many chromosomes do daughter cells have?**
   - **how many daughter cells are produced?**

A photograph is taken of a dividing cell.

The chromosomes in the photograph are cut out and arranged into pairs.
The pairs are arranged so that Pair 1 has the longest chromosomes; Pair 22 the shortest
Pair 23 is the sex chromosomes.

Figure 1.19 A profile of a set of chromosomes, called a karyotype

MAKING CONNECTIONS

To come up with a figure for how many cells there are in the human body, scientists must *estimate* the number by adding up cell counts from different organs.

So that the daughter cells produced are identical to the parent cell, the DNA must first copy itself. Each of the 46 chromosomes then consists of two molecules of DNA.

DNA molecule in the nucleus

The DNA replicates to form a double chromosome Each half has an identical set of genes

The DNA condenses to form a recognisable chromosome. The DNA is now compacted to 1/50 000 of its original length

Figure 1.20 It is these 'double' chromosomes that we always see in micrographs or illustrations of chromosomes.

During mitosis, the double chromosomes are pulled apart as each new set of 46 chromosomes moves to opposite ends of the cell (Figure 1.21). Two nuclei then form. The cytoplasm and cell membrane then divides and two identical cells are produced.

5 **Why do chromosomes appear double, or X-shaped, in micrographs?**

The cell cycle

A cell that is actively dividing goes through a series of stages called the cell cycle. The cycle involves the growth of the cell and the production of new cell components and division.

Figure 1.21 Mitosis in an onion cell

1. The cell grows. The number of sub-cellular structures, e.g. mitochondria and ribosomes, increases.

2. The DNA replicates to form two copies of each chromosome.

3. Further growth occurs and the DNA is checked for errors and any repairs made.

4. Mitosis – the chromosomes move apart and two nuclei form.

5. The cytoplasm divides into two and the new cell membrane separates off to give two new, identical cells.

6. Temporary cell resting period, or the cell no longer divides, e.g. a nerve cell.

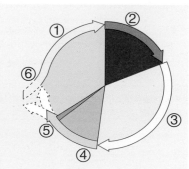

Figure 1.22 The cell cycle

In actively dividing human cells, the whole cell cycle lasts 1 hour.

6 **Using Figure 1.22, calculate the proportion of the cell cycle spent in mitosis. You will need a protractor.**

7 **If the cell cycle lasts 2 hours, estimate the time spent in mitosis.**

8 **Mitosis occurs rapidly in a newly formed fertilised egg. Suggest another situation in the body where you might expect cells to be actively dividing by mitosis.**

Cell differentiation

KEY WORDS

differentiation
organ
organ system
specialised
tissue

Learning objectives:

- explain the importance of cell differentiation
- describe how cells, tissues, organs and organ systems are organised to make up an organism
- understand size and scale in relation to cells, tissues, organs and organ systems.

Cell division makes up only part of our growth and development.

For the first four or five days of our lives, the cells produced as the fertilised egg divides are identical. Then, some of our cells start to become specialised **to do a particular job.**

Figure 1.23 By this stage in its development, this human embryo has developed many of the 200 different cell types in the human body.

Cell adaptations

In a multicellular organism, many different types of cell take on different roles to ensure that the organism functions properly and as a whole.

As cells divide, new cells acquire certain features required for their specific function. This is **differentiation**. A cell's size, shape and internal structure are adapted for its role. Most animal cells differentiate at an early stage.

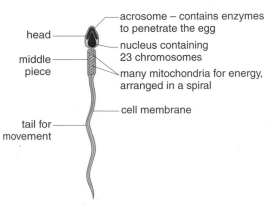

head

middle piece

tail for movement

acrosome – contains enzymes to penetrate the egg

nucleus containing 23 chromosomes

many mitochondria for energy, arranged in a spiral

cell membrane

Figure 1.24 The function of a sperm cell is to swim in the female reproductive system with the aim of fertilising an egg. (Cell length 55 μm; width at widest point 3 μm)

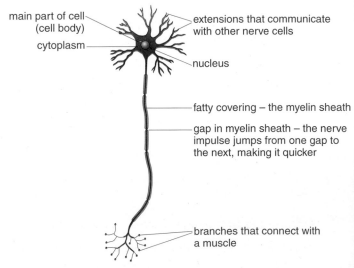

main part of cell (cell body)

cytoplasm

extensions that communicate with other nerve cells

nucleus

fatty covering – the myelin sheath

gap in myelin sheath – the nerve impulse jumps from one gap to the next, making it quicker

branches that connect with a muscle

Figure 1.25 Nerve cells carry messages, or electrical impulses, from one part of the body to another. This type of cell brings about movement of the skeleton. (Motor nerve cell length: up to 1 m or more; diameter 1–20 μm) mitochondria – provide the energy for muscle contraction

heart muscle cells

skeletal muscle

protein filaments – slide over each other to produce muscle contraction

The cells that make up a skeletal muscle fibre physically join together during their development.

smooth muscle cells

Type of muscle cell

Protein filaments give the cells of heart and skeletal muscle a striped appearance. In smooth muscle, found, for instance, in the circulatory system, there are fewer filaments, which are thinner and less well-organised.

Figure 1.26 There are three types of muscle cell. Muscle cells contain protein filaments which move to make the muscle contract. Muscle cells link with each other so a muscle contracts as a whole.

1 **How are the following cells adapted to their functions:**

- **a sperm cell**
- **a muscle cell**
- **a nerve cell?**

2 **Cells of the pancreas produce the hormone insulin. Insulin is a protein. Suggest how pancreatic cells are adapted for their function.**

Cells, tissues and organs

Some cells work in isolation, like sperm cells. Others are grouped as **tissues** and work together.

A tissue is a group of cells with a particular function. Many tissues have a number of similar types of cell to enable the tissue to function.

Tissues are grouped into **organs**. Organs carry out a specific function.

Different organs are arranged into **organ systems**, for example the circulatory system, digestive system, respiratory system, and reproductive system.

3 **Arrange the following in increasing order of size:**

system   cell   human body   organ   tissue

4 **Name two other types of cell and one other type of tissue in the circulatory system.**

5 **Red blood cells have a biconcave shape which gives them a large surface area. How is this shape related to its function?**

cell – heart muscle cell

tissue – heart muscle

organ – the heart

organ system – the circulatory system

Figure 1.27 The organisation of the human circulatory system

Cancer

Learning objectives:

- describe cancer as a condition resulting from changes in cells that lead to their uncontrolled growth, division and spread
- understand some of the risk factors that trigger cells to become cancerous.

KEY WORDS

benign
carcinogen
malignant
mutation
secondary tumour

Every year, over 300 000 people in the UK are diagnosed with cancer. It is estimated, however, that four in ten cases of cancer could be prevented by lifestyle changes.

What is cancer?

Normally, cells grow and divide by mitosis when the body needs new cells to replace old or damaged cells. When a cell becomes cancerous, it begins to divide uncontrollably. New cells are produced even though the body does not need them.

The extra cells produced form growths called tumours. Most tumours are solid, but cancers of the blood, for instance leukaemia, are an exception.

Figure 1.28 A CT scanner, used to detect cancer

1 What is cancer?

2 Name one type of cancer that does not form a solid tumour.

Types of tumour

Type of tumour	Characteristics
Benign	• slow growing • often have a capsule around them, so can be removed easily • not cancerous and rarely spread to other parts of the body • they can press on other body organs and look unsightly.
Malignant	• grow faster • can spread throughout other body tissues • as the tumour grows, cancer cells detach and can form **secondary tumours** in other parts of the body.

Malignant cells develop.

The malignant cells divide and can invade normal tissues.

Malignant cells can detach from the tumour and spread to other parts of the body.

The tumour secretes hormone-like chemicals.

Blood vessels are stimulated to grow around the tumour; the blood vessels supply the tumour with food and oxygen.

Malignant cells detach from the tumour and are transported away in the blood.

The malignant cell squeezes through the capillary wall.

The cell divides to produce a secondary tumour.

Figure 1.29 The growth and spread of a tumour

3 Name two types of tumour.

4 Explain why a tumour needs a blood supply.

5 What is the name of the type of tumour formed when a cancer spreads?

What triggers cancer?

Chemicals and other agents that cause cancer are called **carcinogens**.

Carcinogens cause cancer by damaging DNA. A change in the DNA of a cell is called a **mutation**. Mutations can also occur by chance as a cell is dividing.

There are natural checks for such errors during the cell cycle. Some of our genes suppress developing tumours.

Several mutations, not just one, are necessary to trigger cancer. This is why we are more likely to develop cancer as we get older.

Mutations that lead to cancer can be caused by several agents:

- viruses (see Figure 1.30).
- chemicals in the home, industry or environment
- ionising radiation
- ultraviolet radiation
- lifestyle choices, such as alcohol intake or diet (see Figure 1.31).

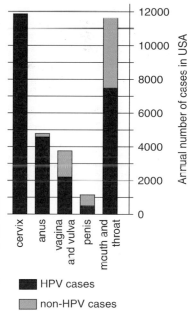

Figure 1.30 Cancers caused by the human papilloma virus (HPV)

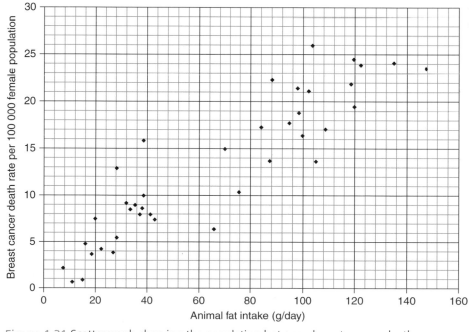

Figure 1.31 Scattergraph showing the correlation between breast cancer deaths and animal fat intake. Each data point represents a different country.

6 Which type of cancer is caused *only* by HPV?

7 Describe the pattern shown by the scattergraph and draw a conclusion.

Stem cells

Learning objectives:

- describe the function of stem cells in embryonic and adult animals
- discuss potential benefits and risks associated with the use of stem cells in medicine.

KEY WORDS

adult stem cell
cell lines
culture
embryonic stem cell
ethical
in-vitro fertilisation
moral

The UK has a shortage of blood donors.

In the summer of 2015 the NHS announced that it planned to start giving people blood transfusions using artificial blood by 2017.

What are stem cells?

Stem cells are unspecialised cells that can produce many different types of cells.

Stem cells are found in the developing embryo and some remain, at certain locations in our bodies, as adults.

Figure 1.32 The red blood cells in the artificial blood will be produced using stem cells.

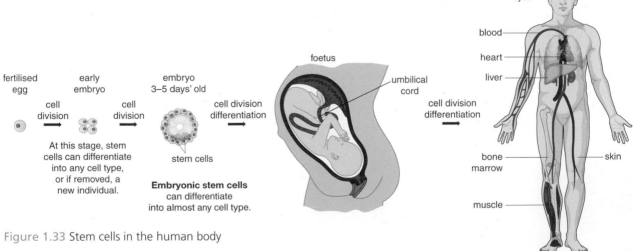

fertilised egg — early embryo — embryo 3–5 days' old — cell division differentiation

cell division — cell division

At this stage, stem cells can differentiate into any cell type, or if removed, a new individual.

stem cells

Embryonic stem cells can differentiate into almost any cell type.

foetus — umbilical cord

cell division differentiation

adult
brain
eyes
blood
heart
liver
bone marrow — skin
muscle

Figure 1.33 Stem cells in the human body

Adult stem cells are rare and found at certain locations only. Their role is to replace body cells that die through injury and disease. They can differentiate only into cells from the type of tissue where they are found, e.g. blood, muscle.

1. **What is the function of adult stem cells?**

2. **Which type of stem cell can differentiate into more cell types?**

Stem cell transplants

Transplanting stem cells, or transplants of specialised cells grown from stem cells, could help people with:

- injuries, e.g. spinal injuries leading to paralysis
- conditions in which certain body cells degenerate, e.g. Alzheimer's disease, diabetes and multiple sclerosis
- cancers, or following treatments for cancer such as chemotherapy or radiation, e.g. people with leukaemia.

Stem cell transplants also enable chemotherapy patients, who have had their bone marrow destroyed, to produce red blood cells.

The hope is that we will be able to **culture** stem cells in limitless numbers. Stem **cell lines** produced from patients with rare and complex diseases could transform the health service.

Figure 1.34 Embryonic stem cells

3 Name two conditions that could be treated with stem cell transplants.

4 Why are stem cell transplants important for people who have had chemotherapy?

Stem cell research and therapy is controversial

Stem cell research is necessary to find out more about stem cell development, and the best types to use in treatments.

The use of **embryonic stem cells**, which are removed from a living human embryo, is especially controversial.

Until recently, the embryos providing the stem cells were usually those left over from fertility treatments involving *in-vitro* **fertilisation** (IVF). Spare embryos would be destroyed if they had not been donated by the IVF couples for research.

British law now allows embryos to be created purely for scientific research. Some people object to this. Some religious beliefs argue that new life begins at the point of conception, so an embryo has rights. And who should decide when a human life ends?

These are **moral** and **ethical** questions. A moral question looks at whether something is right or wrong. An ethical question discusses the reasons why something might be right or wrong.

5 Why do some people object to stem cell transplants?

6 Write down one ethical objection to stem cell research.

7 What are the potential benefits and drawbacks of using stem cells in medicine?

DID YOU KNOW?

Stem cell transplants are not new. Transplants of bone marrow, which contain stem cells, have been carried out since 1968. But there are very few stem cells in bone marrow (only 1 in 10 000 bone marrow cells). We currently isolate these from blood, rather than bone marrow.

KEY INFORMATION

Current potential for adult stem cell use in therapies is restricted to certain cell lines, but it may be greater than once thought. Scientists are trying to induce them to differentiate into a wider range of tissues, a process called transdifferentiation.

Stem cell banks

Learning objectives:

- discuss potential benefits and risks associated with the use of stem cells in medicine.

KEY WORDS

donor
gene
mutation
therapeutic
 cloning
umbilical cord

Scientists predict that, in the future, vast banks of stored stem cells will be available to treat many medical conditions.

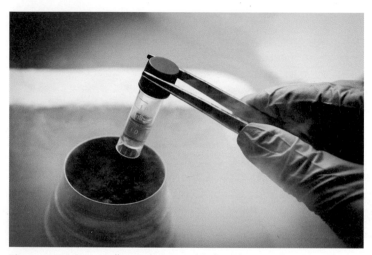

Figure 1.35 Stem cells can be stored in liquid nitrogen.

Rejection of stem cell transplants

The stem cells from a bank originate from many different people. Rejection of stem cell transplants by a patient's immune system is, therefore, a problem.

One current solution is to find as close a match as possible between **donor** and patient cells. Another is to give the patient drugs to suppress their immune system. Scientists are looking for other ways to avoid transplant rejection.

One possible source of stem cells is blood left in the **umbilical cord** and placenta after a baby is born. Cord blood is easy to collect and store.

1. Suggest sources of stem cells that would give the best match between donor and patient.

2. Suggest some possible advantages and disadvantages of having a baby's blood stored to treat possible disease or injury in later life.

Therapeutic cloning

The idea of **therapeutic cloning** is to produce stem cells with the same **genes** as the patient. They would not be rejected by the patient's immune system.

The process involves nuclear transfer. The nucleus of a body cell from the patient is transferred to an egg cell that has had its nucleus removed.

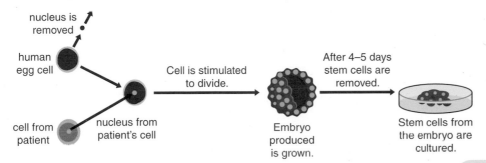

nucleus is removed

human egg cell

cell from patient

nucleus from patient's cell

Cell is stimulated to divide.

Embryo produced is grown.

After 4–5 days stem cells are removed.

Stem cells from the embryo are cultured.

Figure 1.36 Therapeutic cloning

The stem cells are used to treat the patient. The embryo is discarded.

3 What is therapeutic cloning?

4 When are stem cells removed from the embryo?

Scientific, ethical and social questions

Many questions arise from therapeutic cloning and stem cell therapy.

The first scientific question is how successful might these therapies be? Others consider safety: stem cells kept in culture can show similarities to cancer cells. After about 60 cell divisions, **mutations** have been observed. It is also possible for viruses to be transferred with stem cells, leading to infection.

There are also ethical questions:

- Is it morally right to create an embryo with the intent of destroying it?
- Could an embryo simply become a resource for researchers?

There are also important social questions. What are the potential benefits from successful stem cell treatment and do these outweigh the objections? And should patients be given false hope based on a currently unproven treatment? Public education on this issue is important.

5 Suggest two questions scientists might have about therapeutic cloning.

6 Evaluate the risks and benefits as well as the ethical concerns associated with therapeutic cloning.

DID YOU KNOW?

Scientists have succeeded in removing human skin cells and reprogramming them to become cells similar to embryonic stem cells. This removes some of the ethical concerns over stem cell transplants.

Figure 1.37 Blind patients have had their sight restored by stem cells. It has been possible to safely treat the part of the eye responsible for central vision.

MAKING CONNECTIONS

You should be able to evaluate information from a variety of sources regarding practical, social and ethical issues relating to stem cell research and treatment.

KEY CONCEPT

Cell development

Learning objectives:

- give examples of where mitosis is necessary to produce identical daughter cells
- understand the need for the reduction division, meiosis
- describe the use and potential of cloned cells in biological research.

KEY WORDS

asexual
 reproduction
differentiation
gamete
meiosis
mitosis
placenta
zygote

Cell development involves the processes of cell growth, division and differentiation. These processes are closely linked, and are a key focus for current biological research.

Cells

The cell is the basic unit of life. You will have looked at cells with a microscope in school, probably cheek cells and onion skin cells. These illustrate the basic cell pattern, but most cells in all but the simplest of organisms are much more varied in their structure.

helically coiled
nucleic acid
molecule

nucleic acid

lipoprotein envelope

virus

protein
coat

protein
molecule

protein
molecule

Figure 1.38 Viruses are not made up of cells. They consist simply of nucleic acid surrounded by a protein coat. Some have an outer envelope.

1 **Name one example of a human tissue where cells have merged.**

2 **Suggest why viruses can only live in other cells.**

Cell division

Human life begins as a fertilised egg cell, or **zygote.** This cell develops into an adult with trillions of cells. As new cell components are added, and the cell reaches a certain size, it divides by **mitosis**. Mitosis occurs in several other situations:

- to replace cells when they die or become damaged

- when single-celled, eukaryotic organisms reproduce by **asexual reproduction**, for example yeast
- when cancer cells divide
- when eukaryotic cells are cloned.

When an organism reproduces sexually, the sex cells, or **gametes**, cannot be produced by mitosis. If they were, the number of chromosomes in our cells would double every generation! We need another type of cell division, called **meiosis**.

3 Give three examples of situations in which mitosis occurs.

4 Name one type of cell that does *not* divide by mitosis.

Cell differentiation

Cells must become specialised for the development of complex, multicellular organisms.

Cells that can differentiate into other cell types are called stem cells. Embryonic stem cells, found after four to five days, can develop into *almost* any cell type. We can't say *'all'*, as they can't develop into cells of the **placenta**.

Stem cells have the potential to produce an unlimited amount of tissue for transplants. They are also important in medical research such as on how cells differentiate, and in the testing of drugs.

Stem cell research and treatments will require the cloning of cells. Some people object to the idea of these techniques for moral and ethical reasons.

Cancer cells divide uncontrollably by mitosis and do not differentiate into mature, specialised cells. Cancer cells early in the development of the disease can look almost normal, but in advanced cancers, differentiation in most cells is very limited.

5 Why are some news articles that suggest that embryonic stem cells can differentiate into all cell types, strictly speaking, incorrect?

6 Stem cells are being used to test new drugs. What are the advantages of using human stem cells over using rats to test drugs?

KEY SKILLS

For each chapter in the book, map out how different concepts you have learnt link with each other. Use a large sheet of paper or computer software.

Cells at work

Learning objectives:

- explain the need for energy
- describe aerobic respiration as an exothermic reaction.

KEY WORDS

active transport
aerobic
  respiration
exothermic
respiration

This runner is using energy to run a marathon. But we all need a continuous supply of energy – 24 hours a day – just to stay alive.

We need energy to live

Organisms need energy:

- to drive the chemical reactions needed to keep them alive, including building large molecules
- for movement
- for keeping warm

Energy is needed to make our muscles contract and to keep our bodies warm. It's also needed to transport substances around the bodies of animals and plants.

In other sections of the book, you will also find out that energy is needed:

- for cell division
- to maintain a constant environment within our bodies
- for **active transport**. Plants use active transport to take up mineral ions from the soil, and to open and close their stomata
- to transmit nerve impulses.

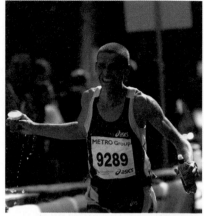

Figure 1.39 An average runner uses around 13 000 kJ of energy for a marathon.

1 List four uses of energy in animals.

2 List four uses of energy in plants.

Aerobic respiration

Respiration is the process used by all organisms to release the energy they need from food.

Respiration using oxygen is called **aerobic respiration**. This type of respiration takes place in animal and plant cells, and in many microorganisms.

Glucose is a simple sugar. It is the starting point of respiration in most organisms. The food that organisms take in is, therefore, converted into glucose.

This chemical reaction is **exothermic**. A reaction is described as exothermic when it releases energy. Some of the energy transferred is released as thermal energy.

Figure 1.40 Birds and mammals maintain a constant body temperature.

3 What is the purpose of respiration?

4 How do birds and mammals make use of the waste thermal energy?

Bioenergetics

This is the equation for aerobic respiration:

glucose + oxygen → carbon dioxide + water (energy released)

$$C_6H_{12}O_6 + 6O_2 \rightarrow 6CO_2 + 6H_2O$$

This equation describes the overall change brought about through each of a series of chemical reactions. A small amount of energy is actually released at each stage in the series.

The first group of steps occurs in the cytoplasm of cells, but most of the energy is transferred by chemical reactions in mitochondria.

5 Where and when does respiration occur?

6 Give one characteristic feature of actively respiring cells.

7 Why do we often get hot when we exercise?

Figure 1.41 Insect flight muscles have huge numbers of well-developed mitochondria.

DID YOU KNOW?

The muscle an insect uses to fly is the most active tissue found in nature.

COMMON MISCONCEPTIONS

Don't forget that *all* organisms respire. The equation is the reverse of photosynthesis, but don't confuse the two. Photosynthesis is the way in which plants make their food.

Living without oxygen

Learning objectives:

- describe the process of anaerobic respiration
- compare the processes of aerobic and anaerobic respiration
- explain how the body removes lactic acid produced during anaerobic respiration

KEY WORDS

anaerobic respiration
fermentation
oxygen debt

Stewart is a brewer. He adds yeast to a mixture of malted barley and hops in water.

Figure 1.42 Yeast converts sugar into alcohol, or ethanol. The process is completed in around 3 days.

Anaerobic respiration

The yeast respires using the sugary liquid. The yeast cells divide rapidly. After a few hours there are so many yeast cells that the oxygen runs out. The yeast is able to switch its respiration so that it can obtain energy *without* oxygen. Many microbes such as yeast can respire successfully without oxygen.

This is **anaerobic respiration** – respiration without oxygen.

Anaerobic respiration in yeast cells and certain other microorganisms is called **fermentation**.

Anaerobic respiration occurs in the cytoplasm of cells.

1 What is meant by anaerobic respiration?

2 Why do yeast cells switch from aerobic to anaerobic respiration in the process of making ethanol?

DID YOU KNOW?

Yeast is unable to use the starch in barley for respiration. Maltsters germinate the barley grains first to break down the starch into sugar.

Figure 1.43 Yeast cells divide rapidly by mitosis. Many of the cells do not separate from each other.

Baking

Yeast is also used in baking bread. Yeast is mixed with flour and some sugar. The ingredients are mixed together thoroughly and the dough is left to rise before baking it.

3 Explain why sugar is added to dough.

4 Why does the dough rise?

5 What happens to the alcohol made during bread production?

Figure 1.44 Dough is kneaded to mix the ingredients.

The biochemistry of fermentation

The equation for fermentation is:

glucose → ethanol + carbon dioxide (energy released)

Anaerobic respiration is much less efficient than aerobic respiration. It produces only around a nineteenth as much energy. This is because the oxidation of glucose is incomplete. But in situations where there's little oxygen, it means that cells can stay alive, and the amount of energy produced is still enough to keep single cells running.

Certain plant cells can also use alcoholic fermentation to obtain their energy. These include plants that grow in marshes, where oxygen is in short supply. Pollen grains can also respire anaerobically.

6 Explain why it is helpful for pollen grains to respire anaerobically.

7 Write down the equation for fermentation.

Oxygen debt

Without oxygen, we would die. But when actively contracting, our muscles run short of oxygen. They are able to respire anaerobically for short periods of time. Lactic acid, and not ethanol, is produced.

glucose → lactic acid (energy released)

The incomplete oxidation of glucose causes a build up of lactic acid and creates an **oxygen debt**. As a result, our muscles become fatigued and stop contracting efficiently.

KEY SKILLS

You must be able to compare aerobic and anaerobic respiration: the need for oxygen, the products and the amount of energy transferred.

HIGHER TIER ONLY

When the period of exercise is over, lactic acid must be removed. The body's tolerance of lactic acid is limited. It is taken to the liver by the blood, and either oxidised to carbon dioxide and water, or converted to glucose, then glycogen. Glycogen levels in the liver and muscles are then restored.

These processes require oxygen. This is why, when the period of activity is over, a person's breathing rate does not return to normal straightaway. Oxygen debt is the amount of oxygen required to remove the lactic acid, and replace the body's reserves of oxygen. Paying back the oxygen debt can take from a few hours, to several days after a marathon.

8 For anaerobic respiration in muscle, write down the word equation, then work out the symbol equation.

9 Compare anaerobic with aerobic respiration.

MATHS SKILLS

Size and number

Learning objectives:

* make estimates for simple calculations, without using a calculator
* be able to use ratio and proportion to calibrate a microscope
* recognise and use numbers in decimal and standard form.

The size of structures is important in biology, from whole organisms to molecules.

Estimating cell size

Accurate measurements are often essential. But estimating cell size or number is sometimes sufficient and may be quicker.

To estimate cell size, we can count the number of cells that fit across a microscope's field of view.

$$\text{Size of one cell} = \frac{\text{diameter of field of view}}{\text{number of cells that cross this diameter}}$$

If the field of view of this microscope, at this magnification, is 0.3 mm, or 300 µm, we can do a quick calculation without a calculator.

Each cell must be roughly (300 ÷ 5) µm, or 60 µm across. This is an approximation, but could be important.

1 **Suggest how to estimate the field of view of a microscope.**

2 **State one advantage of estimating cell size over exact measurement.**

Figure 1.45 In this image, *approximately* five cells fit across the field of view. We round numbers up or down to make calculations straightforward.

Measuring cell size

To make accurate measurements of cell size a scientist **calibrates** their microscope. A **graticule** – piece of glass or plastic onto which a scale has been drawn – is placed into the eyepiece of the microscope.

A stage micrometer is placed on the microscope stage. This is simply a microscope slide onto which an accurate scale has been etched.

In Figure 1.46, 36 divisions on the eyepiece graticule are equivalent to 100 µm on the stage micrometer: 1 division is equivalent to $\frac{1}{36}$ × 100 µm = 2.8 µm

The cell highlighted in the right-hand diagram is 20 eyepiece divisions across: the width of the cell = (20 × 2.8) µm = 56 µm.

DID YOU KNOW?

Scientists *estimate* cell or organism numbers when it is impossible or unnecessary to count them all.

REMEMBER!

The digital point remains fixed. It is the digits that move as a number is multiplied or divided by powers of 10. So, as a number gets larger, the digits move to the left (and vice versa).

3 **What would be the diameter of a cell that was 65 divisions on this graticule?**

4 **How many graticule divisions would a cell that was 35 μm across take up?**

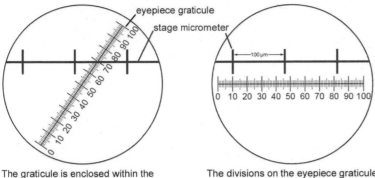

The graticule is enclosed within the eyepiece.
A stage micrometer is placed on the stage of the microscope.

The divisions on the eyepiece graticule and stage micrometer are lined up.

The calibrated eyepiece graticule can be used to make measurements of any cells or other structures viewed with that microscope

Figure 1.46 Calibrating, then using an eyepiece graticule

Numbers written in standard form

When writing and working with very large or very small numbers, it is convenient to use **standard form**. Standard form shows the magnitude of numbers as powers of 10.

Standard form numbers are written as: $A \times 10^n$

where: A is a number greater than 1 but less than 10. This could be a decimal number such as $A = 3.75$, or an integer number such as $A = 7$.
n is the index or power.

We use standard form with large numbers, small numbers and calculations. In standard form:

- when multiplying: multiply numbers and add powers (see example in Figure 1.47).
- when dividing: divide numbers and subtract powers.

Blood cell type	Width of an average cell in m
Lymphocyte (small)	7.5×10^{-6}
Macrophage	5.0×10^{-5}
Megakaryocyte	1.5×10^{-4}
Neutrophil	1.2×10^{-5}

The sizes of different types of blood cell, written in standard form.

5 **Look at the table of cell sizes. Arrange the cell types in descending order of size.**

6 **How many times larger is a megakaryocyte than a lymphocyte?**

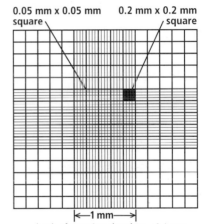

0.05 mm x 0.05 mm square

0.2 mm x 0.2 mm square

←1 mm→
depth of counting chamber = 0.1 mm

For a 0.2 × 0.2 mm counting chamber:

Dimensions:

top length: $0.2 \text{ mm} = 2.0 \times 10^{-1} \text{ mm}$
side length: $0.2 \text{ mm} = 2.0 \times 10^{-1} \text{ mm}$
depth: $0.1 \text{ mm} = 1.0 \times 10^{-1} \text{ mm}$

∴ volume of counting chamber =

add

$(2.0 \times 10^{-1}) \times (2.0 \times 10^{-1}) \times (1.0 \times 10t^{-1}) \text{ mm}^3$

multiply
$= 4.0 \times 10^{-3} \text{mm}^3$

Figure 1.47 Calculating the volume of a counting chamber. The counting chamber is a hollow on a microscope slide which holds a set volume of fluid. It has a grid ruled onto it, and a depth of 0.1 mm. The number of cells in a given volume can be calculated.

Check your progress

You should be able to:

describe the functions of the sub-cellular structures found in eukaryotic cells → understand the size and scale of cells and be able to use and convert units → carry out order of magnitude calculations when comparing cell size; calculate with numbers in standard form

calculate magnification of a light microscope using eyepiece and objective lens magnifications → calculate the magnification of a light or electron micrograph → explain limitations of light microscopy and advantages of electron microscopy

describe the structure of a prokaryotic cell → describe the differences between eukaryotic and prokaryotic cells → explain why scientists have now separated organisms into three domains using evidence from chemical analysis

recall that cells must divide for growth and replacement of cells → describe how chromosomes double their DNA and are pulled to opposite ends of the cell, before the cytoplasm divides, during mitosis → describe the events of the cell cycle and explain the synthesis of new sub-cellular components and DNA

recall that organism development is based on cell division and cell specialisation → explain the importance of differentiation and explain how cells are specialised for their functions → understand size and scale in the components of organ systems

recall where stem cells are found → understand the potential of stem cell therapies → evaluate scientific and ethical issues involved with stem cell therapies

recall that organisms can respire with oxygen (aerobic respiration) or without oxygen (anaerobic respiration) → use word equations to describe the processes of aerobic and anaerobic respiration → use symbol equations for aerobic and anaerobic respiration and be able to compare the two processes

Worked example

Some students see a newspaper article on a European stem cell clinic. The clinic uses stem cell therapy to treat diabetes and other conditions.

1 **What is a stem cell?**

An unspecialised cell that can differentiate, or can be made to differentiate, into many different cell types.

> The part about differentiation is important.

2 **The article contains some information on the clinic's treatment of diabetes.**

It includes data on the 55 patients the clinic has treated so far, which it claims is a success.

Type of diabetes	One month after treatment, number of patients who...		
	showed an improvement	showed no change	became worse
Type 1	8	13	2
Type 2	20	9	3
Total	28	22	5

a **Calculate the overall percentage of patients who:**

- showed an improvement   *50.9%*
- showed no change   *40%*
- became worse   *9.1%*

> The calculations are correct.
>
> The answers have not been recorded consistently, however. Think about significant figures. All the numbers in the table have a maximum of two figures, so you cannot have more in the answer.

b **Does the data support the newspaper article's claims? Explain your answer.**

My percentages show there is no difference between the overall percentage of patients who showed an improvement and those who did not.

The article is certainly untrue for Type 1 diabetes, where only 34.8% improved.

It might be true for Type 2, because 62.5% improved.

> The answer draws correct conclusions from the table and uses data to support these.
>
> With the small number of patients (23 for Type 1; 32 for Type 2), we cannot draw any firm conclusions from the small differences in numbers. Sample size is important in any scientific study.
>
> The heading of the table says 'one month after treatment...'. This may be too early to draw any conclusions. Also, the patients may believe they feel better because they've had treatment. Importantly, we do not know how the 'improvement' was judged, another point to make in your answer.

You will notice that this question draws on your knowledge of scientific methods as well as stem cells.

You may also have to use relevant knowledge from another topic.

When you've learnt about diabetes, you will be aware that Type 2 diabetes can usually be controlled by diet and exercise, so the 'improvements' suggested by the data may be the result of this.

End of chapter questions

Getting started

1 The diagrams below show an animal cell and a bacterial cell.

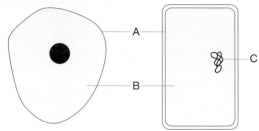

   a Name the cell part shown by:

     i A   `1 Mark`

     ii B   `1 Mark`

   b What is the name of chemical C?   `1 Mark`

     i cellulose   **iii** DNA

     ii chlorophyll   **iv** protein

   c What is the function of the nucleus?   `1 Mark`

2 Explain how you know that the cell shown here is a plant cell.   `2 Marks`

3 The diagrams below show some different objects. The length of each is included on the diagram. List them in order of size.   `1 Mark`

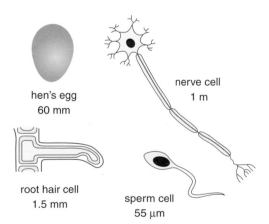

        hen's egg
        60 mm

                         nerve cell
                           1 m

        root hair cell
         1.5 mm

              sperm cell
              55 μm

4 A bacterium divides into two every 30 minutes.

   Starting with one bacterium, how many cells will there be after $1\frac{1}{2}$ hours?   `1 Mark`

5. **Gemma is using Feulgen stain to stain some dividing cells.**

   The label on the bottle of stain is shown.

   IRRITATING TO EYES,
   RESPIRATORY SYSTEM
   AND SKIN

   Explain two safety precautions she should take when using the stain.

   `2 Marks`

Going further

6. **Draw lines to match the two cell structures with their function.**

   `1 Mark`

Cell structure	Function

   Cell structure: Mitochondrion, Ribosome

   Function: Controls what enters and leaves cells, Respiration, Protein synthesis

7. **Use words from the box to complete the word equation for aerobic respiration.**

   `1 Mark`

alcohol	carbon dioxide	glucose	lactic acid

   .... + oxygen → .... + water   (+ energy)

8. **Explain how the features of a sperm cell help it to fertilise an egg cell.**

   `2 Marks`

9. **A scientist is investigating the effect of different sugars on the anaerobic respiration of yeast.**

   carbon dioxide collects
   in gas syringe

   plunger

   plunger is pushed out

   5 cm³ of yeast suspension
   + 25 cm³ of 10% sugar solution

   **She measures the volume of carbon dioxide produced over a 2-hour period.
   She investigates two types of sugar: sucrose and lactose.**

a **Suggest ways in which she can be sure that the readings she takes are the result of using the two different types of sugar and not from other factors.** `4 Marks`

b **Her results are shown below.** `2 Marks`

Type of sugar	Volume of carbon dioxide produced (cm³)						
	Time (min)						
	0	20	40	60	80	100	120
sucrose	0	0.2	1.8	5.6	7.6	7.9	7.9
lactose	0	0	0	0	0	0	0

Suggest reasons for the scientist's results.

More challenging

10 **Give the names of the *two* forms of tumour.** `1 Mark`

11 **Write down the name of the technique that could be used to produce embryonic stem cells from a person's body cells.** `1 Mark`

12 **Explain why mitosis is important in plants and animals.** `2 Marks`

13 **Below are some data on the link between viruses and neck cancer over a number of years.**

Year	Percentage of neck cancer cases where virus DNA was detected in tumours
1965	20
1975	23
1985	28
1995	57
2005	68

Plot a graph of the data. Connect the points with a smooth curve. `4 Marks`

14 **Gemma is using Feulgen stain to stain some dividing cells. One of the images she sees is shown in the micrograph.** `2 Marks`

Describe what is happening in the micrograph.

Most demanding

15 Describe how anaerobic respiration differs from aerobic respiration.

2 Marks

16 Some companies offer to store the stem cells found in the umbilical cord of a new born baby. These stem cells can be used for transplants or therapy for blood diseases. Suggest two possible advantages of using stem cells from an umbilical cord over using stem cells from bone marrow.

2 Marks

17 The graph below shows the correlation between colon cancer incidence and daily meat consumption. What conclusions can you draw from the graph? Evaluate the evidence for meat consumption affecting the incidence of colon cancer in females.

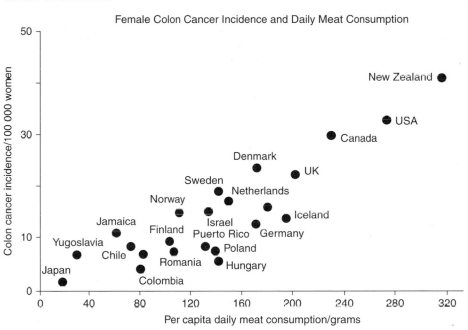

6 Marks

Total: 40 Marks

PHOTOSYNTHESIS

PLANT CELLS ARE ADAPTED TO CARRY OUT THEIR FUNCTIONS.

- Plants have adaptations that allow them to survive and grow, such as air pores in the leaves.
- Cells have specific adaptations so that they can carry out a specialised function in the plant.
- Photosynthesis happens in the mesophyll cells in leaves. Water is absorbed through root hair cells.

PLANTS MAKE THEIR FOOD WITH THE HELP OF SUNLIGHT.

- Green plants use water and minerals from the soil to grow. They use light, carbon dioxide and water to produce carbohydrates in their leaves by photosynthesis.
- The amount of photosynthesis can be affected by a range of different factors.
- The useful product of the photosynthesis reaction is glucose.

light from Sun

PHOTOSYNTHESIS IN CELLS

oxygen released into the air via the stomata

water from soil taken in through root hair cells on roots

carbon dioxide enters the leaf from the air via the stomata

PLANTS CAN MOVE NUTRIENTS AND WATER TO WHERE THEY ARE NEEDED.

- Plants have a network of vessels that transport water and minerals to their leaves and flowers.
- All cells contain watery cytoplasm. Plants need water so that the chemical reactions needed to sustain life can occur.

THE STRUCTURE OF A LEAF ALLOWS MOLECULES TO BE TAKEN IN FROM THE ENVIRONMENT, AND TO BE PASSED OUT.

- Diffusion is the movement of molecules from a higher concentration to a lower concentration until they are equally distributed.
- Substances that plants need diffuse into the plant. Other substances pass out of plants by diffusion.

film of water

spongy mesophyll cells

lower epidermis

carbon dioxide enters leaf due to low concentration inside

guard cell

wax cuticle

IN THIS CHAPTER YOU WILL FIND OUT ABOUT:

HOW DO PLANTS' SPECIAL ADAPTATIONS HELP THEM SURVIVE AND GET ALL THEY NEED FROM THE ENVIRONMENT?

- Adaptations of cells and tissues in leaves allow them to photosynthesise efficiently.
- Stomata are adapted to control the exchange of gases.
- Cells and tissues in leaves, stems and roots are designed for the maximum exchange of substances in and out of the plant.

WHAT FACTORS AFFECT THE PHOTOSYNTHESIS REACTION? HOW DO THEY AFFECT IT?

- The useful products of photosynthesis are simple carbohydrates, for example glucose and sucrose.
- Different environmental factors interact to limit the rate of photosynthesis in different habitats at different times.
- The environment in which plants are grown can be artificially manipulated.

HOW IS THE SUPPLY OF WATER TO A PLANT AFFECTED BY ENVIRONMENTAL CONDITIONS?

- There are two transport systems in plants: xylem transports water up the plant and phloem transports substances up and down the plant.
- Water movement through the plant is affected by different environmental factors.
- Water loss in plants is a consequence of adaptations for photosynthesis.

DIFFUSION ALSO ALLOWS SUBSTANCES TO PASS IN AND OUT OF CELLS. WHICH SUBSTANCES DIFFUSE INTO PLANTS?

cross-section of part of leaf

air spaces

high concentration of oxygen

low concentration of carbon dioxide

carbon dioxide diffuses in through stomata

oxygen diffuses out through stomata

- Different factors that affect the rate of diffusion in plant systems.
- Concentration gradients can affect the rate of photosynthesis.
- Substances move in and out of the leaf during different processes, for example, photosynthesis, respiration and transpiration.

Explaining photosynthesis

Learning objectives:

- identify the raw materials and products of photosynthesis
- describe photosynthesis using an equation
- explain gas exchange in leaves.

Plants and algae are amazing organisms. They transfer energy from outer space into chemical energy in glucose. Without plants, there would be no life! How do plants harness this energy?

Describing the process

Photosynthesis is the chemical reaction that plants use to produce glucose, so essentially, they are able to make their own food. Photosynthesis needs two raw materials:

- carbon dioxide (absorbed through leaves)
- water (absorbed through roots and transported to leaves).

The reaction also needs light and **chlorophyll** in the leaves. The equation is:

$$\text{carbon dioxide} + \text{water} \xrightarrow{\text{light} + \text{chlorophyll}} \text{glucose} + \text{oxygen}$$

$$6CO_2 + 6H_2O \longrightarrow C_6H_{12}O_6 + 6O_2$$

This is an endothermic reaction. It requires energy in the form of light.

The products of photosynthesis are **carbohydrates**, for example, glucose and starch. When iodine solution is added to a leaf, it will turn blue/black if starch is present. If starch is present, it shows that photosynthesis has happened.

DID YOU KNOW?

Some leaves have green parts and yellow/white parts. They are called variegated leaves. Variegated leaves only photosynthesise in the green parts where the chlorophyll is found.

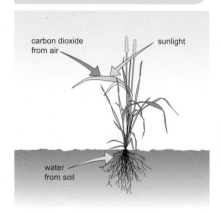

Figure 2.1 A plant needs light, water and carbon dioxide for photosynthesis.

1. Leaf in boiling water to soften it.

2. Leaf in methylated spirits (removes chlorophyll).

3. Leaf washed. Few drops of iodine solution added.

4. Blue/black colour indicates starch produced by photosynthesis.

Figure 2.2 Testing a leaf for starch

Oxygen is made during photosynthesis and released into the air. It is a waste product on which animals depend.

1. Which raw materials are used in photosynthesis and what are the products of the reaction?

2. A leaf was tested for starch. The iodine solution stayed orange.

   a What does this tell you about the leaf?
   b Suggest what conditions it was kept in.

Gas exchange in leaves

Leaves take in carbon dioxide from the air and release oxygen when they photosynthesise. This is called gas exchange.

Some students investigated gas exchange in leaves. They used the same sized leaf in Tubes 1 and 2 and left them in a rack in bright light for an hour. Look at their method in the table.

Tube	Control	Tube 1	Tube 2
Set up		aluminum foil	
	2 cm^3 hydrogencarbonate indicator		
Results	no change in colour	turns yellow	turns red

Figure 2.3 Investigating gas exchange in leaves

Hydrogencarbonate indicator is an orange solution.

- In more acidic conditions it turns yellow.
- In less acidic conditions it turns red.

Carbon dioxide dissolves in water to form an acidic solution.

3. Describe the results of the investigation and explain why a control was used.

4. Explain what the results tell you.

5. Why are light and chlorophyll needed for photosynthesis?

6. Predict what would happen to the hydrogencarbonate indicator if you removed the aluminium foil. Explain your answer.

COMMON MISCONCEPTION

Remember: light does not make food, but light is needed for the reactions to occur.

Looking at photosynthesis

KEY WORDS

endothermic
veins

Learning objectives:

- explain the importance of photosynthesis
- explain how plants use the glucose they produce.

Plants make carbohydrates (for example, sucrose and glucose) and oxygen when they photosynthesise. The plants release the oxygen that they do not need.

Learning about photosynthesis

Photosynthesis is a series of reactions that require energy. Reactions that need energy are called **endothermic** reactions. You will learn more about endothermic reactions in chemistry. In photosynthesis, energy is transferred from the environment to the chloroplast by light.

76.7 kg of plant

2.3 kg of plant

5 years pass only water is provided

90.7 kg of soil

soil is then dried and weighed

90.6 kg of soil

Figure 2.4 What do the results of van Helmont's investigation show?

Early scientists thought that plants grew just by using minerals in the soil.

In 1600, Jan Baptist van Helmont showed that the increase in the mass of a willow tree was not just due to the soil minerals.

In 1771, Joseph Priestley put a plant in a glass container with a lit candle (to use up the oxygen). He then left the investigation for 27 days. Priestley found the candle then burned again. This showed that oxygen was present again.

COMMON MISCONCEPTION

Leaves look green because they only reflect the green light. They do not absorb green light for photosynthesis.

1. What did van Helmont's investigation show?

2. How could you investigate whether plants need light to photosynthesise?

Using sugars

Glucose and sucrose molecules produced by photosynthesis are used in a number of ways. Sugars are soluble molecules that dissolve to be transported to wherever they are needed. **Veins** transport sugar to parts of plants shown in Figure 2.5 that do not photosynthesise.

Glucose is used by cells for respiration. Plants cannot make glucose at night so it is converted into insoluble starch for when it is needed. Starch is the main energy store in plants. It is found in every cell, where it is used for respiration in low light levels or the dark.

Plant cells respire sugars to provide energy, and produce carbon dioxide and water. The energy released is used for chemical reactions in cells, for example:

- building glucose into starch for storage
- building sugars into cellulose for cell walls
- combining sugars with nitrate ions and other minerals to make amino acids for protein synthesis
- building fats and oils for storage.

3 When and why do plants respire?

4 List five ways that plants use glucose.

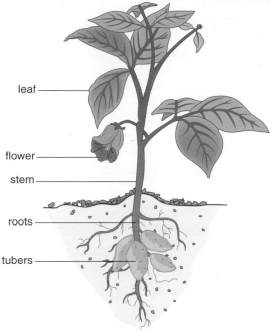

Figure 2.5 Why do plant organs need glucose?

starch is insoluble and is made up of many glucose molecules joined together

glucose molecules are soluble

Figure 2.6 Starch is a large molecule and glucose is a small molecule.

Plant respiration

Oxygen is a waste product of photosynthesis. When plant cells respire they use some of this oxygen. Plants respire continually, as they need a constant supply of energy to keep them alive.

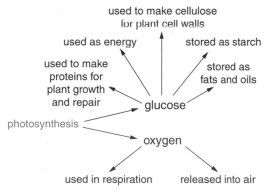

Figure 2.7 How plants use the products of photosynthesis

The rest of the oxygen is released through the stomata, back into the air.

5 Explain the relationship between photosynthesis and respiration in leaves.

6 Explain what is incorrect about the statement 'plants make oxygen for us to breathe'.

DID YOU KNOW?

Some sea slugs eat algae but do not digest it fully. The algae photosynthesise inside the slugs to give them more food and energy.

KEY INFORMATION

Stomata are tiny opening structures found on the outer leaf skin layer. Stomata consist of two specialised guard cells that surround the stoma, a tiny pore (hole).

Investigating leaves

Learning objectives:

- identify the internal structures of a leaf
- explain how the structure of a leaf is adapted for photosynthesis
- recall that chloroplasts absorb energy from light for photosynthesis.

Leaves work to manufacture glucose. Chloroplasts in leaves absorb the light needed for photosynthesis. How do the organelles inside the leaf work together to do this?

The structure of a leaf

Leaves of green plants are plant organs that are adapted to allow them to photosynthesise efficiently. Most leaves:

- are broad, with a large surface for light to be absorbed
- are thin, so that carbon dioxide has a short distance to diffuse
- have **vascular bundles** (veins). These support the leaf and transport:
  › water to the leaf
  › glucose away from the leaf.

1 How does the shape of a leaf help photosynthesis to happen?

2 What is the function of vascular bundles?

Inside the leaf

Figure 2.8 shows the internal structure of a leaf. Each part has a specific function.

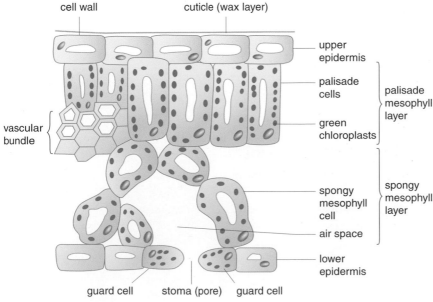

Figure 2.8 A diagram of a vertical section through a leaf

The upper surface is covered by a cuticle to protect it. Under the cuticle are layers of different cells:

- **epidermal tissues** cover the leaf, letting light penetrate
- **palisade mesophyll** carries out photosynthesis, absorbing most of the light
- **spongy mesophyll** has air spaces for diffusion of gases
- lower epidermal tissue protects the underside of the leaf.

Chloroplasts in the mesophyll are where light is absorbed for photosynthesis.

The lower epidermis has small pores called stomata. Each stoma allows gases to diffuse in and out of the leaf.

3 Describe the function of mesophyll cells.

4 Explain why leaf cells contain chloroplasts but root cells do not.

5 Why is the cuticle thin, transparent and waxy?

Adaptations for effective working

Using a microscope, look at a slide of a section through a leaf.

Identify the layers of cells. Calculate the magnification you used.

Each type of leaf cell has features that make it adapted for its function.

Figure 2.9 A micrograph of a section through a leaf. Compare what you can see here with the diagram in Figure 2.8.

> **DID YOU KNOW?**
>
> Meristem tissue is found at the growing tips of roots and shoots. It differentiates into different types of plant cells.

Layer	Adaptation	Function
upper epidermal tissue	thin and transparent waxy cuticle	allows light to pass to the mesophyll to protect the leaf and stop water loss
palisade mesophyll	regular-shaped cells, arranged end-on, near upper surface; most chloroplasts at the top of the cells	absorb the maximum amount of light possible
spongy mesophyll	irregular-shaped cells; many air spaces	increases surface area for CO_2 absorption; allows gases to diffuse
lower epidermal tissue	many stomata; surrounded by guard cells	allow gases to diffuse; guard cells open and close stomata
vascular bundles	contain xylem and phloem tubes	transport substances around the plant

6 Suggest why stomata are found on the lower epidermal tissue.

7 Explain how the adaptations of the palisade mesophyll allow it to photosynthesise efficiently.

REQUIRED PRACTICAL

Investigate the effect of light intensity on the rate of photosynthesis using an aquatic organism such as pondweed

KEY WORDS

photosynthesis
hypothesis
chloroplasts
mesophyll cells

Learning objectives:

- use scientific ideas to develop a hypothesis
- use the correct sampling techniques to ensure that readings are representative
- present results in a graph.

Photosynthesis is the process by which green plants produce food. When plants photosynthesise they absorb light to power the reaction. The equation for photosynthesis is:

$$\text{carbon dioxide} + \text{water} \xrightarrow{\text{light}} \text{glucose} + \text{oxygen}$$
$$6CO_2 + 6H_2O \longrightarrow C_6H_{12}O_6 + 6O_2$$

These pages are designed to help you think about aspects of the investigation rather than to guide you through it step by step.

Developing a hypothesis

Laura and Amy are investigating how light intensity affects the rate of **photosynthesis** in pondweed. They will measure how much gas is released by the pondweed in 1 minute when they put a lamp at 10 cm, 15 cm, 20 cm, 25 cm and 30 cm away from the beaker containing the pondweed.

Before they begin the investigation they are going to make a **hypothesis**. Hypotheses are developed using previous knowledge or observations. Laura and Amy know that:

- photosynthesis produces glucose and oxygen
- the oxygen will be released as bubbles of gas in the water
- light is absorbed by chlorophyll found in the **chloroplasts** in the **mesophyll cells**
- photosynthesis can be limited by different factors.

Figure 2.10 An oxygenating plant photosynthesising

1. **When will the light intensity be greatest?**

2. **How will increasing the light intensity affect the rate of photosynthesis?**

3. **When the rate of photosynthesis increases, what will happen to the amount of oxygen produced?**

4 What other variables could affect this investigation?

5 Suggest a hypothesis for the investigation that Laura and Amy are going to do.

Improving accuracy

Amy and Laura decided that they would check that their data were repeatable by taking repeat readings at each light intensity. Look at their results.

Distance of lamp from pondweed (cm)	Number of bubbles per minute		
	Test 1	Test 2	Test 3
10	105	121	124
15	58	50	54
20	26	30	32
25	15	17	16
30	12	13	14

6 What do you notice about the results in Test 1 compared with the results in Tests 2 and 3?

7 Suggest why this happened.

8 Suggest what Laura and Amy should do with the Test 1 results.

9 Why is it important to take repeat readings when carrying out investigations?

Presenting results

Amy and Laura used a table to record their results because it was quick and the results were organised, but they found it difficult to analyse them in this form. Their teacher said that they should think of a better way to present their results to help them. Laura thought that using a bar chart would be the best method but Amy disagreed. She presented her results as a line graph.

10 Which would be the correct way to present these results? Explain why.

11 Plot the graph of Amy and Laura's results using only Test 2 and Test 3 data.

Increasing photosynthesis

Learning objectives:

- identify factors that affect the rate of photosynthesis
- interpret data about the rate of photosynthesis
- explain the interaction of factors in limiting the rate of photosynthesis.

Plants grow faster in summer than in winter. This means that they must produce more food to allow them to grow in summer. Some factors can increase the rate of photosynthesis.

DID YOU KNOW?

Pine trees grow in a cone shape to expose more needles to the sun, increasing the rate of photosynthesis.

Plants in different habitats

Plants are found in every ecosystem, but their size, appearance and adaptations mean that they look very different. Tropical rainforests have dense plant life. In contrast, few plant species grow in **tundra** (Arctic regions with permanently frozen subsoil) and desert regions.

Figure 2.11 What are the environmental conditions in these habitats?

1. **How would you describe the environmental conditions in tropical forest, tundra and desert ecosystems?**

2. **Suggest how the conditions you have described affect photosynthesis in each habitat.**

Limiting factors

Some students investigated the effect of light on the rate of photosynthesis. Look at their results (Figure 2.12). The students found that:

- Between A and B, the rate of photosynthesis increases as the light intensity increases. Because the rate depends on the light intensity, light intensity is called the **limiting factor**.
- Between B and C, increasing the light intensity has no effect on the rate of photosynthesis. Another factor is now the limiting factor.

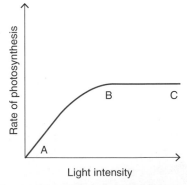

Figure 2.12 Can you explain the shape of the graph between B and C?

KEY INFORMATION

Remember that enzymes denature at temperatures greater than 40 °C.

3 What other factors might limit the rate of photosynthesis between B and C?

Plants need carbon dioxide to photosynthesise but there is only 0.04% in the atmosphere. It is often the limiting factor that controls the rate of photosynthesis.

Carbon dioxide levels around plants rise when there is no light. This is because the plants are respiring but not photosynthesising. As light levels increase, the plants use the carbon dioxide up.

HIGHER TIER ONLY

Interacting limiting factors

Over one day, light, temperature and carbon dioxide levels change. Carbon dioxide may be the limiting factor when plants are crowded on a sunny day. Temperature may be the limiting factor in cooler months. Light may be the limiting factor at dawn.

Plants living in continual shade can adapt. They have a higher ratio of leaves to roots than other plants. The leaves are thinner, have a larger surface area and contain more chlorophyll to absorb light. A shortage of chlorophyll can limit the rate of photosynthesis.

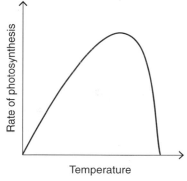

Figure 2.13 Explain what this graph shows.

Figure 2.14 Photosynthesis in normal (A) and shade-adapted (B) leaves

The graph shows that shade-adapted leaves (B) are more efficient at absorbing low-intensity light than normal leaves (A).

4 Suggest the limiting factors for photosynthesis over one complete warm summer's day.

5 Describe and explain adaptations for photosynthesis shown by some shade-tolerant plants.

6 Suggest one advantage and one disadvantage of a tree having needles rather than flat, broad leaves.

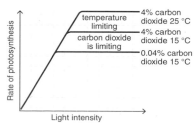

Figure 2.15 In the laboratory, we can see how different factors work in combination.

Increasing food production

Learning objectives:

- explain how factors that increase food production can be controlled
- evaluate the benefits of manipulating the environment to increase food production
- understand and use the inverse square law in the context of light intensity and photosynthesis.

Farmers use their knowledge of the limiting factors of photosynthesis to increase crop *yields*. How can this be done? How do they change the factors?

HIGHER TIER ONLY

Greenhouses

Growing crops in greenhouses gives a large yield for a given area. This is intensive farming. Conditions in the greenhouse can be controlled to optimise the rate of photosynthesis. Greenhouses protect plants from weather conditions and from being damaged or eaten by animals.

shades removed from ceiling to allow maximum light

ventilation

carbon dioxide source

heater

watering system

Figure 2.17 A greenhouse system

Figure 2.16 Why are dull cold days in winter not good for growing plants?

- Sunlight heats up the inside of greenhouses, causing the temperature to rise.
- A carbon dioxide source can be used to increase the concentration of the gas.
- Paraffin heaters are used in greenhouses. As the fuel inside them burns, they produce carbon dioxide. They can also be used to increase the temperature on cooler days and nights.
- Watering systems deliver a regular supply of water.
- Blinds can be used to control the amount of light.
- Humidifiers are used to add moisture to the air.

1 Why do many greenhouses have vents in the roof?

2 Explain why paraffin heaters are used in greenhouses.

3 How do greenhouses increase yield?

Optimising conditions

Farmers need to grow large fruits and vegetables without excessive leaf or root production. By optimising photosynthesis, and reducing effects of limiting factors, farmers can increase yields of crops. Using technology, commercial greenhouses increase yields by over twenty times, compared with traditional farming.

Glucose produced by photosynthesis that is not used for respiration, or stored, in the form of starch, is converted to other essential molecules such as cellulose, and amino acids and proteins. Mineral ions are required for these conversions. The mineral ions provided to plants can be optimised using a technique called **hydroponics**. Plants are grown in nutrient-rich liquid medium, which can be formulated for the type of plant, supported on a material such as rock wool.

Figure 2.18 Hydroponics is growing plants in mineral nutrient solutions, without soil.

Computer systems control conditions.

- Nutrients are monitored and concentrations adjusted as needed.
- Temperature is controlled by sensors to within 0.1°C.
- Weather detection systems monitor external conditions and adjust vents and blinds to suit.
- Floors are covered in white plastic to reflect light.
- The glass used has a low iron content to ensure maximum light levels, and even the metal supports are as thin as possible.
- Special lights are used to increase the hours of light. These are switched off for about 7 hours, allowing plants to transport the glucose that has been made.

4 What are the benefits and drawbacks of changing conditions inside a greenhouse?

KEY INFORMATION

Remember that greenhouses optimise carbon dioxide concentrations, light levels, water levels, temperature and nutrient availability.

DID YOU KNOW?

The biggest threats to crops in commercial greenhouses are viruses. Workers wear protective clothing to prevent contamination of plants.

Inverse square law

As the distance between the light source and a photosynthesising plant increases, the light intensity will decrease. This is described as being an inverse relationship. Light intensity obeys the **inverse square law**. The inverse square law states that if the light distance is doubled, the light intensity decreases by the square of the distance.

For example, if the distance between the light source and the plant is doubled, the light intensity is quartered (see Figure 2.19).

5 Look back at Amy and Laura's data on page 67. Draw a graph of rate of photosynthesis against $1/d^2$.

Figure 2.19 Light intensity obeys the inverse square law: if the distance between the light source and the plant is doubled, the light intensity is quartered.

KEY CONCEPT

Diffusion in living systems

Learning objectives:

- describe the conditions needed for diffusion to occur
- calculate and compare surface area to volume ratios
- explain how materials pass in and out of cells.

KEY WORDS

passive transport
random
concentration gradient
equilibrium

In all living organisms, the transfer of many materials occurs by the process of diffusion. Diffusion is essential in living systems in the supply of important substances and in the control of certain processes.

Diffusion in living systems

Diffusion is sometimes called **passive transport**. This is because it happens due to the **random** motion of particles. No energy is required.

All that is needed for diffusion to happen is a **concentration gradient**. Diffusion can be defined as the net movement of particles from an area of high concentration to an area of lower concentration due to the random movement of particles, until **equilibrium** is reached. This is the point at which the net movement of the particles stops changing.

1 **What effect do you think increasing the concentration gradient will have on the speed of diffusion?**

2 **What other factors will affect the speed of diffusion?**

Photosynthesis and diffusion

Leaf cells need carbon dioxide for photosynthesis and oxygen for respiration. The waste products of these processes must leave the leaf cells too.

high concentration

low concentration

Figure 2.20 In diffusion, particles move from a higher concentration to a lower concentration.

Carbon dioxide diffuses into leaves through the stomata. During photosynthesis, the palisade cells use carbon dioxide; the concentration of carbon dioxide in the leaf is low but the concentration outside the leaf is relatively high. This results in a large concentration gradient, and carbon dioxide diffuses into the leaf.

The rate of diffusion in living systems can be increased by:

- increasing the surface area
- decreasing the distance the particles have to travel
- increasing the concentration gradient.

External conditions can also affect the rate of diffusion.

- Wind increases the concentration gradient of carbon dioxide between inside and outside, and the rate of diffusion increases.
- High humidity decreases the concentration gradient of water vapour between the inside and outside of the leaf, and diffusion slows down.

3 **Explain how oxygen produced during photosynthesis passes out of the leaf.**

4 **Look back at section 2.3, 'Investigating leaves'. How are leaves adapted for maximum diffusion? Explain why this is important.**

5 **How does external temperature affect the rate of diffusion from a leaf?**

Diffusion and cells

Cells are made largely of water containing many dissolved substances. These substances and water enter and leave the cells through cell membranes. Cell membranes allow some particles through, but block others. They are called *partially (or selectively) permeable membranes.*

Cells need continual supplies of dissolved substances, for example, oxygen and glucose, for cellular activities. Waste products, for example, carbon dioxide, need to be removed. To enter or leave a cell, dissolved substances have to be small enough to pass through the partially permeable cell membrane. Diffusion allows this to happen.

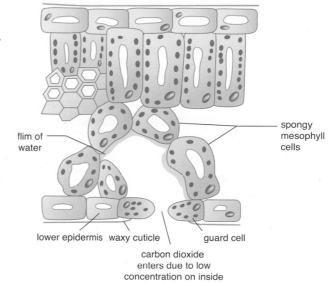

Figure 2.21 Why are the stomata spaced out?

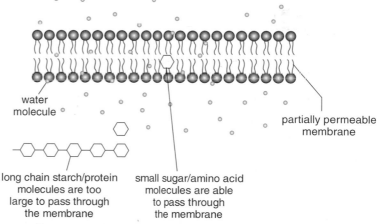

Figure 2.22 A cell membrane model. What is happening to the particles?

Cell membranes are similar to football nets. Large footballs cannot pass through the netting, but small golf balls easily pass through. In the same way, large particles, for example, starch, cannot pass through the cell membrane. However, small glucose particles can pass through the membranes easily. Cell membranes are very thin to allow substances to diffuse through them easily.

6 **Explain how materials pass in and out of cells. Use a diagram to help you.**

7 **Will diffusion ever stop completely? Explain your answer.**

Looking at stomata

Learning objectives:

- describe transpiration in plants
- describe the function of stomata
- explain the relationship between transpiration and leaf structure.

KEY WORDS

guard cell
transpiration
xylem

Gases continually pass in and out of leaves through tiny openings found on the lower surface of each leaf. The openings are called stomata. They control the exchange of gases in plants. Do all leaves have the same concentration of stomata?

Water movement in plants

Plants absorb water from soil through root hairs. The water passes into the root, up the stem and into the leaves. Water on the surface of the spongy mesophyll evaporates and diffuses out of leaves via the stomata. This movement of water through the plant and leaves is called **transpiration**.

Transpiration rate is affected by temperature, light availability, wind and humidity.

1. What is transpiration?

2. Describe the path of water through a plant.

3. Predict what conditions will cause the rate of transpiration to increase.

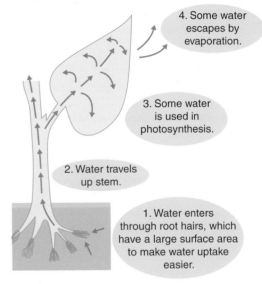

4. Some water escapes by evaporation.

3. Some water is used in photosynthesis.

2. Water travels up stem.

1. Water enters through root hairs, which have a large surface area to make water uptake easier.

Figure 2.23 Where does the water in the leaf come from?

Transpiration

Plants need a constant flow of water. Water is transported in tubes called **xylem** in the veins. Evaporation of water from the leaf causes water to be drawn up the plant, just like a child sucking through a straw. Transpiration is important because:

- evaporation of water cools leaves
- water is a reactant in photosynthesis
- cells full of water support the plant
- water carries dissolved materials around the plant.

If too much water is lost through the stomata, plants may wilt and die. Surrounding each stoma are two **guard cells**. Guard cells open and close to control the exchange of gases and water loss.

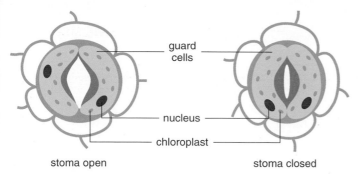

Figure 2.24 Open and closed stomata

4 **Predict why stomatal density may differ for different species.**

Figure 2.25 Make stomatal impressions of two different leaves using clear nail varnish. Use a microscope to calculate the stomatal density of each leaf.

The effect of adaptations

A disadvantage of stomata is that while they are open for gas exchange, water loss occurs. Leaves are broad and thin to increase surface area. Water only has a short distance to diffuse out.

Marram grass grows on beaches. It has rolled leaves with thick cuticles and stomata are sunk into pits. Interlocking hairs hold water vapour. These features all reduce water loss.

5 **Explain how water loss in plants is a result of the adaptations for photosynthesis.**

6 **Explain how marram grass is adapted to prevent water loss.**

DID YOU KNOW?

Water lilies have stomata on the upper leaf surface so that they are not under water.

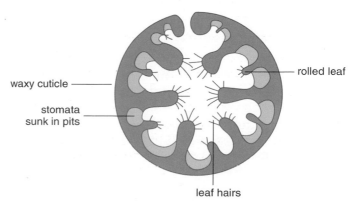

Figure 2.26 Marram grass grows on exposed sand dunes. What conditions have the greatest effect on transpiration?

Moving water

Learning objectives:

- describe the structure and function of xylem and roots
- describe how xylem and roots are adapted to absorb water
- explain why plants in flooded or waterlogged soil die.

KEY WORDS

lignin
lumen
phloem
translocation
xylem

Plants do not have a heart or blood, but they still need a transport system to move food, water and minerals to every cell. The roots, stem and leaves form a plant organ system for the transport of substances.

Transport systems

Plants have two transport systems:

- **xylem** tissue carries water and minerals from the roots around the plant, especially to the leaves
- **phloem** tissue transports dissolved sugars made in the leaves around the plant. This is called **translocation**.

Xylem and phloem are found in continuous vascular bundles.

Water enters plants through the roots. Root hair cells near the root tip have hair-like projections that grow between soil particles to absorb water.

1 Why is water needed in the leaves?

2 What are the functions of xylem and phloem?

3 State what is meant by translocation.

COMMON MISCONCEPTION

Many students confuse xylem and phloem. Remember that **phloem** carries **food**.

Adaptions for transport

Roots are narrow structures with a large surface area. Root hair cells also increase the surface area for water absorption. The water has only a short distance to travel to the xylem to be moved up and around the plant (Figure 2.27).

Xylem tubes are made from long cells with thick, reinforced walls containing **lignin**. This makes them strong. The cell walls are waterproof, which makes the cells die. The contents and end walls break down to form a vessel with a hollow centre or **lumen**. Water and minerals flow through the tubes. Xylem cells form the wood in a tree.

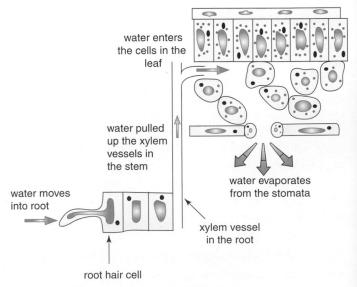

Figure 2.27 Use a microscope to observe root hair cells.

Figure 2.28 shows the vascular bundles (xylem and phloem) in the different parts of the plant.

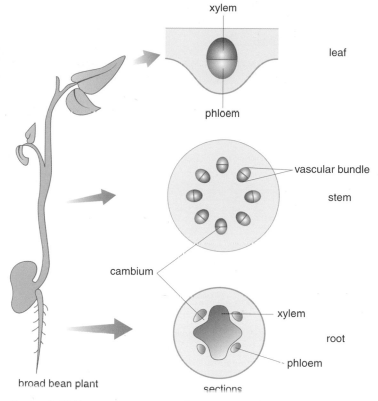

Figure 2.28 Use a microscope to draw sections through a root, stem and leaf to show xylem and phloem.

4 How are root hairs adapted to absorb water?

5 How is xylem adapted for its function?

Water effects

Healthy plants balance water uptake and loss. If plants lose water faster than it is replaced, they wilt. Wilting protects the plant. Leaves droop and hang down to reduce the surface area for water loss by evaporation. The stomata close and photosynthesis stops to prevent water loss. The disadvantage is that the plant may overheat. Plants stay wilted until they get water, the temperature drops or the Sun goes off them.

Plants can have too much water. Waterlogged soil contains very little air. This means that the root cells do not receive the oxygen they need for respiration. They die and rot if the waterlogging lasts a long time.

6 Describe the changes in a plant that help to prevent water loss.

7 A plant grown in a pot with no drainage is prone to dying. Explain why this might happen.

Figure 2.29 Why has this plant wilted?

DID YOU KNOW?

Plant transport systems are found in the bark of trees. Some animals chew this away, causing the tree to die because it cannot transport water and glucose to where it is needed.

Investigating transpiration

Learning objectives:

- describe how transpiration is affected by different factors
- explain the movement of water in the xylem.

KEY WORDS

potometer

Water is an essential constituent of all plant tissues. Plants absorb large amounts of water but only use 2–5% of it for metabolic processes. Why do plants lose so much water?

Environmental factors and transpiration

Water for photosynthesis is transported to leaves in xylem vessels. Diffusion out of the spongy mesophyll causes a film of water to cover the cell surfaces. Water evaporates into the spaces between cells and the water vapour moves along the concentration gradient towards the stomata, and escapes from the leaf. When transpiration increases, water uptake by the plant increases.

Factors that increase the rate of transpiration are:

- an increase in temperature
- an increase in wind speed
- a decrease in humidity.

When plants photosynthesise, the stomata are open to allow carbon dioxide to diffuse into the leaf. Factors that increase photosynthesis will increase transpiration.

Some students investigated how light intensity affected the rate of transpiration (Figure 2.31).

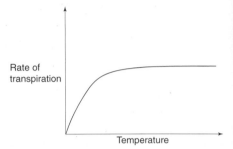

Figure 2.30 How does temperature affect transpiration rate?

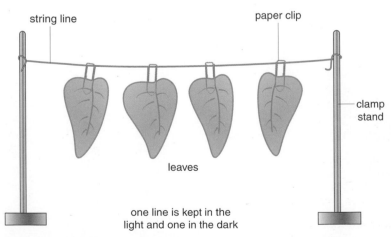

Figure 2.31 Experiment to show the effect of light on transpiration

1   **In Figure 2.31, why were leaves put in the dark and the light?**

2   **What measurements could the students take?**

3   **Predict what you think will happen to the leaves that are put in the dark, and those put in the light. Give a reason for your prediction.**

How plants control water loss

Potometers are used to measure the uptake of water by plants in different conditions. The movement of the air bubble in the tube shows how much water is taken up.

Different plants control water loss in different ways:

- waxy cuticle: in hot environments it can be very thick
- most stomata are on the underside of leaves, protected from environmental factors
- needle-like, spiny or rolled-up leaves
- stomata in pits on the leaf surface.

4 Describe an experiment to show that transpiration rate is affected by air movement.

5 Describe what happens to transpiration rate as humidity decreases.

6 Describe how a leaf is adapted to reduce water loss.

Explaining changes in transpiration

On still days when water vapour diffuses out of the leaf, the diffusion and evaporation concentration gradients decrease until the water vapour concentrations inside and outside the leaf are equal and transpiration stops.

On windy days, water vapour is blown away. The concentration gradients are maintained and the transpiration rate increases.

Figure 2.32 A potometer

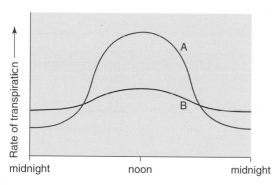

Figure 2.33 Explain how light intensity affects the rate of transpiration for plant A and plant B.

7 Explain how the structure of a leaf is adapted to reduce water loss.

8 Why is water uptake rate not the same as transpiration rate?

9 Predict and draw graphs to describe and explain how transpiration rate is affected by:

a cold conditions   c dull cloudy conditions

b windy conditions   d still, humid conditions.

10 'Plants grow best in cooler, cloudy and humid conditions because they lose less water.' Discuss this statement. Do you agree with it? Explain why.

Moving sugar

Learning objectives:

- describe the movement of sugar in a plant as translocation
- explain how the structure of phloem is adapted to its function in the plant
- explain the movement of sugars around the plant.

KEY WORDS

companion cells
sieve plates
translocation

Sugars are needed by all cells for respiration. They are transported from the leaves for immediate use or storage. Amino acids are needed by all growth areas.

Phloem vessels

Phloem cells are elongated, thin-walled living cells that form columns or tubes.

The movement of sugars in plants is called **translocation.** Translocation happens in the phloem. Cell sap containing sugars and amino acids is moved from where these substances are produced to where they are needed.

1 Why are carbohydrates and proteins transported as sucrose and amino acids in the phloem vessels?

2 What is translocation?

The structure of phloem vessels

The end cell walls of phloem cells do not break down, but they do have many small pores in them. These perforated walls are called **sieve plates**.

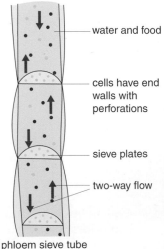

phloem sieve tube

Figure 2.34 How is phloem different from xylem? Make a model of phloem cells.

Figure 2.35 Use a microscope to observe and draw phloem tubes.

Phloem cells contain cytoplasm but have no nucleus. They have a **companion cell** next to them. The companion cell controls the activities of the phloem but does not help with translocation. Substances in phloem vessels are moved by a process that requires energy.

Substances are transported in any direction in the phloem. Glucose made by photosynthesis is converted into a complex sugar called sucrose. Sucrose and amino acids are transported to all tissues in the plant. Different tissues use the substances in different ways.

3 Describe the structure of phloem cells.

4 Compare and contrast phloem and xylem cells.

How are phloem tubes adapted for their function?

Phloem tubes have:

- companion cells with a nucleus and many mitochondria, which provide the energy needed to move substances in the phloem
- limited amounts of cytoplasm and no nucleus, to allow efficient movement of substances
- perforated sieve plates to allow the movement of substances through the phloem
- two-way flow of substances so that they are transported all over the plant.

5 Design a diagram to show how the plant uses the glucose made in photosynthesis.

6 Why do phloem tubes have companion cells?

7 Explain the function of the sieve plates.

KEY INFORMATION

Phloem is living, has thin walls and has sieve plates. Xylem is dead, has strengthened walls and no sieve plates.

DID YOU KNOW?

The strings that go up and down the length of bananas are phloem vessels.

MATHS SKILLS

Surface area to volume ratio

Learning objectives:

- be able to calculate surface area and volume
- be able to calculate surface area to volume ratio
- know how to apply ideas about surface area and volume.

KEY WORDS

ratio
sphere

In science, we use mathematical skills to help us understand what is happening. Surface area to volume ratio is very important in living things.

Finding the area of a surface

Alveoli provide a large surface area for gas exchange between the air and the bloodstream. If our lungs were smooth on the inside, like balloons, the surface area would be much less and materials would not be exchanged fast enough.

We can calculate surface area in different ways. For a rectangular shape, we multiply the length by the width. For example, an area of skin 4 cm long and 7 cm wide has a surface area of (4 cm × 7 cm) = 28 cm².

Living things are not generally made up of regular shapes, such as rectangles, so we have to use other ways of finding the area. One way is to use squared paper and to count how many squares are covered (or are largely covered) by the specimen.

Figure 2.36 Elephants have wrinkled skin to increase their surface area.

KEY INFORMATION

Note that both the length and the width have to be measured in the same units and that the answer is in those units, squared.

 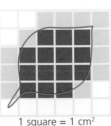

1 square = 1 cm²   1 square = 1 cm²

Figure 2.37 Counting squares that are largely covered is (approximately) balanced by not counting squares that are slightly covered.

1. Estimate the surface area of the leaf in Figure 2.38.

2. Calculate the surface area of:
   a a piece of tree bark that is 30 cm long and 3 cm wide
   b a razor shell that is 50 mm long and 8 mm wide.

Figure 2.38 One square is 1 cm².

Working out the volume

It is easier for warm-blooded animals to keep warm on cold days if their volume is large, but then it is harder for these same animals to lose heat on a hot day. We calculate the volume of a cube by multiplying length by width by height. A die with a side of 2 cm has a volume of (2 cm × 2 cm × 2 cm) = 8 cm³. Again, all the distances need to be in the same units and the volume is also in those units, cubed.

3 **What Is the volume of:**
a **a science laboratory 10 m wide, 15 m long and 3 m high?**
b **a block of wood 2 cm wide, 3 cm long and 4 cm high?**

4 **Finding the volume of a tree branch is tricky, but one way is to immerse the branch in a tank full of water. Suggest how the volume is measured.**

Surface area to volume ratio

In science it is useful to compare the surface area with the volume. We do this by finding the **ratio** of one compared with the other. To find the ratio, divide the surface area by the volume. For example, for a cube with sides 2 cm long:

surface area = 2 cm × 2 cm × 6 = 24 cm²;
volume = 2 cm × 2 cm × 2 cm = 8 cm³;
surface area to volume ratio = 24:8 = 3:1

The shape of an organism also affects its surface area to volume ratio. **Spheres** have the smallest surface area compared with their volumes. Many small mammals have a shape that is almost spherical – for example, a mouse – and puppies and kittens curl up into a ball to sleep. As small animals, they want to minimise their surface area to volume ratio so as to minimise heat loss.

5 **Compare how surface area, volume, and surface area to volume ratio change as the size of a cube increases. Use cubes with sides of 1, 2, 3, 4, 6 and 8 cm.**

6 **Imagine the shapes below are animals. Look at A, B and C in Figure 2.39.**

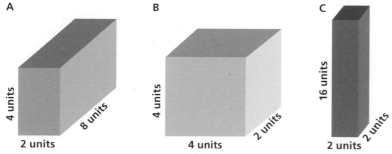

Figure 2.39 What do you notice about the surface area to volume ratios of these 'animals'?

Which animal will have problems keeping:
a **cool? Explain your answer.**
b **warm? Explain your answer.**

7 **Devise a method to measure the volume of the air you breathe out in one breath.**

Check your progress

You should be able to:

☐ use the word equation to describe photosynthesis → ☐ recall and use the symbol equation for photosynthesis → ☐ recall and use the balanced symbol equation for photosynthesis

☐ know that chloroplasts absorb light and convert it to chemical energy → ☐ describe the use of light and chloroplasts in photosynthesis → ☐ explain that chloroplasts absorb energy to drive chemical reactions

☐ understand that photosynthesis is an endothermic reaction → ☐ explain why photosynthesis is an endothermic reaction

☐ understand that plants respire and photosynthesise → ☐ explain why plants carry out respiration → ☐ describe the difference in gas exchange in plants between day and night

☐ name the factors that affect photosynthesis → ☐ describe how the rate of photosynthesis can be increased → ☐ explain the effects of limiting factors on photosynthesis

☐ identify the parts of a leaf and their function → ☐ describe how leaves are adapted for efficient photosynthesis → ☐ explain how the leaf's structure is adapted for photosynthesis

☐ know the definition of diffusion → ☐ explain diffusion using the idea of particles → ☐ explain how substances pass in and out of cells

☐ describe how water travels in plants → ☐ describe adaptations in xylem and phloem → ☐ explain adaptations of xylem and phloem

☐ describe experiments on the rate of transpiration → ☐ describe how different factors affect transpiration → ☐ explain how different factors affect transpiration

☐ recall that the movement of sugars is called translocation → ☐ describe how proteins and carbohydrates are transported in plants → ☐ explain how concentration gradients affect processes

Worked example

Laura is growing tomatoes in her greenhouse.

Laura knows that to increase her crop of tomatoes, she must increase photosynthesis.

1 **Complete the equation for photosynthesis.**

$$CO_2 \; + \; H_2O \; \rightarrow \; C_6H_{12}O_6 \; + \; H_2O$$

> Water (H_2O) has been correctly identified as a reactant, but has also been given as the product. The equation has not been balanced. The correct answer is:
> $$6CO_2 + 6H_2O \rightarrow C_6H_{12}O_6 + 6O_2$$

2 **Laura heats her greenhouse. She wants to know the best temperature to grow the tomatoes. Look at the graph.**

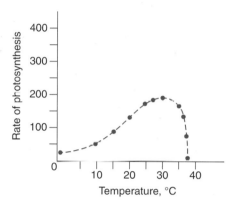

Explain what the graph shows.

The rate increases from 5–30°C and then decreases to 0 at 37°C because the enzymes denature.

> The pattern has been given (increases and then decreases) and the explanation for the decrease in rate is correct.
>
> An alternative answer would be to explain that the rate increases from 5–30°C as the enzymes gain more energy or collide more often.

3 **What is the best temperature for Laura to grow the tomatoes?**

30 °C

> Correct answer given.

How does water for photosynthesis get to the leaves?

Through the xylem by osmosis.

> One correct answer is given (xylem).
>
> A better answer would be '…by transpiration'.

4 **Laura notices that when she turns the heaters up, she needs to water the plants more often. Explain why.**

More water evaporates.

> One correct answer is given
>
> Another answer could be: Transpiration increases because more water evaporates through the stomata.

End of chapter questions

Getting started

1   **a**   Why do plants photosynthesise?

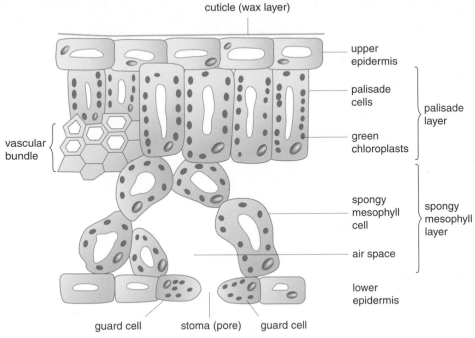

cuticle (wax layer)

upper epidermis

palisade cells

palisade layer

green chloroplasts

vascular bundle

spongy mesophyll cell

spongy mesophyll layer

air space

lower epidermis

guard cell   stoma (pore)   guard cell

b   What structures inside plant cells absorb energy from light?

c   What is the name of the solution used to test leaves for starch?

d   What type of cells carry dissolved sugars around the plant?

e   What are the products of photosynthesis?

2   Jenna is investigating the effect of light on leaf growth. To do this she needs to calculate the surface area of each leaf.

    a   Estimate the surface area of this leaf:

1 square = 1 cm^2 1 square = 1 cm^2

Jenna's results are shown below:

Leaf	South facing tree (most sun)	North facing tree (most shade)
	Area (cm³)	
1	14.0	29.0
2	18.0	19.5
3	13.5	28.0
4	21.5	29.5
5	15.5	23.0
Mean	16.5	

b Calculate the mean area for the north facing tree.   `1 Mark`

c Explain the difference in the results.   `2 Marks`

Going further

3 Give two uses of sugars in plants.   `1 Mark`

4 Describe how xylem vessels are adapted to their function.   `2 Marks`

5 Give a disadvantage of growing crops in greenhouses.   `1 Mark`

6 Why does Sally put her tomato plants in a greenhouse?   `4 Marks`

7 A scientist measured water uptake and transpiration in a tree over 18 hours. The graph shows her data.

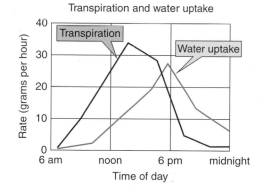

a Transpiration is highest between 1 and 2pm. When is water uptake highest?   `1 Mark`

b What conclusion can you make about water loss and uptake in this tree?   `1 Mark`

More challenging

8 **a** If you are investigating the effect of light intensity on the rate of
photosynthesis, what other variables must you control? `2 Marks`

 b Draw a diagram to show how you could measure the effect of light intensity
on photosynthesis using equipment you would find in a school laboratory.
Show how you would set up the equipment and label each part. `2 Marks`

9 The images below show plants growing in the Sahara Desert in Africa.

Explain the adaptations that these Saharan plants have that allow them to
survive in this extreme environment. `6 Marks`

Most demanding

10 Write the balanced equation for photosynthesis. `2 Marks`

11 Suggest two reasons why loss of water is important for a plant. `2 Marks`

12 Some students were investigating how light intensity affects the rate of photosynthesis. The graph shows their results:

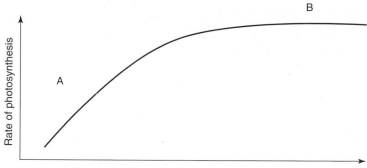

a Explain what is happening at A and at B.

2 Marks

b Predict what would happen if the temperature was increased from 25 °C to 35 °C. Give reasons for your prediction.

2 Marks

c Explain the relationship between light intensity and distance from the light source.

2 Marks

Total: 40 Marks

MOVING AND CHANGING MATERIALS

IDEAS YOU HAVE MET BEFORE:

MOLECULES MOVE BY DIFFUSION.

- Molecules in gases and liquids move from a high concentration to a lower concentration until all areas have an equal concentration.
- Different factors can affect the rate of diffusion.
- The steepness of a concentration gradient affects the rate of diffusion.

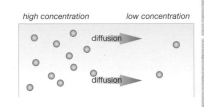

ANIMALS AND PLANTS TRANSPORT SUBSTANCES TO WHERE THEY ARE NEEDED.

- There are two transport systems in plants: xylem transports water up the plant from the roots to the leaves, and phloem transports substances up and down the plant.
- The circulatory system moves substances around the body in the blood.

BLOOD IS USED TO TRANSPORT OXYGEN TO BODY TISSUES.

- Oxygen is taken from the lungs to the body. Carbon dioxide is returned from the body to the lungs.
- The function of the heart is to pump blood around the body.
- Blood is made up of red blood cells, white blood cells, plasma and platelets.

ENZYMES ARE IMPORTANT FOR THE REACTIONS THAT OCCUR IN OUR BODY.

- Enzymes speed up reactions inside the body.
- Different enzymes are used to speed up different reactions.
- The digestive system uses enzymes to digest food.

IN THIS CHAPTER YOU WILL FIND OUT ABOUT:

DO ALL MATERIALS MOVE BY DIFFUSION?

- Water moves from a high concentration of water to a lower concentration of water in living tissues by osmosis.
- The movement of water can affect the turgidity of living cells.
- Some substances that living cells need can be moved against a concentration gradient.

WHY DO SOME ORGANISMS NEED ORGAN SYSTEMS?

- Size affects the ability and efficiency of diffusion alone to supply cells with nutrients.
- Membrane surfaces and organ systems are specialised for exchanging materials to ensure that all body cells get the nutrients that they need.
- An example of an efficient exchange surface is root hair cells in plants.

DO ALL ORGANISMS MOVE MATERIALS IN THE SAME WAY?

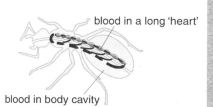

blood in a long 'heart'

blood in body cavity

- Small organisms do not have specialised organs for gas exchange or transport of some materials.
- Fish and mammals have evolved specialised exchange surfaces for gaseous exchange.
- Fish and mammals have specialised transport systems.
- The heart is an efficient pump for the transport system.

HOW DO ENZYMES WORK?

- All reactions in cells are controlled by enzymes.
- The lock-and-key and collision theories are used to explain enzyme function and specificity.
- There are specific enzymes in the digestive system; their action is affected by different factors.
- The small intestine is adapted to make it an efficient exchange surface.

Explaining water movement

Learning objectives:

- describe how water moves by osmosis in living tissues
- identify factors that affect the rate of osmosis
- explain what the term 'partially permeable membrane' means.

Some examples of substances that are transported in and out of cells by diffusion are carbon dioxide and oxygen. Living cells contain a lot of water. How does water move in and out of cells?

The diffusion of water

Osmosis is the diffusion of water through a **partially permeable membrane**. Partially permeable membranes have tiny holes in them.

A solution is dilute when there is a high water concentration. A dilute sugar solution has a high water concentration (the solvent) and a low sugar concentration (the solute). A solution is concentrated when there is a low water concentration. Most solute particles are too large to pass through the partially permeable membrane, but water molecules can pass through. Osmosis is the diffusion of water molecules from a dilute solution to a concentrated solution through a partially permeable membrane.

dilute solution (high water concentration)   partially permeable membrane   concentrated solution (low water concentration)

Key ⦾ water molecule   ⬤ solute

Figure 3.1 Describe the movement of water particles.

1 How does water move in and out of living cells?

2 Suggest why potatoes become soft when boiled.

Osmosis and cells

Look at the diagram in Figure 3.2.

In (a) the cell has a concentrated solution. Water molecules enter by osmosis from the surrounding dilute solution.

In (b) the cell has a dilute solution. Water molecules move out to the surrounding concentrated solution.

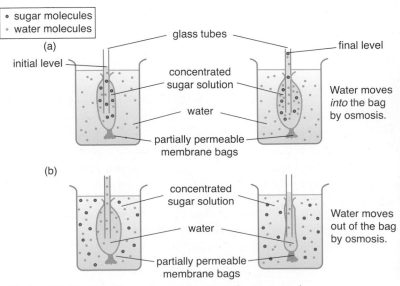

- sugar molecules
- water molecules

(a)

glass tubes

initial level

final level

concentrated sugar solution

water

Water moves *into* the bag by osmosis.

partially permeable membrane bags

(b)

concentrated sugar solution

water

Water moves out of the bag by osmosis.

partially permeable membrane bags

Figure 3.2 Model cells can be used to investigate osmosis.

Living cells must balance their water content to work efficiently. Chemical reactions in cells use water. If the cytoplasm becomes concentrated, water enters by osmosis. If the cytoplasm becomes too dilute, water leaves the cell by osmosis.

Problems occur in animal cells when the external solution is more dilute than that inside the cell. Water enters; the cells swell and may burst.

When the external solution is more concentrated than that inside the cell, water moves out by osmosis. The cell shrinks and shrivels.

Plant cells have inelastic cell walls. Water enters the cell by osmosis and fills the vacuole. This pushes against the cell wall, making the cell **turgid.**

If water moves out of the cell by osmosis, the vacuole shrinks and the cell becomes **flaccid.**

If too much water leaves the cell, the cytoplasm moves away from the cell wall.

Figure 3.3 What will happen if red blood cells are placed in a very dilute or a very concentrated solution?

Figure 3.4 Explain the movement of water in these plant cells.

3 **How are osmosis and diffusion similar and different?**

4 **Describe how osmosis affects animal cells.**

Explaining osmosis

Water molecules and sugar molecules in a solution move around randomly. When a sugar molecule hits the membrane, it bounces away. When a water molecule hits the membrane, it can pass through a hole to the other side.

In the Figure 3.5, there are more water molecules on the left, so more water molecules can pass through the membrane to the right-hand side than can pass in the opposite direction. The water molecules move both ways, but the net movement is from left to right.

5 **Explain why there are differences in the effects of water on plant and animal cells.**

6 **Explain osmosis.**

> **REMEMBER!**
>
> **Osmosis is only the movement of water across a partially permeable membrane. No other molecules move by osmosis.**

Figure 3.5 Water particles move both ways across the membrane.

> **DID YOU KNOW?**
>
> Giant redwood trees grow to over 90 m tall. The water pressure in the cells and the strong, lignified cell walls keep the plant upright.

REQUIRED PRACTICAL

Investigate the effect of a range of concentrations of salt or sugar solutions on the mass of plant tissue

KEY WORDS

osmosis
partially permeable
  membrane
plasmolysed

Learning objectives:

* use scientific ideas to develop a hypothesis
* plan experiments to test a hypothesis
* draw conclusions from data and compare these with hypotheses made.

Osmosis regulates the water content in living cells. Maintaining the internal concentration of a cell is important so that necessary reactions to keep the cell alive can take place.

These pages are designed to help you think about aspects of the investigation rather than to guide you through it step by step.

Developing a hypothesis

Gill and Aidan are going to investigate the effect of putting onion cells into water and then into salt solution. They will examine the cells through a microscope. If the cell is short of water the cytoplasm comes away from the cell wall. It is said to be **plasmolysed**.

Before they do the investigation they are going to produce a hypothesis. Hypotheses need to be developed using previous knowledge or observations. They know that:

* the concentration gradient between the solutions inside and outside a cell causes water to move by **osmosis**
* water moves towards a higher solute concentration through a **partially permeable membrane**
* the salt solution is more concentrated than the cytoplasm in the onion cells.

REMEMBER!

You choose how to change the independent variable and measure the changes in the dependent variable.

1. When the onion cells are put in water, how will the concentration inside the cell compare with that outside?

2. When the cells are put into salt solution, how will the concentration inside the cell compare with that outside?

3. When the cells are put into salt solution, in which direction will the water move?

4. Suggest a hypothesis for the experiment that Gill and Aidan are about to do.

Planning an investigation

Lily and Ahmed investigated the effect of a range of salt solutions on potato cylinders. They weighed the cylinders, placed them in salt solutions of various concentrations and then reweighed them. Before they reweighed the potato cylinders, they carefully dried them using a paper towel.

5 What were the independent and dependent variables in the investigation?

6 Why did Lily and Ahmed dry the potato cylinders?

7 Lily and Ahmed collected these results:

Concentration of NaCl solution (mol dm^{-3})	Starting mass (g)	Final mass (g)	Change in mass (g)	Percentage change in mass (%)
0.00	15.9	17.0		
0.15	19.2	20.1		
0.30	24.1	23.3		
0.45	20.7	19.2		
0.60	24.1	22.0		
0.75	14.9	13.5		

a Complete the table by calculating the change in mass and percentage change in mass of each cylinder.

b Are any of the results anomalous?

c How should anomalous results be dealt with?

d Why do Lily and Ahmed use percentage change in mass?

e Suggest what conclusion Lily and Ahmed can make from this data.

Evaluating the experiment

Lily and Ahmed had written a hypothesis before they did their experiment. They thought that 'the more concentrated the salt solution was that the potato was put in, the greater the loss of mass from the potato would be'.

8 What conclusion would you draw from their data?

9 Was their hypothesis proved or disproved?

10 Explain why they got the result that they did.

Learning about active transport

KEY WORDS

active transport

Learning objectives:

- describe active transport
- explain how active transport is different from diffusion and osmosis
- explain why active transport is important.

Diffusion and osmosis explain how gases and water move down a concentration gradient to enter (and sometimes exit) living things. Minerals are taken up into the root hair cells of a plant by another method.

Active transport

Cells can absorb substances that are at low concentration in their surroundings by **active transport**. These substances move against the concentration gradient, for example, when plants absorb nitrate ions through their root hairs from the soil water. The concentration of nitrate ions in soil water is usually less than the concentration of nitrate ions inside the root hair cells.

Nitrate ions naturally diffuse down their concentration gradient, out of the cell and into the soil, but plants transport the nitrates into their cells using active transport.

Active transport moves substances from a more dilute solution to a more concentrated solution (against a concentration gradient). This requires energy from respiration.

1 **Describe how minerals are absorbed by plants.**

2 **How is active transport different from diffusion and osmosis?**

More active transport

Investigations have shown that a plant can absorb different minerals in different amounts. The plant can select which minerals it needs. Look at the graph. Algae absorb a lot of chlorine, but only a little calcium in comparison.

In 1938, scientists discovered that an increase in mineral uptake by a plant happened at the same time as an increase in its respiration rate. This shows that the process needs energy – because the minerals are absorbed against the concentration gradient.

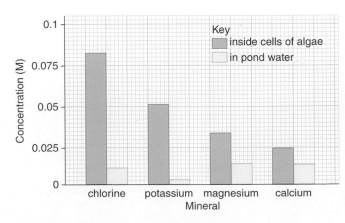

Figure 3.6 What does the graph show?

The greater the rate of cellular respiration, the more energy is available for active transport to happen.

Different cells use active transport for different purposes:

- Marine fish have cells in their gills that can pump salt back into the salty sea water.
- Cells in the thyroid gland take in iodine to use in the production of hormones.
- Cells in the kidney reabsorb sodium ions from urine.
- The villi in the small intestine absorb glucose and amino acids into the blood.
- Crocodiles have salt glands in their tongues that remove excess salt from their bodies.

3 **Suggest how cells that carry out active transport are adapted to do this.**

4 **Explain why it is important for a plant to transport actively only the minerals that it needs.**

Figure 3.7 Villi in the small intestine

Figure 3.8 Explain the relationship between active transport and respiration.

	Substances moved:	Conditions:	Requirements:	Energy needed:
Diffusion	any dissolved substance or any gas	high concentration to low concentration	down a concentration gradient	No
Osmosis	water	dilute solution to concentrated solution	through a partially permeable membrane	No
Active transport	dissolved substances	more dilute solution to more concentrated solution	against a concentration gradient through a partially permeable membrane	Yes

KEY CONCEPT

Investigating the need for transport systems

Learning objectives:

- describe how the size of an organism affects the rate of diffusion
- explain how changes in conditions affects the rate of diffusion
- explain the need for exchange surfaces and transport systems using surface area to volume ratio.

> **KEY WORDS**
>
> surface area
> exchange surfaces

Many chemical reactions happen inside living cells. Substances must enter the cell to fuel these reactions and the waste products of the reactions need to be removed. Larger cells have greater chemical activity, so need more substances, for example, nutrients and oxygen, and more substances have to be removed, for example, carbon dioxide.

Size matters

Most cells are no more than 1 mm in diameter. This is because in small cells nutrients, oxygen and waste substances can diffuse quickly in and out. As the volume of a cell increases, the distance between the cytoplasm at the centre of the cell and the cell membrane increases. In cells bigger than 1 mm diameter, the rate of exchange with the surrounding environment may be too slow for diffusion to meet the cell's needs. The cell would probably not survive.

Figure 3.9 Which will have the faster diffusion rate?

1 How does the size of a cell affect the chemical activity inside the cell?

2 Describe one chemical activity that takes place in cells.

Looking at surface area to volume ratio

The **surface area** of a cell affects the rate at which particles can enter and leave the cell.

The volume of the cell affects the rate of chemical reactions within the cell (how quickly materials are used in reactions and how fast the waste products are made).

Look at the diagram. The cubes represent cells.

- Cubes have 6 faces, so the surface area = length × width × 6
- the volume of a cube = length × width × height
- surface area to volume ratio = surface area ÷ volume

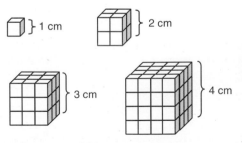

Figure 3.10 Cubes of increasing size

3 Calculate the surface area, volume and surface area to volume ratio (SA:V) for each of the cubes. Cube A has been done for you.

Cube	Number of internal cubes	Surface area (cm²)	Volume (cm³)	SA:V
A	1	6	1	6
B	8			
C	27			
D	64			

KEY INFORMATION

The feathery projections in a fish's gills are used to increase surface area. Water is continually taken in through the mouth and forced over the gills to maintain the concentration gradient.

4 What happens to the surface area and volume as the size increases?

5 What happens to the surface area to volume ratio as the size increases?

6 What does a decrease in surface area to volume ratio make it more difficult to do?

Transport systems and exchange surfaces

With a small surface area to volume ratio, multicellular organisms need surfaces and organ systems specialised for exchanging materials. Once an organism is multicellular and has several layers of cells, the oxygen and nutrients take longer to diffuse in and are all used up by the outer layers of cells. Exchange systems allow transport into and out of all cells for the organism's needs. As well as exchanging substances, cells also have to lose thermal energy fast enough to prevent overheating.

To function efficiently, **exchange surfaces** need the following features:

- a large surface area to maximise exchange
- a thin membrane to provide a short diffusion path
- a method of transporting substances to and from the exchange site, for example, a blood supply to carry nutrients around the body, and lungs to take oxygen into the body.

7 How are efficient exchange surfaces adapted to carry out their function?

8 Explain why large organisms need transport systems but small organisms do not.

Organism		SA:V
bacterium		6 000 000
amoeba		60 000
fly		600
dog		6
whale		0.06

Explaining enzymes

Learning objectives:

- describe what enzymes are and how they work
- explain the lock-and-key theory
- use the collision theory to explain enzyme action.

KEY WORDS

biological catalyst
collision theory
denatured
lock-and-key theory
metabolism
optimum

Chemical reactions happen all the time. *Metabolism* **describes all the reactions in a cell or the body. The energy transferred by respiration in cells is used for the continual enzyme-controlled processes of metabolism that synthesise new molecules.**

A special catalyst

A catalyst is a chemical that speeds up a reaction without being used up itself. This means it can be reused. Different reactions need a different catalyst.

Enzymes are **biological catalysts**. Enzymes catalyse most chemical reactions that happen in cells, for example, respiration, protein synthesis and photosynthesis. Enzymes help to:

- break down large molecules into smaller ones
- build large molecules from smaller ones
- change one molecule into another molecule.

1 **What is an enzyme?**

2 **Explain what enzymes do in a living organism.**

How do enzymes work?

Enzymes are large protein molecules made from folded, coiled chains of amino acids. Each enzyme has a unique sequence of amino acids. The active site, the area that attaches to the substrate (reactant), has a very specific shape that fits its substrate exactly. Enzymes catalyse specific reactions due to the shape of their active site.

Figure 3.11 The **lock-and-key theory** is a simple explanation of how enzymes work.

Only one type of substrate can fit into the active site of an enzyme, like a key fits into a lock. Once the substrate is attached to the active site, it is changed into a product.

If the shape of the active site changes, the enzyme is **denatured** and cannot catalyse the reaction. This is an irreversible change. The enzyme cannot work because the substrate cannot fit into the active site.

Enzyme-controlled reactions are affected by:

* pH
* temperature.

Every enzyme has an **optimum** pH and an optimum temperature, and these vary from one enzyme to another. Above or below these levels, the rate of reaction will slow down. Extremes of pH or temperature can denature an enzyme.

KEY INFORMATION

Enzymes are chemicals. They are not living and, therefore, cannot be killed. They are denatured.

Figure 3.12 Graphs to show how (a) pH and (b) temperature affect the rate of the washing powder enzyme reaction. What is the optimum pH for the reaction in (a)?

3 **Biological washing detergents contain enzymes. Explain why clothes washed at 60 °C will not be as clean as those washed at 40 °C.**

4 **How does the lock-and-key theory explain the specificity of enzymes?**

Explaining enzyme action

Look at the graph in Figure 3.13. It shows the amount of product produced during an enzymic reaction.

1 Reactants start to collide; as collisions increase more product is made.

2 Enzyme is added, holding the reactant in place.

3 There is an increase in collisions between the reactants: the rate of reaction also increases.

4 Reactants are being used up and there are fewer collisions, so the rate of reaction decreases and the amount of product made levels off.

This is known as **collision theory**.

5 **Use the collision theory (Figure 3.13) and particle diagrams (Figure 3.11) to explain how enzymes work.**

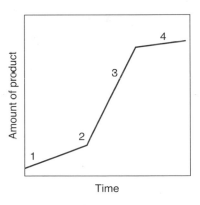

Figure 3.13 How do enzymes affect a reaction?

DID YOU KNOW?

Some bacteria live in hot springs. Their enzymes have an optimum temperature of over 80 °C. Other bacteria live on the ocean floor. Their enzymes have optimum temperatures of below 0 °C.

REQUIRED PRACTICAL

Investigate the effect of pH on the rate of reaction of amylase enzyme

Learning objectives:

- describe how safety is managed, apparatus is used and accurate measurements are made
- explain how representative samples are taken
- make and record accurate observations
- draw and interpret a graph from secondary data using knowledge and observations.

Amylase is an enzyme that controls the breakdown of starch in our digestive systems. Starch turns a blue-black colour when iodine (an orange solution) is added.

Making accurate measurements and working safely

In this investigation digestion is modelled, using solutions of starch and **amylase** in test tubes, to find the optimum pH required for the reaction. Amylase and **starch** solution are each added to a different test tube and put in a water bath or a beaker of water at 25 °C and left for 5 minutes. The pH buffer solution is added to the amylase, before adding the starch. To carry out this method, small volumes of chemicals and enzymes (less than 10 cm³) must be accurately measured. To do this a 10 cm³ measuring cylinder or a 10 cm³ calibrated dropping pipette could be used.

The iodine test is used to indicate the presence of starch. Iodine solution is added to the food being tested and if starch is present the result is a strong blue/purple colour. The investigation involves taking samples from the mixture at timed intervals and adding them to **iodine solution** in a spotting tile. To do this a glass rod or a dropping pipette could be used. The time at which the solution no longer turns a blue-black colour with iodine solution (the iodine solution remains orange) is recorded.

The procedure is repeated for buffer solutions of different pH values.

> These pages are designed ❶ to help you think about aspects of the investigation rather than to guide you through it step by step.

starch
amylase
water

Figure 3.14

Drop of starch/amylase mixture added at zero time

Spotting tile containing drops of iodine solution

Figure 3.15

❶ **Which piece of apparatus would you use to:**

    a   measure small volumes accurately?
    b   add drops of solution to the iodine?

② To calculate the time taken for the reaction to occur, the teacher has told the students to count the drops of iodine solution used. Explain how this is an accurate measurement of the time taken.

③ Give two safety precautions that should be taken when doing the investigation.

Planning your sampling

Tom carries out a trial run of the procedure before starting his investigation. Tom found that at pH7 the colour change took 40 seconds to happen. He then decided when to take samples of the solution.

④ What colour will Tom see in the spotting tile when all the starch has been broken down by the amylase?

⑤ Explain why Tom will need to take continuous samples throughout his investigation.

⑥ Why did Tom carry out a trial before starting the investigation?

⑦ From the result of the trial run, suggest suitable time intervals for Tom to take the continuous samples in his investigation.

Using results to draw and interpret a graph

Tom completed the investigation. He sampled the test solutions every 10 seconds. The table shows his data.

pH of solution	Time for colour change to occur (seconds)		
	Test 1	Test 2	Test 3
5	150	160	160
6	70	70	80
7	40	50	40
8	80	80	60
9	130	90	140

Tom decided to draw a graph of the data in his table to make it easier for him to see trends in the data.

⑧ Should Tom draw a bar chart or a line graph? Give a reason for your answer.

⑨ Tom repeated each pH test three times.

   a Why did he repeat the tests?
   b Tom thought he had an anomalous result. Which result do you think it was?
   c What should Tom do with the anomalous result?

⑩ Calculate the mean time for the colour change to happen at each pH.

⑪ Plot the graph of Tom's data.

⑫ Use the graph to calculate the rate of reaction at each pH.

⑬ Use your knowledge of enzymes to help you identify patterns, make inferences and draw conclusions.

> **REMEMBER!**
>
> A measurement is repeatable if you repeat the investigation using the same method and equipment and obtain the same results.
> A measurement is reproducible if the investigation is repeated by someone else or by using different equipment or methods, and the same results are obtained.

Learning about the digestive system

Learning objectives:

- identify and locate the organs in the digestive system, and describe their functions
- describe how the products of digestion are absorbed into the body
- explain why the small intestine is an efficient exchange surface.

KEY WORDS

absorption
emulsify
lymphatic system
peristalsis

Our body breaks down the food we eat, so that all cells can receive the nutrients that they need to survive. How does this happen?

The digestive system

The digestive system is a long tube that runs from the mouth to the anus. It consists of several organs working together to digest and absorb food. Each organ is adapted to perform a different function.

Digestion is completed in the small intestine. The soluble food passes through the small intestine wall into the blood. This is called **absorption**. The blood transports the products of digestion to the body cells.

1 Why do we digest food?

2 What is 'absorption'?

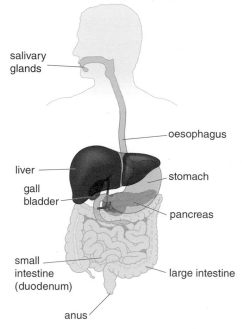

Figure 3.16 The human digestive system

Organs in the digestive system

Each part of the digestive system carries out a specific function.

Part	Adaptation/substance produced	Function
salivary gland	produces saliva	moistens food; has enzymes to digest food
oesophagus	muscular walls	moves food to the stomach by **peristalsis**
stomach	strong muscles produces hydrochloric acid produces enzymes	mix food kills harmful microbes; provides optimum pH for stomach enzymes digest food
liver	produces bile (alkaline)	neutralises stomach acid stores carbohydrates (as glycogen) emulsifies fats
gall bladder	small bag-like structure	stores bile
pancreas	produces enzymes	provides enzymes to digest food in the small intestine
small intestine (duodenum)	large surface area produces enzymes	digestion of food **absorption** of soluble food
large intestine	special cells to absorb fluids	absorbs water; solidifies waste
anus	strong muscle	releases waste

Proteins are digested into amino acids. Carbohydrates are digested into glucose. These soluble products pass from the small intestine to the blood capillaries.

Bile **emulsifies** fats into smaller droplets to increase the surface area. The alkaline pH of bile and large surface area of fat droplets increase the rate of fat digestion into fatty acids and glycerol. Fatty acids and glycerol diffuse into the **lymphatic system**.

How the products of digestion are used:

- Glucose is used for respiration and to make new carbohydrates.
- Amino acids are synthesised (built) into proteins in the ribosomes. Protein synthesis is catalysed by enzymes.
- Fatty acids and glycerol are used:
    › for energy
    › to build cell membranes
    › to make hormones.

3 Explain the difference between emulsification and digestion.

4 Suggest why fatty acids are not absorbed into the blood.

5 Why is digestion important?

A special exchange surface

The small intestine is an effective exchange surface because:

- at about 7 m long, there is ample time for absorption of soluble molecules as food travels along
- it has a very thin, permeable membrane for easy diffusion
- there are many small projections called villi, with tiny projections called microvilli, increasing the surface area for absorption
- blood capillaries transport molecules away, maintaining the concentration gradient for diffusion.

Between meals, the concentration of dissolved food molecules in the blood can be higher than in the intestine. At this time, the molecules are moved into the blood using active transport.

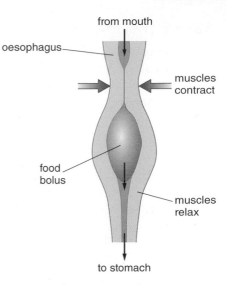

Figure 3.17 Explain how food is moved along the digestive system by peristalsis.

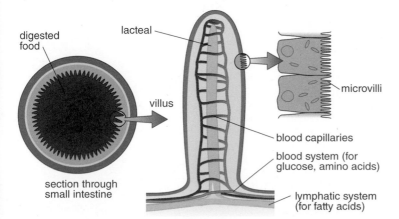

Figure 3.18 Villi help make the small intestine an effective exchange surface.

6 Explain how the small intestine is an effective exchange surface.

COMMON MISCONCEPTION

Remember that emulsification breaks fats into smaller drops but enzymes *digest* fats into fatty acids and glycerol.

DID YOU KNOW?

The flattened surface of the small intestine is about 250 m² (the size of a tennis court).

Explaining digestion

KEY WORDS

carbohydrase
lipase
protease

Learning objectives:

- describe how physical digestion helps to increase the rate of chemical digestion
- name the sites of production and action of specific enzymes
- interpret data about digestive enzymes.

In 1822, Alexis St Martin was shot. Dr William Beaumont saved his life, but the wound did not heal. Dr Beaumont used the hole to watch what happened in Alexis's stomach after he ate food!

Figure 3.19 Pieces of meat in the stomach were much smaller after a few hours. What had happened?

Physical or chemical digestion?

In the mouth, teeth are used to cut and grind food into smaller pieces. This is physical digestion. It allows food to pass through the digestive system more easily. It increases the surface area of the foods to speed up chemical digestion.

Muscles in the stomach wall also help to physically digest food by squeezing it. Muscles in other parts of the digestive system also squeeze the food to keep it moving by peristalsis.

Even small pieces of food cannot pass into the blood. Enzymes are produced in some parts of the digestive system. Enzymes break down food into very small soluble molecules, so they can be absorbed by the blood. This is chemical digestion.

1 **Why is physical digestion important?**

2 **How is chemical digestion different from physical digestion?**

Digestive enzymes

Most enzymes work inside cells, but the digestive enzymes work outside cells. They are produced by cells in glands and in the lining of the gut. The enzymes pass into the gut to mix with the food. There are three groups of enzymes in digestion:

- **Carbohydrases** break down carbohydrates into simple sugars. Amylase is a carbohydrase that breaks down starch.
- **Proteases** break down proteins into amino acids.
- **Lipases** break down fats into fatty acids and glycerol.

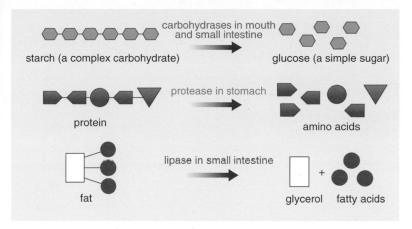

Figure 3.20 Why is chemical digestion important?

Different parts of the gut produce different enzymes, as shown in the table.

Enzyme	Site of production	Reaction
carbohydrase	salivary glands, pancreas, small intestine	carbohydrates → simple sugars
protease	stomach, pancreas, small intestine	proteins → amino acids
lipase	pancreas	lipids (fats) → fatty acids + glycerol

3 Where are proteases produced and what reaction do they catalyse?

4 Suggest why digestive enzymes do not work inside cells.

COMMON MISCONCEPTION

Remember that bile is not an enzyme and it does not *digest* fat molecules. Bile *emulsifies* fat droplets to increase their surface area to speed up their digestion by lipase enzymes.

DID YOU KNOW?

Your stomach produces about 3 litres of hydrochloric acid a day.

Speeding up digestion

Enzymes are affected by temperature and pH. Our body temperature is kept nearly constant at 37 °C. That is the optimum temperature of enzymes in our body.

Enzymes also have an optimum pH. Salivary amylase in the mouth works best at pH 6·7–7·0. The protease enzyme in your stomach works best in acidic conditions, so the stomach produces hydrochloric acid. The stomach also produces mucus which coats the stomach wall to protect it from the acid and enzymes. Protease enzymes that are made in the pancreas and small intestine need alkaline conditions. Bile, made in the liver, neutralises the stomach acid so that these enzymes can work effectively.

5 Look at Figure 3.21a. What does this graph tell you about pepsin and trypsin enzymes?

6 Explain Figure 3.21b using the collision theory.

(a)

(b)

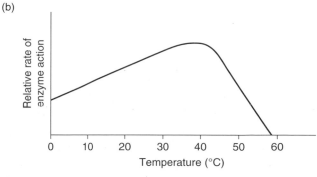

Figure 3.21

REQUIRED PRACTICAL

Use qualitative reagents to test for a range of carbohydrates, lipids and proteins

KEY WORDS

Benedict's test
carbohydrates
qualitative
reagents

Learning objectives:

- suggest appropriate apparatus for the procedures
- describe how safety is managed and apparatus is used
- describe how accurate measurements are made
- interpret observations and make conclusions.

Foods can contain carbohydrates (starch and sugars), protein, fat and small amounts of minerals and vitamins.

Describing how apparatus is used and working safely

Qualitative tests can be used to test for the presence of different food groups using ground-up food. The food is added to distilled water, stirred and filtered.

The **Benedict's test** is used to test for sugars: the filtrate is transferred to a test tube, Benedict's reagent is added and the tube is placed in a water bath of boiling water for five minutes to see if a colour change occurs.

To test for lipids, the filtrate is added to a test tube and shaken gently with Sudan III stain.

The Biuret test is used to test for protein.

These pages are designed ❶ to help you think about aspects of the investigation rather than to guide you through it step by step.

Figure 3.22 Test for glucose

Figure 3.23 Test for protein (Biuret test)

❶ Which piece of apparatus could be used to:

a grind the food up?
b add drops of indicator solution?
c measure small volumes of liquids?

2 Why is the ground-up food stirred with the distilled water and then filtered?

3 Describe the test that could be carried out to show if protein was present in the food.

4 State two safety precautions that should be taken for each test.

Making and recording observations

Ravi is going to test three different foods to see which food groups, including starch, are present. She needs to design a table for the results that all the data will fit into. It needs to be fully labelled and include units. Ravi is going to test each food for each food group twice and is also going to use a control tube, using water.

5 Why is Ravi going to repeat the test for each food group?

6 Why is a control tube set up?

7 Construct a table that Ravi can use that will fit all the data she is going to collect.

Interpreting observations

Food samples A, B and C were tested for different food groups.

Complete this table to show the initial colour of the reagent and the colour change of a positive test.

Food group	Colour change of a positive test	
	Initial colour	Final colour
Glucose		
Protein		
Fat		

ADVICE

Always use a measuring cylinder to measure liquid volumes. The smaller the volume, the narrower the measuring cylinder or pipette you should use.

In the first test, the foods were boiled with Benedict's reagent, in the second test Biuret reagent was added and in the third test Sudan III reagent was added.

Food sample	Colour with Benedict's reagent	Colour with Biuret reagent	Colour with Sudan III reagent
A	brick red	blue	red layer at top of tube
B	blue	purple-pink	no red layer
C	brick red	purple-pink	no red layer

8 Which food/foods contained these different food groups? Explain your answers.

   a   No protein

   b   Glucose

   c   Lipids

Learning about plants and minerals

KEY WORDS

fertiliser
nitrates
phosphates

Learning objectives:

- describe how mineral ions from the soil help plants to grow
- explain how root hair cells are adapted for efficient osmosis
- describe the function of different mineral ions in a plant.

Like animals, plants also need to exchange materials. Leaves are exchange surfaces that are specialised for photosynthesis. Plants also need minerals and water. The root hair cells are adapted for the uptake of these materials.

Roots and minerals

Root hair cells are found on plant roots, just behind the root tip. Root hair cells help to anchor the plant, and absorb water and mineral ions from the soil.

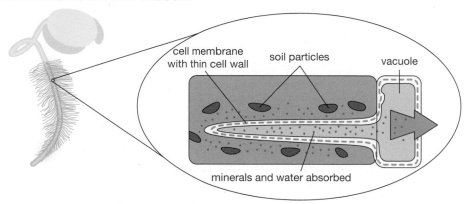

Figure 3.24 Root hair cells are specialised exchange surfaces.

Fertilisers containing minerals can be added to the soil to improve plant growth. Fertilisers contain **nitrates, phosphates**, potassium and magnesium. It is the root hairs that absorb the water and the minerals.

Each root hair cell has a long thin exchange surface reaching out between the soil particles. Water is absorbed by osmosis and mineral ions are absorbed by active transport.

1. **What are the functions of root hairs?**

2. **How do plants absorb the minerals they need?**

Root hair cells

Plants need water to maintain the shape of their cells and for photosynthesis. Minerals are needed to make proteins and other chemicals to help the plant grow.

root hair cell

root cortex cell

xylem vessels

water and minerals

Figure 3.25 Roots are adapted for the transport of water and minerals.

Root hair cells are an efficient exchange surface for osmosis because they:

- provide a large surface area for absorption of water
- have no cuticle, just a thin membrane to allow absorption
- have a thin cell wall to reduce the distance for osmosis
- have a large permanent vacuole to absorb as much water as possible
- are close to the xylem, so that materials can be moved around the plant.

These adaptations mean that a lot of water and mineral ions can get into the cell very quickly and then pass around the plant efficiently.

3 **How are root hair cells adapted for osmosis?**

4 **Why do plants need minerals?**

Looking at minerals

Mineral ions are only found in low concentrations in the soil, compared with the concentration inside the root hair cell. They need to be taken in by active transport. Root hair cells contain many mitochondria to supply the energy needed for this.

The table lists some of the minerals that you might hear about. You only need to remember about nitrates and magnesium for your examinations.

Mineral	Use in the plant
nitrates, containing nitrogen (N)	to make amino acids for protein synthesis
phosphates, containing phosphorus (P)	in respiration to make DNA and new cell membranes
potassium (K)	in respiration in photosynthesis to make enzymes
magnesium (Mg)	needed to make chlorophyll for photosynthesis

5 **Why are enzymes important in plants?**

6 **A farmer adds fertiliser to the soil to make his plants grow better. It is a warm, windy day. Describe how the plants take in and transport the fertilisers, and why this happens more quickly on a windy day. (Hint: look at Chapter 2, 'Photosynthesis'.)**

COMMON MISCONCEPTION

Do not think that water is absorbed through the leaves; it is only through the roots.

DID YOU KNOW?

Roots can grow 1 cm every day. The roots absorb most of their water and minerals just behind the growing tip.

Investigating how plants use minerals

KEY WORDS

culture solution
deficiency

Learning objectives:

- describe why plants need different mineral ions
- explain the effects of mineral deficiencies on plant growth
- explain the importance of fertilisers.

Plants need minerals to grow and stay healthy. What happens if plants do not get the minerals they need?

Fertilisers and plant growth

Many years ago, people cut down trees and burned them so that they could plant crops. After a few years, the crops had used up all the minerals in the soil, and the plants did not grow well. The farmers would then cut down more trees to have new land to grow their food.

trees cut down and burned | wheat seeds planted in the warm ash and covered with soil | crops harvested after six weeks

Figure 3.26 This is the 'slash-and-burn' method of farming.

Over the years, farmers found they could replace soil minerals using fertilisers. This means the same crop can be grown in the same field for several years. Fertilisers help increase the yield of crops. If a plant does not get enough of any of the minerals that it needs, its growth is poor.

1. **Why are fertilisers important?**
2. **Why do gardeners add fertiliser to water before watering their plants?**

Investigating minerals

Plants can be grown, without soil, in special aerated solutions to investigate the effect of a lack of a mineral. A control plant is grown with all the essential minerals a plant needs. Other plants are grown in different **culture solutions**, each one missing only one mineral at a time. The minerals investigated are nitrates, phosphates, potassium and magnesium.

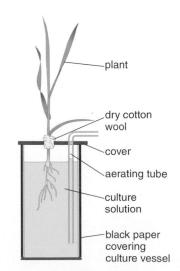

plant

dry cotton wool

cover

aerating tube

culture solution

black paper covering culture vessel

Figure 3.27 Culture solutions contain known amounts of specific minerals.

A mineral **deficiency** happens when a plant cannot get enough of a mineral from the soil or culture solution for healthy growth. Plants only need minerals in small amounts. Mineral deficiencies are easy to analyse and treat.

3 How would you know when a plant has a mineral deficiency?

4 Describe the effect of:

   a a magnesium deficiency

   b a phosphate deficiency.

Food production

Intensive farming methods use machines and chemicals to produce as much food as possible, quickly and cheaply. The use of fertilisers has increased crop yields but the area of land used has stayed the same or decreased.

Farmers use two types of fertilisers:

- inorganic fertiliser
- organic fertiliser.

Inorganic fertilisers are man-made. They come from concentrated sources of minerals, are used in small amounts and can be absorbed immediately. They do not smell, and they are easy to apply and store.

Organic fertilisers come from animal or plant matter. They take time to break down in the soil and slowly release the minerals. They can reduce soil erosion and improve water retention in the soil.

5 Describe the similarities and differences between inorganic and organic fertilisers.

6 What are the advantages and disadvantages of using fertilisers in farming?

KEY INFORMATION

Each mineral has different deficiency symptoms that can be used to identify why a plant is not growing well.

DID YOU KNOW?

In hydroponics systems, the plant roots are in water that contains the correct amounts of fertiliser and oxygen.

Learning about the circulatory system

Learning objectives:

- identify the parts of the circulatory system
- describe the functions of the parts of the circulatory system
- explain how the structure of each part of the circulatory system relates to its function.

KEY WORDS

double circulation
lumen

Very small animals have no need for a transport system. But as the distance from the internal cells to the animal's surface increases, a transport system becomes vital to supply cells with oxygen and nutrients, and to take away waste materials.

Transport systems

Insects have an open circulation system with no blood vessels. The blood flows slowly round the body cavity.

In closed circulatory systems, blood flows in vessels. There are two types of closed circulatory systems:

- a single circulation (for example, in fish); the blood flows in one circuit around the body
- a **double circulation** (for example, in humans); the blood flows in two circuits around the body:
  - › from the heart to the lungs
  - › from the heart to the rest of the body.

double circulatory system

lungs   heart   body

Figure 3.28 Why does blood travel to the lungs?

Blood is pumped out of the heart into arteries under high pressure. As the blood flows from the arteries, through capillaries and then veins, the pressure decreases.

1. **What is a double circulation system?**
2. **Why do closed circulation systems need a heart?**

How does the system work?

Each type of blood vessel is adapted to carry out slightly different functions.

Arteries	Veins	Capillaries
thick, elastic wall / small lumen	thin wall / large lumen / valve	wall is one cell thick
carry blood from the heart	carry blood to the heart	carry blood from arteries to veins
blood under high pressure with a pulse	blood under low pressure, flows smoothly	pressure falls and pulse disappears
thick walls, not permeable	thinner walls, not permeable	walls are one cell thick and permeable
small **lumen**	large lumen	
no valves	valves along their length prevent backflow of blood	no valves
carry oxygenated blood (except pulmonary artery)	carry deoxygenated blood (except pulmonary vein)	blood slowly loses its oxygen

Blood flows from the heart to arteries, arterioles (small arteries), capillaries, venules (small veins), veins and then back to the heart.

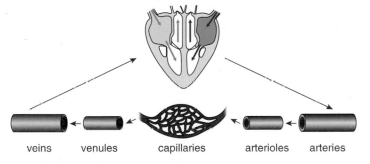

veins   venules   capillaries   arterioles   arteries

Figure 3.29 The sequence of blood flow

3 Describe how blood is transported around the body.

Explaining adaptations

The advantages of the double circulation system include:

- blood pressure is higher, especially to the body
- there is a higher blood flow to body tissues
- oxygenated blood is separate from deoxygenated blood.

Adaptations of the blood vessels include:

- the thick elastic walls of arteries withstand the high pressure of the blood
- capillary networks have a large exchange surface area
- the thin permeable walls of capillaries mean that substances have only a short distance to diffuse
- large lumen in the veins gives the least flow resistance
- valves in the veins prevent the backfow of blood.

4 Explain how the structure of blood vessels is adapted to their function.

5 Why is a double circulation an advantage to an active animal?

> **KEY INFORMATION**
>
> Arteries carry blood away from the heart.

> **DID YOU KNOW?**
>
> Every cell in your body is 0.05 mm away from a capillary, so substances have a very short distance to diffuse.

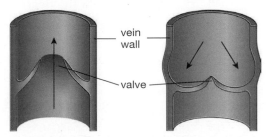

vein wall

valve

Figure 3.30 How do valves prevent backflow?

Exploring the heart

Learning objectives:

- describe the structure and function of the heart
- identify the functions and adaptations of the parts of the heart
- explain the movement of blood around the heart.

KEY WORDS

aorta
atrium (plural: atria)
coronary artery
pacemaker
vena cava
ventricle

Active or larger animals need a transport system with a pump. This is to maintain a constant supply of materials to meet the demand of all cells throughout the body, and to remove waste.

The heart

The heart is made of muscle. Heart muscle continually contracts and relaxes. It uses a lot of energy. Heart muscle receives oxygen and glucose for respiration from the blood brought by the **coronary artery**.

The heart has two pumps (a double circulation) that beat together about 70 times every minute of every day.

Each pump has an upper chamber (**atrium**) that receives blood and a lower chamber (**ventricle**) that pumps blood out. Both **atria** fill and pump blood out at the same time, as do both ventricles. The natural resting heart rate is controlled by a group of cells located in the right atrium that act as a **pacemaker**.

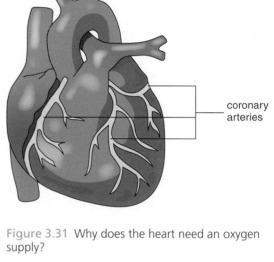

coronary
arteries

Figure 3.31 Why does the heart need an oxygen supply?

Blood from the lungs contains oxygen and enters the heart at the left atrium. It passes into the left ventricle and is pumped out to the body.

Blood from the body contains very little oxygen and enters the heart at the right atrium, passes into the right ventricle and is pumped to the lungs to be oxygenated.

1. **What is the function of the heart?**
2. **Describe how blood flows through the heart.**

The parts of the heart

The heart has four main blood vessels:

- The pulmonary vein transports oxygenated blood from the lungs to the left atrium.
- The **aorta** (main artery) transports oxygenated blood from the left ventricle to the body.

Figure 3.32 Blood flow through the heart

- The **vena cava** (main vein) transports blood from the body to the right atrium.
- The pulmonary artery transports deoxygenated blood from the right ventricle to the lungs.

Ventricles have thicker walls than atria because they pump blood further. The left ventricle pumps blood around the body. It has a thicker wall than the right ventricle, which only pumps blood to the lungs. Valves between the atria and the ventricles prevent the backflow of blood. They open to let blood through and then shut.

3 **Describe the functions of the different chambers of the heart.**

4 **Describe how the atria and ventricles move blood through the heart.**

pulmonary artery · to lungs · to body · aorta · from body · from lungs · vena cava · pulmonary vein · right atrium · left atrium · right ventricle · valve · deoxygenated blood · oxygenated blood · left ventricle

Figure 3.33 Why does the heart need two pumps?

Explaining blood flow

In the second century, Galen thought blood was made in the liver. He said it flowed round the body, but was used as fuel for the muscles. Galen also thought there were holes in the septum, which allowed blood to flow from one side of the heart to the other. In the seventeenth century, Galen's ideas were disproved by William Harvey, who explained heart structure and described the blood vessels.

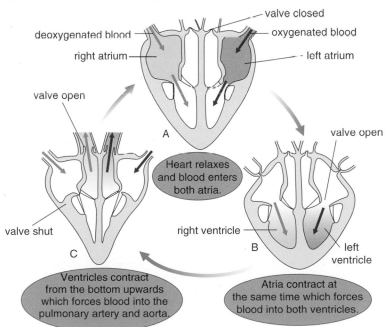

valve closed · deoxygenated blood · oxygenated blood · right atrium · left atrium · valve open · A · Heart relaxes and blood enters both atria. · valve open · valve shut · right ventricle · C · B · left ventricle · Ventricles contract from the bottom upwards which forces blood into the pulmonary artery and aorta. · Atria contract at the same time which forces blood into both ventricles.

Figure 3.34 The cardiac cycle

KEY INFORMATION

Atria receive blood, ventricles pump it out.

DID YOU KNOW?

The complete cardiac cycle normally takes 0.8 seconds.

5 **Explain the sequence of contractions and valve openings as blood passes through the heart.**

6 **If a coronary artery supplying the left ventricle becomes blocked, what effect does this have on the functioning of the heart? Explain your answer.**

Studying blood

Learning objectives:

- identify the parts of the blood and their functions
- explain the adaptations of red blood cells
- explain how red blood cells and haemoglobin transport oxygen efficiently.

KEY WORDS

haemoglobin
oxyhaemoglobin
plasma
red blood cells

Effective exchange systems in animals need a method of transporting substances to and from the exchange site; for example, mammals have an efficient circulatory system.

What is blood?

Blood is a tissue. It is a mixture of cells, solutes and a liquid. The liquid part of blood is **plasma**. It is straw coloured.

Red blood cells, white blood cells and platelets are suspended in the plasma. Each part of the blood has a specific function:

- Plasma transports substances around the body, for example, carbon dioxide.
- Red blood cells carry oxygen from the lungs to body cells.
- White blood cells help to protect the body against infection.
- Platelets are cell fragments which help the clotting process at wound sites.

There are millions of red blood cells in the plasma. This is why blood looks red.

Figure 3.35 Why does blood look red?

1 **Look at the scanning electron micrograph of blood (Figure 3.35). Identify which type of blood cell is visible.**

2 **What is the function of:**

   a red blood cells

   b white blood cells?

Looking closer

The blood parts can be separated by spinning them very fast in a machine called a centrifuge. About 55% of blood is plasma; plasma consists of roughly 90% water and 10% solutes. It is very important because it transports many substances, for example:

- hormones
- antibodies
- nutrients, such as glucose, amino acids (proteins), minerals and vitamins
- waste substances, like carbon dioxide and urea.

plasma (55%)

buffy coat (white blood cells and platelets)

red blood cells (45%)

Figure 3.36 Blood looks like this if it is separated in a centrifuge.

Red blood cells transport oxygen from the lungs to tissues all over the body. Blood is able to transport oxygen efficiently because in 1 mm³ of blood there are about 5 million red blood cells. Red blood cells:

- are tiny, allowing them to pass through the narrow capillaries
- have a biconcave disc shape, giving them a large surface area to volume ratio which increases the efficiency of diffusion of oxygen into and out of the cell, and reduces the diffusion distance to the centre of the cell
- contain **haemoglobin** which binds to oxygen to transport it from the lungs to the body tissues
- have no nucleus, increasing the space available for haemoglobin.

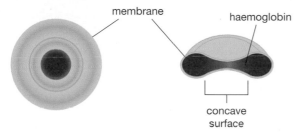

membrane   haemoglobin

concave
surface

Figure 3.37 Red blood cells are adapted to carry oxygen.

3 Describe the role of plasma.

4 How are red blood cells adapted to their function?

How the blood carries oxygen

Haemoglobin binds with oxygen at high concentration to form a bright red compound called **oxyhaemoglobin**. The bonds between the haemoglobin and oxygen are weak, and oxyhaemoglobin dissociates to haemoglobin and oxygen in low oxygen concentrations.

oxygen + haemoglobin ⇌ oxyhaemoglobin

5 Describe how haemoglobin transports oxygen.

6 Use SA:V to explain how red blood cells are adapted to their function.

7 Sickle cell anaemia is a serious inherited blood disorder where the red blood cells develop abnormally and contain defective haemoglobin.

Explain why somebody with sickle cell anaemia is likely to feel very tired and breathless when exercising.

Investigating gas exchange

Learning objectives:

- identify the parts of the human gas exchange system and know their functions
- explain how gas exchange occurs in humans
- explain the adaptations of the gas exchange surfaces.

KEY WORDS

alveolus (plural: alveoli)
ventilate

Our body needs a constant supply of oxygen for cellular respiration. Mammals have evolved a specialised exchange surface to provide a continuous supply of oxygen and to remove carbon dioxide.

The breathing system

The lungs are in the thorax. They are surrounded by the ribcage to protect them. Between the ribs are the intercostal muscles. These help to **ventilate** (move air into and out of) the lungs. Gas exchange happens in the **alveoli**.

Under the lungs is the muscular diaphragm. This also helps to ventilate the lungs.

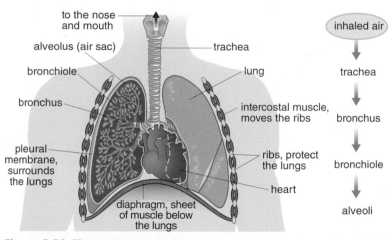

Figure 3.38 The respiratory system

Air is filtered, warmed and moistened in the mouth and nasal passages. It passes into the trachea, through one of the bronchi into the lungs. In the lungs, air passes through the many bronchioles until it reaches an **alveolus** (air sac). Oxygen then passes across the specialised cell membrane of the alveolus into the blood.

1. Describe how air reaches the alveoli.

2. What is gas exchange and where does it happen?

Gas exchange

Oxygen is used to release energy from food during respiration. Carbon dioxide is a waste product of the reaction. Gas exchange is:

- taking in oxygen
- releasing carbon dioxide.

Gas exchange happens in the alveoli. Blood transports the gases to and from the surface of each alveolus through the capillaries that cover the alveoli.

Air entering the alveoli has a greater oxygen concentration than the deoxygenated blood flowing through the lungs. This steep concentration gradient allows efficient diffusion to happen.

Deoxygenated blood contains a greater concentration of carbon dioxide, so it diffuses out of the blood and into the alveoli to be breathed out.

3 Explain how gas exchange happens in the alveoli.

4 What is the difference between breathing and respiration?

3.15

COMMON MISCONCEPTION

Remember that breathing is gas exchange and respiration is the release of energy from food.

DID YOU KNOW?

The lungs have over 300 million alveoli and the left lung is slightly smaller than the right, so there is room for your heart.

Why are alveoli good exchange surfaces?

Alveoli are efficient exchange surfaces. They have evolved adaptations to ensure maximum gas exchange:

- They are tiny spheres. Smaller spheres have a much larger surface area than larger ones, resulting in efficient diffusion of gases.
- The exchange surface at the alveoli wall is very thin (just one cell thick). This means that the diffusion distance for the gases is very short.
- Each alveolus is surrounded by blood capillaries to ensure a good blood supply. Oxygen is constantly moved into the blood and carbon dioxide is constantly taken to the lungs to be removed. This means that gas exchange happens at the steepest concentration gradients possible.
- The alveoli surfaces are moist. Gases dissolve to allow efficient diffusion across the exchange surface.

Figure 3.39 Gas exchange in the alveoli

5 Describe and explain how alveoli are adapted to their function.

6 Explain how cells located deep in our body can receive the oxygen they need and dispose of carbon dioxide efficiently.

Learning about coronary heart disease

Learning objectives:

- identify the causes and symptoms of coronary heart disease
- describe possible treatments of coronary heart disease
- evaluate the possible treatments of coronary heart disease.

Heart disease is one of the main causes of death in the UK. Cholesterol is made in the liver and transported in the blood. High levels of cholesterol are linked to heart disease.

(a) normal artery   artery wall

normal blood flow

artery cross section

Heart problems

In **coronary heart disease**, fatty material builds up inside the coronary arteries. Blood flow is reduced and less glucose and oxygen reach the heart for respiration. Less energy is available for the heart to contract. If cells are starved of nutrients, they can die and a heart attack may happen. Factors that contribute to coronary heart disease include genetic factors, gender, age, diet and smoking.

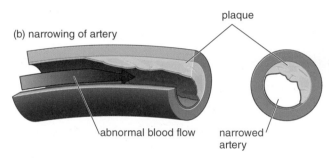

(b) narrowing of artery   plaque

abnormal blood flow   narrowed artery

Heart valves prevent the backflow of blood. They can become faulty due to heart attack, infection or old age. Faulty valves may not open fully or can leak. Symptoms of leaky valves include:

Figure 3.40 How does coronary heart disease affect blood flow?

- tiredness and lack of energy
- breathlessness.

1 Describe the symptoms of coronary heart disease.

2 What causes coronary heart disease?

1. Stent pushed through catheter into position using X-rays.

Treatments for heart problems

- Some people cannot control their heart rate. **Artificial pacemakers** can be fitted under the skin. A wire is passed from a vein to the right atrium. This sends electrical impulses to the heart to control heartbeat.
- Faulty heart valves can be replaced using biological (from humans or other mammals) or mechanical valves.
- High cholesterol levels are treated with drugs called **statins** which stop the liver producing as much cholesterol. Patients can also change their diet to help reduce cholesterol.
- **Stents** are used to treat narrow coronary arteries. If the coronary artery is too damaged, bypass surgery is used. A vein is transplanted from the leg to bypass the blockage.

2. Balloon inflated, expanding stent.

3. Catheter taken out, leaving stent to open up artery.

Figure 3.41 Inserting a stent

When heart failure occurs, the only effective treatment is a donor heart transplant. An artificial heart can be used in the short term, while the patient is waiting for a heart transplant, or to allow the heart to rest to help recovery.

3 How is coronary heart disease treated?

4 What are artifical valves and what do they do?

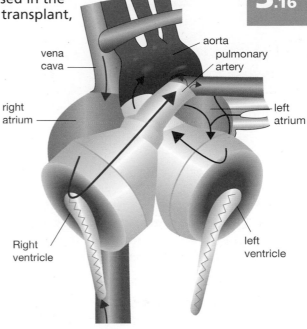

Figure 3.42 An artificial heart

Evaluating heart treatments

All treatments help keep patients alive.

Treatment	Advantage	Disadvantage
artificial valves	no rejection	can damage red blood cells patient needs anti-clotting drugs
biological valves	red blood cells not damaged	valves can harden and need replacing
stents	little risk	fatty deposits can rebuild
bypass surgery	no rejection	major surgery
statins	reduce cholesterol	possible side effects, e.g. liver damage
artificial pacemakers	major surgery not required	immune system can reject the pacemaker may need replacing
heart transplant	better quality of life	major surgery anti-rejection drugs needed (leading to greater infection risk) shortage of donors

5 Evaluate the advantages and disadvantages of treating cardiovascular diseases by drugs, mechanical devices or transplant.

6 Why are doctors increasingly prescribing statins for their patients?

KEY INFORMATION

The coronary artery takes oxygen and glucose to heart muscles for respiration.

DID YOU KNOW?

Over 300 000 people in the UK have a heart attack every year.

MATHS SKILLS

Extracting and interpreting information

Learning objectives:

- to extract and interpret information from tables, charts and graphs.

KEY WORDS

classify
compare
correlation
trend

Tables, charts and graphs give a lot of information in a small space. Extracting and interpreting data from graphics is a vital skill for all scientists.

Looking at tables

Tables allow us to **classify** and **compare** data. To read a table and extract information from it, you must first read the headings carefully.

Light intensity (units)	Rate of photosynthesis (number of bubbles per minute)
1	2
3	11
6	26
9	48
11	47
14	48

The headings of each column help us to read the table.

Column 1 tells us that this table is about light intensity, and column 2 tells us that the data collected was the rate of photosynthesis, which was measured by counting the number of bubbles released in a minute.

Looking at charts and graphs

The most commonly used statistical diagrams in science are line graphs, bar graphs and pie charts. Pie charts are used to show proportions and the relative importance of different data sets. The size of the angle at the centre of each sector represents the relative size of the data set. Different sectors can be compared without even knowing the numbers in the different groups.

DID YOU KNOW?

Correlations prove a relationship but do not prove cause and effect.

Look at the table.

① **a** What was the light intensity when 26 bubbles were released in a minute?

b What happened to the rate between 9 light intensity units and 14 light intensity units?

② **a** At what light intensity was the rate of photosynthesis highest?

b What trends do you notice in the data?

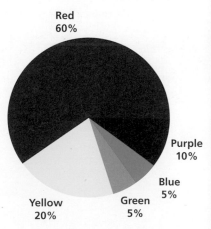

Figure 3.43 Pie chart showing the amount of time that hummingbirds spent at different coloured feeders

In a bar graph each bar represents the number of a specific data set. The height of the bars allow us to compare the quantity of each sub-group within a data set.

Plot one data set against another to show whether or not there is a relationship, or correlation, between them. When the points are more or less in a straight line, it is said that there is a good **correlation** between the two data sets. Correlations can be positive, negative, or zero. Positive correlation shows that as one set of values increases, so does the second set (a 'more:more' relationship). Negative correlation shows that as one set of values increases, the other data set decreases (a 'more:less' relationship). Zero correlation shows that one data set increasing or decreasing has no effect on the other.

Another type of graph is the pictogram, which uses pictorial forms to represent data, for example, statistical data.

3 **What can you deduce from this scatter graph?**

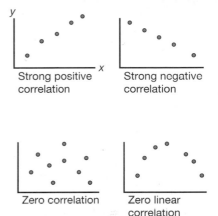

Figure 3.44 Correlations can be positive, negative, or zero.

Figure 3.45 What can you deduce from this scatter graph?

Line graphs

To interpret or read a line graph:

- Look at the labels, scales and units on each axis. What are they telling you?

- Look at the general **trend** or trends on the graph. As factor X increases, what happens to factor Y?

- Pick out specific points of interest. Follow the line along the graph until you find the data point that corresponds with a value on the other axis.

4 **What does the graph in Figure 3.46 tell you?**

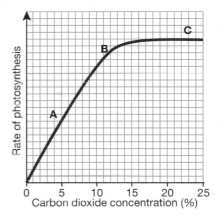

Figure 3.46 This line graph gives information about a factor that is relevant to plants.

KEY INFORMATION

Remember to read table headings and graph axes carefully.

Check your progress

You should be able to:

recall that osmosis describes water movement in and out of cells → explain osmosis as the movement of water through a partially permeable membrane → predict water movement during osmosis / explain the words flaccid, plasmolysed and turgid

know that enzymes catalyse reactions in cells / understand that substrate molecules fit into active sites of enzymes → describe how pH and temperature affect enzymes / describe the lock-and-key theory → explain how pH and temperature affect enzyme activity / use collision theory to explain enzyme action

describe the effect of SA:V on the diffusion of substances → describe the features of a range of exchange surfaces in plants and animals → explain the features of exchange surfaces

describe the functions of different parts of the circulatory system → describe how the circulatory system transports substances → explain how the circulatory system is adapted to its function

know that digested food is transported from the small intestine to body cells → describe the adaptations of the intestine as an exchange surface → explain how the small intestine is adapted for efficient food absorption

Worked example

The diagram shows the human heart.

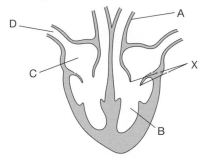

1. **Label parts A–D on the diagram.**

   A *Artery*
   B *Left ventricle*
   C *Right atrium*
   D *Vena cava*

2. a **What is the name of part X?**

   valve

   b **Part X can become damaged or may leak. What effect will this have?**

   Person will have a lack of energy and breathlessness.

   c **How can a damaged or leaky part X be treated?**

   Transplant a valve from another person.

   d **Give an advantage and a disadvantage of the treatment above.**

   It will not be rejected.

3. **The heart pumps blood to the lungs so that gas exchange can happen.**

   Why are alveoli an efficient exchange surface?

   They have a large surface area compared with volume to give a large area for gas exchange. Good blood supply to take oxygen to body cells where it is used for respiration for energy for growth.

B–D correctly identified. Giving 'artery' for A is insufficient.

'Aorta' is an alternative answer.

Valve is correctly identified.

Two symptoms correctly identified.

One treatment has been identified.

Artificial valves are another treatment.

The student has correctly identified an advantage of one treatment but they have only answered half the question for this.

Two correct answers are identified. Then the student forgets the question being asked and moves away from the topic of alveoli.

Overall, this student shows a good understanding of the topic but does not give complete answers. Careful reading of the questions, and consideration of exactly what is being asked for, in addition to more detailed responses, might be helpful.

End of chapter questions

Getting started

1 In what part of the lung does gas exchange take place? `1 Mark`

2 Insects have tiny holes called spiracles along the side of the body. What is the function of the spiracles? `1 Mark`

3 How is glucose absorbed into the blood? `1 Mark`

4 What is the function of the heart? `1 Mark`

5 Describe the difference between respiration and breathing. `1 Mark`

6 Lindsay is investigating the effect of pH on the rate of reaction of amylase enzyme. She wants to find out the time taken to completely digest a starch solution at a range of pH values. She measures out 2 cm³ of amylase solution and puts it in a test tube before adding 1 cm³ of a pH solution. `1 Mark`

Next she adds 2 cm³ of starch solution, starts the stop clock and then stirs the mixture using a pipette.

After 20 seconds she tests the mixture using iodine solution.

a Why should Lindsay use a syringe to measure the solutions? `1 Mark`

b Why is it important that the mixture is stirred? `1 Mark`

c Why does Lindsay use iodine solution? `1 Mark`

The rate of enzyme activity can be calculated using the following equation:

Rate of enzyme activity = 1000/time taken

d Calculate the rate of enzyme activity if the time taken for amylase to break down starch was 125 seconds. `1 Mark`

Going further

7 What is the function of bile? `1 Mark`

8 What does it mean if an enzyme is denatured? `1 Mark`

9 Give two ways in which the small intestine is adapted for efficient absorption. `2 marks`

10 Amoeba is a single-celled organism that lives in fresh water. It has a vacuole that fills with water, moves to the outside of the cell and bursts. A new vacuole starts to form. Use osmosis to explain why amoeba needs a vacuole. `4 Marks`

11 Yeast was allowed to carry out anaerobic respiration at different temperatures. The carbon dioxide produced was collected for 5 minutes. The results are shown in the table:

Temperature °C	Amount of carbon dioxide collected in 5 minutes in cm³		
	Test 1	Test 2	Test 3
20	0.8	0.9	1.0
30	23.4	22.8	22.4
40	39.4	40.8	41.7
50	39.1	31.9	30.8

a Identify the anomalous result.

1 Mark

b Describe the effect of temperature on respiration in yeast shown by the data.

1 Mark

More challenging

12 Explain how plant cells become turgid.

2 Marks

13 How are plant roots adapted for the exchange of materials?

2 Marks

14 The graph shows the effect of temperature on the enzyme amylase. Describe and explain the graph.

2 Marks

Most demanding

15 Define the term 'emulsification' and explain its purpose.

2 Marks

16 What is plasmolysis?

1 Mark

17 Why are molecules in the digestive system sometimes moved by active transport?

1 Mark

18 The table below shows the surface area and volume of a bison and of a prairie dog. Both are herbivores.

	Surface area	Volume	Surface area to volume ratio SA:V
	1128	2016	
	10	2	

Calculate the surface area to volume ratio for both and suggest why the prairie dog needs to eat more comparative to its size than the bison does.

2 Marks

19 What is the disadvantage of having a large volume compared to surface area?

2 Marks

20 Potato cores were cut to the same length. Each core was placed in a different concentration of sugar solution. After 30 minutes they were measured. The results are shown in the diagram. Using the diagram, describe and explain the results.

7 cm

original length

pure water

increasing concentration of sugar solution

6 Marks

Total: 40 Marks

HEALTH MATTERS

HEALTH CAN BE AFFECTED BY DRUGS AND DISEASE.

- Smoking is damaging to health because cigarette smoke contains harmful chemicals.
- Drugs can be medicines and may help people suffering from pain or disease.
- Lack of exercise and a poor diet can lead to a higher BMI.
- Alcohol affects our response time and behaviour.

BACTERIA ARE SINGLE-CELLED LIVING ORGANISMS.

- Bacteria multiply by simple cell division every 20 minutes, if conditions are favourable.
- Temperatures higher than 25°C increase the likelihood that pathogens will grow.
- Antiseptics can kill bacteria.
- A specific antibiotic can kill a specific bacterial colony.

ORGANS WORK TOGETHER IN SYSTEMS TO PERFORM CERTAIN FUNCTIONS.

- Air enters the respiratory system through the nose.
- The trachea and bronchi are organs in the respiratory system.
- The stomach produces hydrochloric acid.
- The skin covers the outside of the body.
- Blood is the transport system in the body; red blood cells transport oxygen from the lungs to all cells.

GREEN PLANTS ALL HAVE ORGAN SYSTEMS THAT HAVE SPECIFIC FUNCTIONS.

- Plants photosynthesise to increase biomass, which is tranferred to animals in higher trophic levels.
- Plants can be damaged by a range of ion deficiency conditions.
- In self-supporting ecosystems plant and animal populations are interdependent.

IN THIS CHAPTER YOU WILL FIND OUT ABOUT:

FACTORS THAT AFFECT OUR CHANCES OF CATCHING A NON-COMMUNICABLE DISEASE.

- Factors in our environment can increase our risk of disease.
- Our lifestyle can increase the chance of us developing a non-communicable disease.
- Sometimes a number of risk factors for developing a disease interact.
- Lifestyle factors can increase the risk of a person developing cancer.

HOW ARE COMMUNICABLE DISEASES SPREAD?

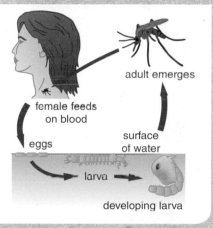

- Pathogens are microorganisms that cause disease in animals.
- Bacteria, viruses, fungi and protists can cause disease.
- Toxins produced by bacteria make us feel ill.
- Understanding the life cycles of some pathogens allows us to control the spread of disease.

HOW DO WE CONTROL THE SPREAD OF DISEASE?

- The skin, nose, respiratory system and stomach all protect us from pathogens.
- The immune system is our major defence system against disease.
- White blood cells protect us from bacterial infections in a number of ways.
- Vaccination protects us from viral and bacterial pathogens.

HOW ARE PLANTS AFFECTED BY DISEASE?

- Plant diseases can usually be detected by visible symptoms.
- Viral, bacterial and fungal pathogens cause plant diseases.

Learning about health

Learning objectives:

- recall the difference between health and disease
- explain how some diseases interact
- evaluate data about lifestyle and health.

KEY WORDS

communicable
depression
immune system
mental health
non-communicable

The **word 'health' can mean many different things, depending on the people involved and their situation.**

Health and disease

Good health is complete physical and mental well-being. It is about feeling good and having a positive frame of mind. **Mental health** is as important as physical health.

The major causes of physical and mental ill health include:

- disease
- diet
- stress
- life situations.

Diseases are disorders that affect part or all of an organism. They can be **communicable**, like measles and HIV, or **non-communicable**, such as cancer and cardiovascular disease.

Different types of disease may interact; for example, viruses living in cells can cause cancers. Cervical cancer is linked to infection with human papilloma virus (HPV), which causes genital warts.

Being overweight is strongly related to having high blood pressure. Having high blood pressure damages the body's arteries in the long term, making the walls thick and stiff, rather than flexible and elastic.

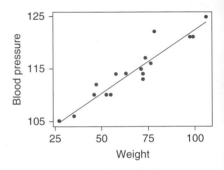

Figure 4.1 What does this data show?

1. **Describe what we mean by 'health'.**

2. **Name the major causes of ill health.**

3. **Name one communicable and one non-communicable disease.**

Diet, life situations and stress

Poor nutrition can contribute to the risk of developing some diseases:

- high-fat or sugar-rich diets can cause high blood pressure, **depression**, heart disease and strokes, eating disorders and Type 2 diabetes.
- low-calcium diets cause osteoporosis.
- red meat and processed meat increase the risk of bowel cancer.

Stress develops when challenging life situations occur, for example, moving home, death in the family or divorce.

When you are stressed, hormones are released, blood vessels constrict and blood pressure rises. Stress often causes depression. It increases the risk of obesity, heart disease, Alzheimer's disease and diabetes; it can also trigger asthma attacks in people who already have asthma.

Different diseases can interact:

- **Immune system** diseases, such as AIDS, can cause an increased risk of contracting infectious diseases.
- Immune reactions initially caused by a pathogen can cause allergies, such as skin rashes. Severe viral respiratory infections in early childhood can trigger asthma as children grow.
- Severe physical ill health, for example, obesity or cancer, can cause depression and other mental illnesses.

Figure 4.2 Name a cause of asthma.

4 **Explain how lifestyle factors affect mental health.**

5 **Give one example of how different diseases interact.**

HPV and cervical cancer

HPV is found in most cervical cancers. People with weak immune systems are less able to resist HPV. Not everyone who gets HPV develops cancer. Worldwide, cervical cancer is the second most common female cancer. It often takes many years to develop after having HPV and does not usually show symptoms until it is quite advanced. It is hard to treat.

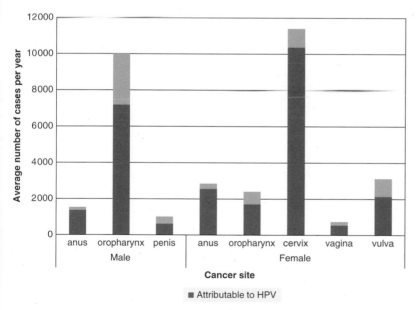

■ Attributable to HPV

Figure 4.3 What do these data show?

6 **Explain the graph in Figure 4.3.**

7 **Discuss the human and financial cost of cancer on individuals, families and nations.**

DID YOU KNOW?

Around 80 000 children aged between 5 and 16 years suffer from severe depression.

KEY INFORMATION

Don't forget that ill health can lead to poor mental health.

KEY CONCEPT

Looking at risk factors

Learning objectives:

- recall the causes of some non-communicable diseases
- describe the impact of lifestyle on non-communicable diseases
- explain the impact of lifestyle on non-communicable diseases.

KEY WORDS

causal
  mechanism
risk factor

In **developed countries, non-communicable disease is the largest cause of death.**

Risk factors

Risk factors increase the chance of having a disease. Risk factors can be aspects of a person's lifestyle, and substances in the person's body or environment. They include diet, exercise, type of workplace, sexual habits, smoking, drinking and drug-taking.

Non-communicable diseases may be caused by the interaction of a number of factors:

- Factors involved in cardiovascular disease may be diet/obesity, age, genetics and exercise.
- Lung disease factors are smoking and cleanliness of the environment.
- Alcohol, diet/obesity, genetics, drugs and viral infection may be involved in liver disease.
- Genetics, diet/obesity and exercise may affect Type 2 diabetes.

We cannot control some risk factors, such as genes and age, but we can control lifestyle factors, like drinking and smoking, to reduce the risk of contracting some diseases.

Figure 4.4 Why is this person at risk of cardiovascular disease?

1. **What factors increase the risk of Type 2 diabetes?**

2. **How could the risk of liver disease be reduced?**

Causal mechanisms

A **causal mechanism** is one risk factor that may be partly responsible for a disease. Research has shown a causal mechanism for some risk factors.

Disease/condition	Risk factor with causal mechanism
cardiovascular disease	poor diet, smoking and lack of exercise
Type 2 diabetes	obesity
liver and brain damage	alcohol
lung disease, cancer	smoking
low birthweight and premature birth	smoking
abnormal foetal brain development	alcohol
cancer	carcinogens (including ionising radiation)

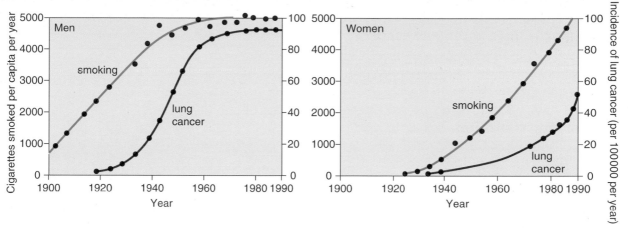

Figure 4.5 Smoking and lung cancer

3 Use the data in Figure 4.5 to describe the smoking habits of men from 1900 to 1990. Describe what happened to the incidence of lung cancer during this time.

Time lag

There is a long time lag between when people start to smoke and the development of cancer. So, it took a long time to compile evidence to prove smoking was the causal mechanism for lung cancer.

Human and financial costs of smoking include:

- serious health problems, possible death, damage to unborn children, dangers of passive smoking
- cost of cigarettes, loss of family income and a depleted workforce
- financial burden of healthcare costs on local, national and global economies.

An isolated case of disease does not provide evidence for or against a risk factor. Large sample groups need to be monitored. Groups are randomly selected, or matched in terms of age and gender.

4 Explain the impact of lifestyle on non-communicable diseases.

5 Explain the human and financial impact of smoking.

Figure 4.6 Smoking does not cause lung cancer immediately.

DID YOU KNOW?

Research shows that teenagers who eat fast food at least once a week are more likely to develop insulin resistance, a risk factor for Type 2 diabetes.

KEY INFORMATION

Remember: smoking is a causal mechanism for lung cancer but cancer is caused by the chemicals in cigarettes.

Exploring non-communicable diseases

Learning objectives:

- identify risk factors for cancer
- explain the differences between types of tumours
- explain the impact of non-communicable diseases.

In the UK, over 33% of people will develop a form of cancer during their life.

Cancer facts

Sometimes cell division can become uncontrolled. This causes **tumours** to form. Tumours can be harmless and **benign**, or **malignant** and cancerous.

Doctors cannot explain why only some people develop cancer. Research shows that certain risk factors increase the chance of a person developing cancer. These include:

- smoking
- obesity
- some common viruses
- UV light
- age
- possible genetic causes.

Figure 4.7 Warts are benign tumours.

1 **How do tumours form?**

2 **Suggest which risk factor may increase the chance of:**

   a skin cancer
   b lung cancer.

Cancer in detail

Benign tumours divide slowly, do not spread and are harmless. Warts are benign tumours. They can be removed by simple surgery.

Malignant tumours divide very quickly. They can invade tissues around them and spread via the blood to different parts of the body, where they form secondary tumours. Malignant tumour cells are cancers.

Substances or viruses that increase the risk of cancer are called **carcinogens**; for example:

- tar in tobacco smoke
- asbestos
- human papilloma viruses (HPV).

Figure 4.8 How are benign and malignant moles different?

Some risk factors that are associated with cancer cannot be changed, for example, aging and family history. Ways to reduce other risk factors include:

- not smoking
- staying out of the sun and using sun screen
- only drinking alcohol in moderation
- healthy diet and exercise.

3 Explain how benign and malignant tumours differ.

4 Describe some lifestyle changes to reduce the risk of cancer.

Smoking and cancer

Figure 4.9 Over 25% of UK cancer deaths are caused by smoking.

Smoking is the biggest preventable cause of cancer worldwide. The link between smoking and cancer was known for many years before being widely accepted. Lung cancer symptoms include a cough, chest pains, shortness of breath, poor appetite and weight loss, and coughing up blood. Each person with lung cancer costs the NHS over £9000 every year. The total workforce is reduced and the economy is weakened.

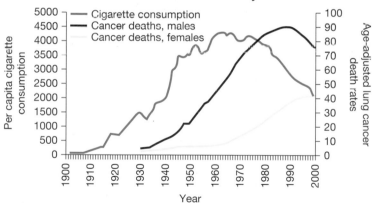

Figure 4.10 Is there evidence for a link between smoking and cancer?

5 Describe and explain the graph in Figure 4.10.

6 Suggest why there is a time lapse between the rise in cigarette consumption and the rise in lung cancer deaths.

7 'The data on the graph prove that smoking causes lung cancer.' Do you agree with this statement? Justify your answer.

DID YOU KNOW?

Breast, lung, prostate and bowel cancers are the most common in the UK. They account for 50% of diagnosed cancers.

KEY INFORMATION

Remember: malignant tumours cause cancer, whereas benign ones do not.

Analysing and evaluating data

KEY WORDS
....
bias
correlation
trend

Learning objectives:

- translate information between graphical and numerical forms
- use scatter diagrams to identify correlations
- evaluate the strength of evidence.

Analysing and evaluating data is a key skill for all scientists, but it is vitally important in medical research.

Looking for patterns

Scientists try to identify links between variables. Sometimes there is no link. When interpreting graphs:

- identify patterns or **trends**
- use axis labels and units when describing the graph; for example, 'as vaccination uptake increases, cases of measles fall'
- look for particular features of the graph, such as maximum and minimum values, the range, outliers and patterns that do not fit trends
- quote numbers to clarify descriptions.

Useful words to describe graphs are: increased, decreased, faster, slower, constant, plateau, maximum, minimum.

① **What do the data in Figure 4.11(a) show?**

② **Describe the trends in the data shown in Figure 4.11(b). Are the two trends linked?**

Exploring links in data

A **correlation** is an association between two sets of random data. A correlation does not prove that A affects B, or that B affects A. Both A and B could be caused by another variable. In medical research, scientists have to determine links between treatments and cures, or risk factors and disease. This is difficult if:

- the proposed cause only sometimes results in the disease
- the disease has many possible causes
- there is a long delay between proposed cause and effect.

If one variable increases as the other increases, this is a positive correlation. If one variable increases as the other decreases, it is a negative correlation. To prove a causal mechanism, an investigation needs to be carried out.

(a)

(b)

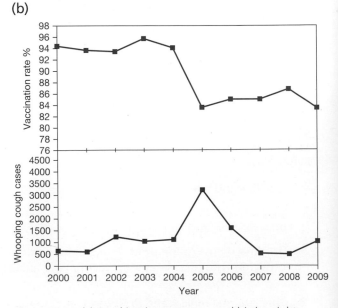

Figure 4.11 (a) Smoking in pregnancy and birthweight (b) Whooping cough incidence and vaccination uptake

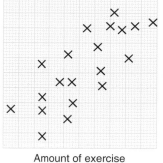

Figure 4.12 Do these graphs show correlation or not?

3 **Explain the data in Figure 4.13.**

4 **Why is it often difficult to determine links between variables?**

Evaluating data

When evaluating data think about these questions:

- Are the data reliable? Was there an appropriate control group?
- Are the data valid?
- Was the sample size sufficient?
- How could better data be collected? (Think about length of study, sample selection, etc.)
- How could more accurate data be collected? Do the data answer the question?
- Are there any anomalies in the data? Can these be explained?

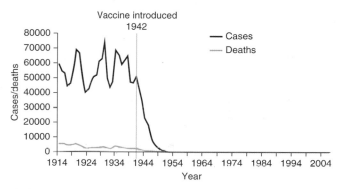

Figure 4.13 Diphtheria cases in the UK

HIGHER TIER ONLY

- How confident are you that the evidence supports the conclusion? Has a causal relationship been proved? Could anyone use the same data to support a different conclusion?
- Are the data **biased**? Who completed the research? Do they have a personal interest in the data?

Figure 4.14 Deaths due to coronary heart disease in Australia

5 **Describe the male trend in Figure 4.14. Compare both trends.**

6 **Evaluate the data in Figure 4.14.**

COMMON MISCONCEPTION

Remember: a correlation is not the same as a causal mechanism.

DID YOU KNOW?

Researchers often need studies with large numbers of people carried out over long periods to detect small, subtle effects.

Studying pathogens

Learning objectives:

- recall the definition of a pathogen
- explain how communicable diseases can be controlled

KEY WORDS

Ebola
pathogen
protist

Ebola haemorrhagic fever (EHF) first appeared in 1976 in two outbreaks. One was in Sudan, and the other was in a village near the Ebola River in the Democratic Republic of Congo.

What are pathogens?

Pathogens are microorganisms that cause infectious diseases. They depend on their hosts to provide the conditions and nutrients they need to grow and reproduce. Pathogens can be

- viruses, for example, measles
- bacteria, such as *Salmonella,* which causes food poisoning
- **protists**, a protist causes malaria
- fungi, like rose black spot.

Pathogens can infect plants or animals. They are spread by direct contact, by water or through the air.

Figure 4.15 What type of pathogen causes rose black spot?

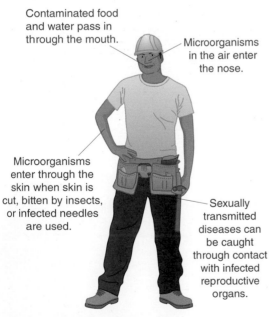

Contaminated food and water pass in through the mouth.

Microorganisms in the air enter the nose.

Microorganisms enter through the skin when skin is cut, bitten by insects, or infected needles are used.

Sexually transmitted diseases can be caught through contact with infected reproductive organs.

Figure 4.16 How are pathogens spread?

1 **Give four examples of pathogens.**

2 **Describe how pathogens spread.**

Pathogens in detail

Bacteria and viruses can reproduce rapidly in the body.

- Bacteria produce toxins that damage tissues and make us feel ill.
- Viruses live and reproduce inside cells, damaging them.

The toxins released by pathogens cause the symptoms of infection. These include high temperatures, nausea, headaches and rashes. People get a communicable disease because they receive the pathogen from someone who has it. Measures to prevent or reduce the spread of diseases include:

- simple hygiene, such as covering your mouth when coughing, using a handkerchief when sneezing and washing your hands after using the toilet
- isolation of infected individuals
- destroying vectors, for example, mosquitoes are the malaria vector
- vaccination.

Figure 4.17 Why do doctors and nurses wear protective clothing?

3 Why do pathogens make us feel ill?

4 Explain how the spread of diseases can be reduced or prevented.

A case study

Ebola haemorrhagic fever (EHF) is a deadly virus: 50–90% of people infected with EHF die. The last outbreak of EHF began in December 2013, in Guinea, and spread to Nigeria, Sierra Leone and Liberia.

Fruit bats carry EHF and may infect animals and humans. The disease is caught by direct contact with body fluids (blood and saliva) of an infected individual. Symptoms include fever, headache, diarrhoea, nausea and rashes. Currently, there is no cure for EHF but two vaccines are under development.

Prevention measures include:

- reducing the risk of contact with infected animals
- wearing protective clothing
- washing hands frequently
- isolation of infected people and safe burials of the dead
- travel restrictions.

5 Evaluate the control measures for EHF.

Figure 4.18 Fruit bat meat is a delicacy in West Africa.

DID YOU KNOW?

In 1918, Spanish influenza killed 40–50 million people.

ADVICE

Remember that pathogens come in many different forms, and that each one causes a different disease.

Learning about viral diseases

Learning objectives:

- describe the symptoms of some viral diseases
- describe the transmission and control of some viral diseases
- explain how some viral diseases are spread.

Communicable diseases are caused by pathogens that pass from one person to another.

Viral diseases

Viruses are very small pathogens. They are not living cells. They have a strand of genetic material inside a protein coat. The genetic material replicates inside host cells to make new viruses, which are then released.

Figure 4.19 How are viruses different from living cells?

Examples of viral diseases are:

- Measles, a serious illness. Symptoms include fever and a red rash over the skin. It can be fatal if there are complications.
- HIV, which initially causes a flu-like illness.
- Tobacco mosaic virus (TMV), which affects over 150 plant species including tomatoes. Leaves have discoloured 'mosaic' patterns. This reduces photosynthesis and affects plant growth, and the quality and number of fruits are affected.

1 **How do viruses reproduce?**

2 **Describe the symptoms of two viral diseases.**

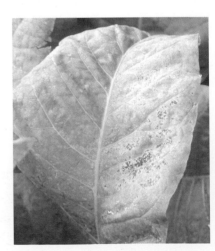

Figure 4.20 Suggest how TMV got its name.

Spread and control

Viruses spread and are controlled in various ways.

Virus	Mechanism for spread	Control
Measles	**Droplet infection** Talking, coughing and sneezing all cause the expulsion of tiny droplets into the air. Inhaling droplets that carry viruses causes measles to spread.	Most young children have **vaccinations** to protect them against this possibly fatal disease.
HIV	**Direct contact** HIV is spread by sexual contact or exchange of body fluids such as blood. This can occur if drug users share needles.	**Antiretroviral drugs** are prescribed to stop the virus entering the lymph nodes.
TMV	**Enters plants via wounds** The virus gains access through a break in the skin or plant epidermis.	It is controlled by: removal of infected plant material, controlling pests, sterilising tools (using heat), washing hands after handling infected plants.

Figure 4.21 Suggest why these commuters are wearing masks.

3 Describe how HIV is spread and suggest control measures.

4 Describe how TMV is spread and controlled.

Counting the cost

Viral diseases are harder to treat than bacterial diseases. Bacteria are living cells that survive outside body cells. They can be treated with prescribed drugs. Viruses are only found inside host cells, where they are protected from drugs. This is why we are vaccinated against some viral diseases.

HIV is very difficult to control. If it is not successfully controlled by antiretroviral drugs, the virus enters the lymph nodes and attacks the body's immune cells. Late-stage HIV, or AIDS, occurs when the body's immune system is no longer able to deal with other infections or cancers.

5 Explain how HIV leads to AIDS.

6 Why is it harder to treat viral diseases than bacterial diseases?

7 Compare the mechanism for the spread of measles with that of HIV. Explain which disease is most infectious.

DID YOU KNOW?

Each type of virus attacks a specific cell. For example, the measles virus attacks skin and sensory nerve cells.

KEY INFORMATION

Remember: viruses are not living things. They have many different shapes (just one of which is shown in Figure 4.19).

Studying bacterial diseases

KEY WORDS

diarrhoea
gonorrhoea
Salmonella

Learning objectives:

- describe the symptoms of some bacterial diseases
- explain how some bacterial diseases can be controlled
- compare and contrast bacterial and viral diseases.

Some pathogens are bacterial. Bacteria can reproduce very quickly in our bodies.

Bacterial diseases

Many bacteria are not harmful and some are actually very useful. We use them to make cheese and yoghurt, to break down our waste and make medicines. Some bacteria, however, are pathogens and cause diseases, infecting both plants and animals.

Examples of bacterial diseases are:

- *Salmonella*, which causes food poisoning. A build-up of toxic bacterial waste products causes symptoms that include:
  - › fever
  - › abdominal cramps
  - › vomiting
  - › **diarrhoea**.
- **Gonorrhoea**, a sexually transmitted disease. The toxic bacterial products cause symptoms that include:
  - › a thick yellow or green discharge from the vagina or penis
  - › pain when urinating.

Figure 4.22 *Salmonella* bacteria cause food poisoning.

1 Name some bacterial diseases.

2 Describe the symptoms of *Salmonella* and gonorrhoea.

Figure 4.23 How are these gonorrhoea bacteria different from *Salmonella* bacteria?

Spread and control

Bacteria are spread and controlled in various ways.

Salmonella is spread by:

- ingesting (eating) food that is contaminated with *Salmonella* bacteria
- preparing food in unhygienic conditions; for example, using contaminated knives or chopping boards.

In the UK, the spread of *Salmonella* is controlled by vaccinating poultry against the bacterium. Food should be prepared in hygienic conditions and cooked thoroughly. Washing hands before and after food preparation and after using the bathroom also help.

Figure 4.24 Why must food be cooked thoroughly?

Gonorrhoea is spread by sexual contact. The spread can be controlled by:

- treatment with antibiotics. In the past, the disease was easily treated with the antibiotic penicillin, but in recent years many resistant strains of the bacteria have appeared
- use of a barrier method of contraception, such as a condom, to prevent contact.

3 Describe how *Salmonella* is spread.

4 Explain how gonorrhoea can be controlled.

HIGHER TIER ONLY

Symptom delay

People with communicable infections do not develop symptoms as soon as they are infected with the pathogen. There are distinct stages of infection:

- The pathogen enters an organism.
- The pathogen reproduces rapidly in ideal conditions to increase numbers. This is the incubation period.
- Pathogens make harmful toxins, which build up. The more bacteria that are present, the quicker the toxins build up.
- Symptoms develop, for example, fever and a headache.

The graph shows *Salmonella* cases over a period of 12 months.

Figure 4.25 *Salmonella* cases over 1 year

5 Describe the pattern of *Salmonella* cases shown in the bar chart and suggest explanations for it.

6 Explain how knowledge of the spread of bacterial diseases can lead to their control.

7 Compare and contrast bacterial and viral diseases.

DID YOU KNOW?

In 2015 there was an outbreak of a highly drug-resistant strain of gonorrhoea bacteria in the UK.

KEY INFORMATION

Remember: bacteria are living things, unlike viruses. Bacterial diseases can be treated with antibiotics, unlike viral diseases.

Looking at fungal diseases

Learning objectives:

- recall the name and symptoms of a fungal disease
- describe the transmission and treatment of rose black spot
- explain how rose black spot affects the growth of the plant.

KEY WORDS

mulch
pruning
spores

Rose black spot is the most serious disease of wild and cultivated roses. It is caused by a fungus.

What is rose black spot?

Diplocarpon rosae is a parasitic fungus that causes black spot on roses. It needs warm, wet conditions to grow and spread; British summers are ideal.

The fungus produces black or purple spots on the upper surface of leaves. The spots spread rapidly and sometimes the string-like fungus can be seen. The leaves often turn yellow around the spots and drop early, even though other plant parts are not affected. Sometimes small, black scab-like spots develop on young stems.

Figure 4.26 Newly sprouted leaves are susceptible to black spot.

Figure 4.27 Black spot can cause black lesions on stems.

In recent years, rose black spot has become more common in urban gardens. Untreated, black spot can quickly affect all the roses in a garden, resulting in plants with bare stems.

1. What are the symptoms of rose black spot?
2. What conditions does the fungus need to grow?

Transmission and treatment

The fungus produces **spores** (similar to seeds). The spores are released in wet, humid conditions, for example, when it rains or the plants are watered. Wind also helps spores to disperse. The optimum temperature for fungal growth is about 24°C. After about 7 hours of wet, hot conditions the spores germinate. Symptoms start to appear on leaves 3–10 days after infection. Spores are then produced every 3 weeks throughout the growing season. They overwinter on shoots, but can survive on dropped leaves and in soil.

Treatments include:

- immediately removing infected dropped leaves from the soil and burning them
- **pruning** shoots in the spring and burning all cut stems
- not composting infected leaves and stems
- treating infections with fungicides to kill the pathogen
- putting manure or **mulch** around the plants in spring to prevent fungal spores reaching the stems.

Figure 4.28 How does pruning help prevent the spread of the fungus?

3 Describe how black spot is transmitted.

4 Explain three treatments for black spot.

How does the pathogen affect growth?

Rose growth is greatly reduced because affected leaves are unable to photosynthesise efficiently. The fungus grows in the mesophyll, penetrating cells and intercellular spaces. This causes irreversible structural changes in affected cells, for example, by damaging cell membranes which causes leakage of essential nutrients into the intercellular spaces. The cells can then no longer photosynthesise to make the food the plant needs to survive.

5 Explain how the black spot fungus affects the growth of roses.

Learning about malaria

Learning objectives:

- recall that malaria is a protist disease
- describe the life cycle of the malarial vector.

Malaria is the most prolific parasitic disease of humans in the world. More children die from malaria than any other communicable disease.

What is malaria?

The pathogens that cause malaria are called **protists**. Protists are single-celled organisms. The protist that causes malaria is called *Plasmodium*. For part of its life cycle it lives in human blood.

sharply-pointed
mouthparts

blood
vessel

Figure 4.29 How do you catch malaria?

The protist is spread by female mosquitoes, which feed on blood. They suck infected blood from someone with malaria and then pass the protists on when they feed on a new person.

Organisms that spread disease, rather than causing it themselves, are called **vectors**. The mosquito is the vector for malaria.

Symptoms of malaria appear from 7–18 days to over a year after infection and include:

- recurrent episodes of fever
- sweats and chills
- muscle pains
- headaches
- diarrhoea
- cough.

Malaria can be fatal if not treated.

1 **What causes malaria?**

2 **What are the symptoms of malaria?**

3 **What is a vector?**

Spreading malaria

The mosquito has a complicated life cycle. Mosquitoes breed and lay eggs in still water. The eggs hatch and each larva develops into a pupa in the water. When an adult mosquito hatches, it rests on the water surface to let its body dry and harden so it can fly.

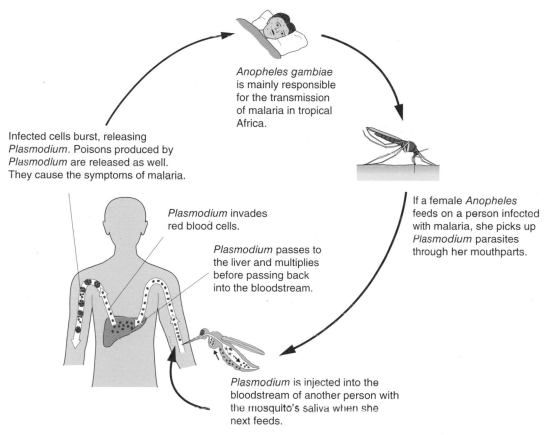

Anopheles gambiae is mainly responsible for the transmission of malaria in tropical Africa.

Infected cells burst, releasing *Plasmodium*. Poisons produced by *Plasmodium* are released as well. They cause the symptoms of malaria.

Plasmodium invades red blood cells.

Plasmodium passes to the liver and multiplies before passing back into the bloodstream.

If a female *Anopheles* feeds on a person infected with malaria, she picks up *Plasmodium* parasites through her mouthparts.

Plasmodium is injected into the bloodstream of another person with the mosquito's saliva when she next feeds.

Figure 4.30 Mosquito life cycle

Malaria is controlled by breaking the life cycle of the vector or by avoiding contact with it. Control measures include:

- spraying pools of water with insecticide to kill the mosquitoes
- draining stagnant water pools
- spraying pools with oil to prevent the larvae from breathing
- using mosquito nets to avoid bites
- taking drugs to kill the protist in the blood.

Malaria can also be spread by using dirty needles for injections or can be passed from a pregnant woman to her baby.

4 **Explain how malaria is spread.**

5 **Describe the life cycle of the malarial vector.**

DID YOU KNOW?

Malaria is not found in the UK, but about 1400 people were diagnosed with it after returning from holiday in 2012. Two people died.

Protecting the body

Learning objectives:

- describe how the body protects itself from pathogens
- explain how the body protects itself from pathogens
- explain how communicable diseases can be spread.

The body has defence mechanisms for each way that pathogens are transmitted.

How does the body defend itself?

Millions of pathogens are around us each day, but your body protects you from being infected:

- Your skin acts as a barrier and produces antimicrobial secretions via glands in the skin.

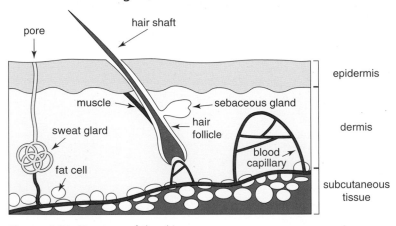

Figure 4.31 Structure of the skin

- The nose traps particles that may contain pathogens.
- Your trachea and bronchi secrete mucus, which traps pathogens.
- The stomach produces acid, which kills the majority of pathogens that enter via the mouth.
- Platelets (cell fragments in your blood) start the clotting process at wound sites. Clots dry to form scabs, which seal the wound.

1 How does the body protect itself from pathogens?

2 Which of these defence mechanisms will protect you against pathogens in water and in food?

Hygiene and wounds

When you cough or sneeze, thousands of tiny drops of liquid are sprayed into the air. If you have a disease, the droplets may contain pathogens. This is why you should use a paper tissue and then put it in the bin. Coughing up phlegm and then spitting it out can also spread infections to those around you. Children playing may fall on it and any pathogens can enter the body through wounds in the skin.

When the skin is cut, platelets in the blood are exposed to the air at the wound site. They make protein fibres (fibrin) that form a mesh over the wound. The platelets and red blood cells get caught in the fibres to form a clot.

3 Explain how coughing and sneezing spread pathogens.

4 How do clots form over wounds? Explain how the formation of a scab helps to protect the body.

Figure 4.32 How are wounds sealed?

HIGHER TIER ONLY

Defence mechanisms in detail

Skin protects the body from physical damage, infection and dehydration. The outer layer of skin cells is dry and dead. Pathogens cannot easily penetrate these dead cells. Sebaceous glands in the skin produce antimicrobial oils.

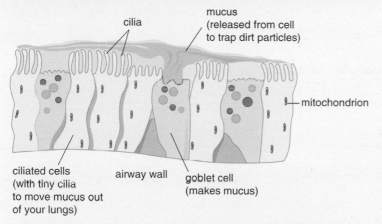

Figure 4.33 How does the respiratory system protect the body?

Every time you breathe, you take in many microbes. Hairs in the nose trap larger microbes and dust particles. The trachea and bronchi have a ciliated epithelium. **Cilia** are tiny hair-like structures. **Goblet cells** in the epithelium produce mucus; mucus traps smaller dust particles and microbes. Cilia beat together to waft mucus to the back of the throat, where it is swallowed. Ciliated cells have many mitochondria to supply the energy needed to do this.

5 How does skin act as a defence against pathogens?

6 Explain the adaptations of the respiratory system to protect us against pathogens.

7 Smoking can damage and paralyse the cilia. Explain why smokers are more susceptible to respiratory infections.

DID YOU KNOW?

It has been estimated that a sneeze expels mucus at 160 km/h.

REMEMBER!

Cilia are like hairs; they are not cells and cannot be killed.

Exploring white blood cells

Learning objectives:

- describe phagocytosis
- explain how antibody production can lead to immunity
- explain the specificity of immune system responses.

Although the body's defence mechanisms prevent many microbes from entering the body, some will succeed.

White blood cells

The immune system recognises and destroys pathogens that enter the body. White blood cells are an important part of the immune system.

They attack invading pathogens. If a pathogen enters the body, white blood cells defend it by:

- ingesting pathogens
- producing antibodies
- producing antitoxins.

There are two main groups of white blood cell: **phagocytes** and **lymphocytes**. Phagocytes can leave the blood by squeezing through capillaries to enter tissues that are being attacked. They move towards pathogens or toxins and ingest them. This is called phagocytosis.

Figure 4.34 White blood cells are the largest blood cells.

1 A phagocyte moves towards a bacterium.

2 The phagocyte pushes a sleeve of cytoplasm outwards to surround the bacterium.

3 The bacterium is now enclosed in a vacuole inside the cell. It is then killed and digested by enzymes.

Figure 4.35 Phagocytes ingest pathogens during phagocytosis

1 **How do white blood cells protect the body?**

2 **What happens to a pathogen during phagocytosis?**

Antitoxins and antibodies

Pathogens make us feel ill because they release toxins into our body. White blood cells, called lymphocytes, produce **antitoxins** to neutralise toxins made by the pathogen. Antitoxins combine with the toxin to make a safe chemical. Antitoxins are specific to a particular toxin.

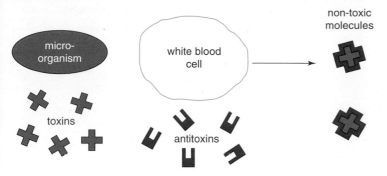

Figure 4.36 Antitoxins neutralise toxins made by pathogens.

Lymphocytes also produce chemicals called **antibodies** that destroy pathogens. Lymphocytes recognise when pathogens are present. They quickly reproduce to make lots of antibodies that:

- cause cell lysis (the pathogens burst)
- bind to the pathogens and destroy them
- cover the pathogens, sticking them together.

Phagocytes then ingest them.

If the same type of pathogen enters the body again, lymphocyte cells recognise it and immediately make lots of antibodies. This is **immunity**: the person is immune to that disease.

3 How do antitoxins work?

4 Explain how antibody production leads to immunity.

5 Explain how phagocytosis and antitoxin production protect the body.

Producing antibodies

Each lymphocyte has a specific antibody to attack a specific pathogen. Pathogens carry chemicals called antigens on their surface. The appropriate antibodies lock onto the matching antigens, sticking the pathogens together to destroy them.

HIV damages white blood cells, meaning that they cannot make antibodies or kill other infected cells. When HIV has destroyed sufficient white blood cells, the body cannot make appropriate immune responses. Then the person has AIDS. They have fewer or no lymphocytes to recognise simple infections and release antibodies. This means that they can die from simple infections that healthy people can overcome.

6 Explain the specificity of antibodies.

7 Why can a person with AIDS die from a simple infection?

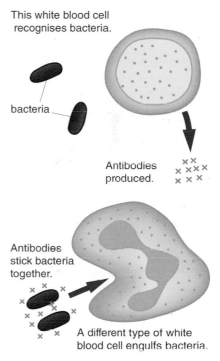

Figure 4.37 How do these white blood cells work?

DID YOU KNOW?

Only 1% of all the cells in blood are white blood cells. There are 5 000–10 000 of them in 1 mm^3 of blood.

COMMON MISCONCEPTION

Remember: white blood cells do not *eat* pathogens; they *ingest* them.

Using antibiotics and painkillers

KEY WORDS

antiviral
aspirin
opiates
penicillin

Learning objectives:

- describe the uses of antibiotics and painkillers
- explain how antibiotics and painkillers can be used to treat diseases
- explain the limitations of antibiotics.

You can take medicines to make you feel better when you have an infectious disease.

Useful drugs

A drug is any chemical that alters how the body works. Medicines contain useful drugs. Many medicines do not affect the pathogen that makes you ill. They just relieve the symptoms caused by the infection, for example, painkillers and cough medicines. Other medicines work inside the body to kill bacterial pathogens: these are antibiotics, for example, **penicillin**.

Antibiotics work by interfering with the pathogen's metabolism; for example, with processes that make bacterial cell walls. Antibiotics do not affect human cells and they do not kill viral, protist or fungal pathogens. They only kill bacterial pathogens.

1. What is a medicine?
2. How are painkillers and antibiotics similar and different?

How do medicines work?

There are many different antibiotics. Some antibiotics work against one type of bacterial infection. Others are used to treat many different bacterial infections. It is important to use the correct antibiotic for a specific bacterium.

If a bacterium cannot be killed by an antibiotic, it is resistant to that antibiotic. A prescribed course of antibiotics has the correct amount to kill the bacterial pathogen completely. This is why you must always take the complete antibiotic course.

The use of antibiotics has greatly reduced deaths from infectious bacterial diseases. But, misuse of antibiotics has led to the emergence of strains of bacteria that are antibiotic resistant (for more on this, see Topic 7.7 Antimicrobial resistance).

Figure 4.38 Antibiotics and painkillers are medicinal drugs

Figure 4.39 Antibiotic test: the size of the clear area around the antibiotic disc indicates the effectiveness of the antibiotic against the bacteria growing on the agar plate.

Figure 4.40 How has the antibiotic affected these bacteria?

When you are injured, sensory nerve endings send pain messages to your brain. Painkillers stop these nerve impulses, so you feel little or no pain. Many painkillers are based on two natural drugs:

- **aspirin**, from willow bark
- **opiates**, from poppies.

3 Explain how painkillers work.

4 Compare the use of painkillers and antibiotics.

Antiviral drugs

Antibiotics cannot be used to kill viral pathogens. This is because viruses live and reproduce inside cells. Antibiotics do not harm body cells and the viruses inside are protected. **Antiviral** drugs are used to treat viral infections. Antivirals are specific to a particular virus. While antibiotics can kill bacteria, antiviral drugs only slow down viral development. It is difficult to develop drugs which kill viruses without also damaging the body's tissues.

5 Explain the limitations of antibiotics.

6 The graph shows the bacteria present during an infection.

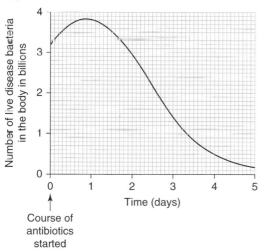

Figure 4.41 Graph showing the effect of an antibiotic on bacterial numbers

Explain

a why the numbers increase after antibiotics were taken
b why the full course of antibiotics needs to be taken.

DID YOU KNOW?

Alexander Fleming discovered penicillin, the first antibiotic, in 1928.

KEY INFORMATION

Remember: painkillers relieve infection symptoms.
Antibiotics kill bacteria.

Building immunity

Learning objectives:

- recall how vaccinations prevent infection
- explain how mass vaccination programmes reduce the spread of a disease
- evaluate the global use of vaccination.

KEY WORDS

immunity
vaccination
vaccine

One in three people who caught smallpox in the 1600s died from it. Smallpox is now almost eradicated globally.

What is vaccination?

A **vaccination** introduces a small quantity of an inactive or dead form of a pathogen into the body to protect us from disease. Lymphocytes produce antibodies to fight the 'infection' but we don't actually become ill. When live pathogens of the same type infect you, your immune system starts to protect you immediately.

Different **vaccines** are needed for specific pathogens. For example, polio, whooping cough, flu and HPV (human papilloma virus) all have a different vaccine. MMR vaccinations contain three vaccines (for measles, mumps and rubella).

Vaccinations are usually given to children and people who are going to travel to countries where there is a risk of serious disease. Vaccines are given by injection, orally or by nasal sprays.

1. What is a vaccination?
2. What do vaccinations do?

Figure 4.42 Suggest why vaccinations are given to children

antibody   antigen

- An antibody is a protein produced by the immune system in response to the presence of a foreign antigen.

- An antibody is specific because its shape will only fit one shape of antigen.

bacterium

Figure 4.43 Antibodies are specific to a particular antigen on a pathogen

How do vaccines work?

After the vaccination:

- lymphocytes detect antigens on the dead or inactive pathogen; they produce a specific antibody for these antigens
- antibodies lock onto the antigens
- lymphocytes 'remember' the shape of the antigens
- when there is a real infection due to a live pathogen entering the body, lymphocytes instantly recognise the pathogen because it has the same antigens as the vaccine
- lymphocytes quickly make many specific antibodies
- antibodies lock onto the pathogens and kill them before they have a chance to make you feel ill. This is **immunity**.

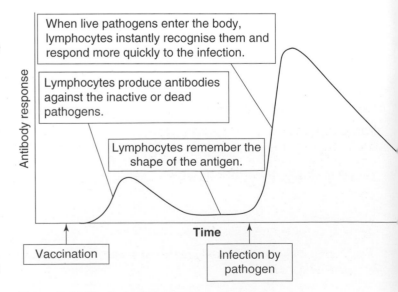

When live pathogens enter the body, lymphocytes instantly recognise them and respond more quickly to the infection.

Lymphocytes produce antibodies against the inactive or dead pathogens.

Lymphocytes remember the shape of the antigen.

Antibody response

Time

Vaccination

Infection by pathogen

Figure 4.44 The immune response

Mass vaccination programmes increase the number of people who are immune to a pathogen, making it difficult for the pathogen to pass to people who are not immunised. If a large proportion of the population is immune to a pathogen, its spread is very much reduced. Global vaccination programmes have eradicated polio, except in Pakistan and Afghanistan. Nigeria did not have any new polio infections in 2015.

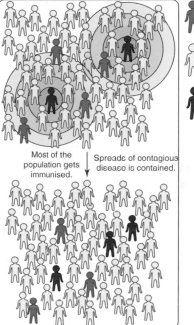

= not immunised but still healthy

= immunised and still healthy

= not immunised, sick and contagious

No one is immunised. | Contagious disease spreads through the population.

Some of the population gets immunised. | Contagious disease spreads through some of the population.

Most of the population gets immunised. | Spread of contagious disease is contained.

Figure 4.45 Mass vaccination programmes reduce the spread of disease

3 **Look at Figure 4.44 on the previous page.**

   a **Why were antibodies produced more quickly after the second infection?**

   b **Will the person be ill after the second infection?**

4 **How do mass vaccination programmes reduce the spread of disease?**

Vaccination and populations

Some viruses frequently mutate into new strains. This means that lymphocytes do not recognise the new strains. As a result, new vaccines are made regularly for some diseases, such as flu.

Some antibodies give lifelong protection, such as those that are active against measles. Sometimes antibodies fall below the critical level needed for immunity, as happens in the case of tetanus. Booster doses are needed to increase the antibodies again.

5 **Explain why new flu vaccines are made each year.**

6 **People now travel widely across the world. Evaluate the global use of vaccination.**

DID YOU KNOW?

Flu vaccine is stored in eggs because it needs to be in a living organism to survive.

ADVICE

Remember: lymphocytes make *antibodies*.
Pathogens have antigens.

Making new drugs

KEY WORDS

dose
efficacy
placebo

Learning objectives:

- recall some traditional drugs and their origins
- describe how new drugs are developed
- explain why 'double-blind' trials are conducted.

Doctors, politicians, drug companies and scientists all have roles in deciding the development of new drugs.

Making new drugs from old

Researchers sometimes use traditional medicines to start developing new drugs. Traditionally, drugs were extracted from plants and microorganisms, for example:

- the heart drug digitalis comes from foxgloves
- the painkiller aspirin comes from willow trees
- penicillin was discovered by Alexander Fleming in *Penicillium* mould.

Chemists working for pharmaceutical companies formulate most new drugs. The starting point is often chemicals that are extracted from plants.

New drugs are tested and trialled before being prescribed to ensure they are:

- effective – able to prevent or cure a disease, or make you feel better; this is the drug's **efficacy**
- safe – not too toxic or with any undesirable side effects
- stable – it must be possible to store any new drug for a period of time.

1. Name three traditional drugs and state the source of each.
2. Why do new medicinal drugs need to tested and trialled?

Figure 4.46 Suggest why research may start with traditional medicines.

Developing new drugs

Stages in drug development are:

- preclinical testing in laboratories (using cells, tissues and live animals) to find out side effects and efficacy
- clinical trials, which use healthy volunteers and other patients. Low **doses** of the drug are given at the start. Then, if the drug is deemed safe, further trials are performed to find the optimum dose. Clinical trials are split into phases, as shown in Figure 4.47.

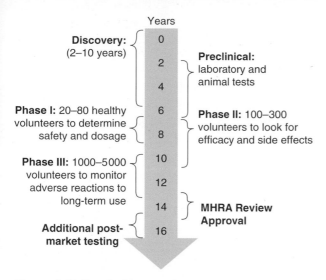

Figure 4.47 Developing new drugs

Trial results are peer reviewed by medical professionals and, only then, are they published.

Clinical trials involve some risk because unexpected side effects can occur.

3 Describe the stages in the development of a drug.

4 Why are potential drugs tested on human cells, animals and healthy human volunteers before being tested on patients?

Double-blind trials

Double-blind trials are when patients are allocated randomly to groups, so that doctors and patients do not know, until the trial is complete, if they are taking:

- the new drug (this is the test group)
- a **placebo** (a treatment that does not contain the drug). This is the control group.

Clinical trials must not be influenced by the people involved in them, whether patients, doctors or employees of pharmaceutical companies. Sometimes, people feel better just because they think they will if they take a medicine. This is the 'placebo effect'.

5 Why are double-blind trials conducted?

6 What is the placebo effect?

7 In a blind trial, the patients do not know which drug they are receiving but the doctors do. Results from such trials are not always reliable. Suggest why this might be the case.

MATHS SKILLS

Sampling and scientific data

Learning objectives:

- understand why sampling is used in science
- be able to explain different sampling techniques
- be able to extract and interpret information from graphs.

When undertaking clinical investigations, scientists are unable to test all people, so sampling is used.

Populations and samples

We cannot study every individual in a population, so we use a sample of the population.

Choosing the right size of sample is important. Carrying out studies costs money so scientists don't want to use sample groups that are large, but the risk with small groups is that they aren't representative enough of the whole population. This is known as a 'sampling error' and it means that the results of the study don't indicate well what the population as a whole is like.

Scientists were investigating the effectiveness of a new antibiotic. For an antibiotic to be effective it should cure 95–100% of the cases of an illness.

Imagine that the population taking the antibiotic is represented by a container of coloured balls. Each ball is a patient. Red balls represent patients who are not cured by the antibiotic. The blue balls represent the patients who are cured.

The scientists take a small sample, of 10 balls. There is 1 red ball and 9 blue balls:

$$\frac{\text{Patients not cured (red balls)}}{\text{All patients (red and blue balls)}} \times 100 = \text{\% chance of not being cured}$$

So:

$$\frac{1}{10} \times 100 = 0.1 \times 100 = 10\% \text{ chance of not being cured.}$$

This suggests that the antibiotic is only effective for 90% of patients treated.

However, in another sample, this time of 100 balls (patients), there are only two red balls:

$$\frac{2}{100} \times 100 = 0.02 \times 100 = 2\% \text{ chance of not being cured.}$$

This larger sample suggests that the antibiotic is 98% effective.

DID YOU KNOW?

Thalidomide relieved morning sickness in pregnant women. Pregnant women were not in the sample used to test thalidomide. Many babies born to mothers who took thalidomide had limb abnormalities.

ADVICE

Remember: a small error in a small sample can mean a large percentage error.

When using a small sample size, a sampling error can easily be made, which makes the outcome unreliable. To avoid this sampling error, large-scale clinical trials that test new drugs in humans are likely to involve thousands of patients.

1 Why do scientists use samples for investigations?

2 Figure 4.48 shows more samples in the antibiotic investigation.
a Calculate the proportion of people who were cured in each sample.
b How does sample size affect the results of the test?

Sampling techniques

Research aims to find consistent patterns in repeat samples, which show relationships. Scientists select samples for clinical trials by:

- using random samples
- grouping individuals by characteristics, then randomly selecting people from each group
- focusing on a particular subset of a population.

The sampling technique used can affect the outcomes.

3 Why must care be taken when selecting the sampling method to be used?

4 Scientists studied 31 000 heart disease patients. They compared patients with high heart rates (more than 80 beats per minute) and low heart rates (less than 58 beats per minute). How could the sampling method be improved?

Figure 4.48 How does sample size affect results?

Looking at bias

Sample size needs to be considered as part of the research process. For a small population, 5–10% is a large enough sample size. For a larger population of size '*n*', sample size = $\sqrt{n}$.

The symbol '$\sqrt{}$' means square root, so

$\sqrt{25}$ means the 'square root of 25'

The square root is the inverse of the square of a number.

For a population of 900, the sample size = $\sqrt{900}$ = 30.

There is a square root key on a scientific calculator.

Bias refers to **systematic** errors, which can give false outcomes. These must be eliminated wherever possible. In clinical trials, control groups are used (these are people with similar diet, weight etc.), along with an approach called blinding (see section 4.13, 'Making new drugs'). Neither the patients nor the doctors can tell which are the test or the placebo drugs, so they do not know which patients get the test drug.

5 Explain fully how bias in clinical trials can be minimised.

6 What sample size would you suggest for trials involving these total populations?
a 36 patients
b 169 patients
c 729 patients
d 136 161 patients

Check your progress

You should be able to:

describe the major causes of ill health → explain how diseases and lifestyle factors affect health → evaluate graphical data about lifestyle and health

recall a number of interacting factors which cause different diseases → explain how risk factors are linked to an increased rate of some non-communicable diseases → evaluate evidence linking risk factors and increased rates of disease

describe different types of tumours → describe lifestyle changes to reduce cancer risk → evaluate evidence linking smoking and cancer

describe the symptoms of some viral, bacterial, fungal and protist diseases → describe the transmission and control of different diseases → compare and contrast bacterial and viral diseases / evaluate control measures for malaria / explain the specificity of antibodies

describe how the body protects itself from pathogens → explain the role of the immune system → explain the impact of antibiotic-resistant bacteria

recall why vaccinations are used → explain how vaccinations trigger an immune response → evaluate the global use of vaccinations

describe the use of antibiotics and painkillers → explain how antibiotics and painkillers treat disease → explain the limitations of antibiotics

Worked example

Viruses are pathogens that cause many diseases. Babies and children are vaccinated to protect them from many viruses.

1 **a Why are antibiotics not used to kill viruses in the body?**

   They cannot kill them.

> The correct answer is that viruses live inside cells, where they are protected from the action of antibiotics.

b What is in a vaccine?

   A weak form of the virus.

> Correct answer identified, although 'weak form' could be improved by replacing it with 'inactive or dead form'.

c What does the vaccine do in the child's body?

   It makes antibodies.

> This is inaccurate. White blood cells/lymphocytes make antibodies.

d Why do pathogens make us feel ill?

   They produce poisons.

> This is partially correct, but the answer should also include the fact that pathogens damage cells.

2 **a One type of tumour is known as benign. Name the other type of tumour and explain how it is different from a benign tumour.**

   Cancer tumour spreads through the body.

> Incorrect tumour type identified. Correct answer is malignant tumour, but the difference is correct.

b Name a risk factor for lung cancer.

   Smoking

> Correct answer identified

3 **a Describe how malaria is spread by mosquitoes.**

   Mosquitoes suck the blood of an infected person.

> Answer should also include how the mosquito then passes the protist pathogen/*Plasmodium* to an uninfected person.

b Explain how malaria is controlled by insecticide.

   Insecticide kills eggs.

> Answer should mention mosquito eggs, and also include that mosquitoes lay their eggs in water.

End of chapter questions

Getting started

① Define the term 'vector'. `1 Mark`

② Describe how the stomach helps defend the body against pathogens. `1 Mark`

③ Name two risk factors for developing cardiovascular disease. `2 Marks`

④ What type of pathogen causes rose black spot? `1 Mark`

⑤ What type of blood cells destroy bacterial pathogens? `1 Mark`

⑥ A blood test reveals that Victoria has a white cell count of 4 000 000 000. `1 Mark`

Write this number in standard form.

⑦ Smoking damages cilia in the bronchi. How does this affect the smoker? `1 Mark`

Going further

⑧ Name a disease that is caused by a protist pathogen. `1 Mark`

⑨ What do vaccines contain? `1 Mark`

⑩ Give two examples of physical defences that help prevent pathogens entering the plant. `2 Marks`

⑪ Shireen has a sore throat caused by a bacterial pathogen, and a headache. What medicines should she take? Explain why. `4 Marks`

⑫ The first plant virus to be identified was tobacco mosaic virus (TMV). The virus causes 'mosaic'-like mottling and yellow spots on the leaves. The virus damages chloroplasts.

Suggest why plants infected with TMV have stunted growth and discoloured leaves. `4 Marks`

⑬ The graph shows the effect of two risk factors on mortality. Describe the patterns in the data.

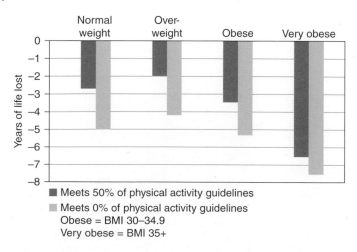

`2 Marks`

More challenging

⑭ Why is an antibody specific? `1 Mark`

⑮ Why is it difficult to develop drugs that kill viruses? `1 Mark`

16 Explain the use of antibiotics against bacteria and viruses.

2 Marks

17 A group of scientists are investigating the effectiveness of a new antibiotic used to treat *Streptococcus pyogenes* bacteria. They test the antibiotic by spreading *Streptococcus pyogenes* bacteria on an agar jelly plate and place a small disc of filter paper containing the antibiotic in the centre of the dish. They then measured the radius of the 'zone of inhibition' shown in the diagram.

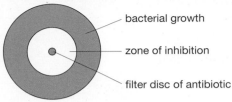

bacterial growth

zone of inhibition

filter disc of antibiotic

a The radius of the zone of inhibition was 12 mm. Calculate the area using the equation: Area = πr^2

Use the value $\pi = 3.14$

1 Mark

b The scientists used aseptic techniques during the investigation in order to avoid contamination. Explain why is this important.

2 Marks

For an antibiotic to be considered effective it should cure 95–100% of the cases of an illness. Out of a sample of 568 patients given the new antibiotic, 483 were cured.

c Calculate the chance of not being cured.

2 Marks

d The patients sampled were all university students aged between 18 and 25. Suggest how this may have affected the results of the investigation.

1 Mark

Most demanding

18 Cholera is a potentially fatal bacterial infection caused by consuming contaminated food or water. In 1997 there were 150 000 cases of cholera and in 1998 there were 290 000.

Calculate the percentage increase in cases between 1997 and 1998. Give your answer to 1 decimal place.

2 Marks

19 The graph below shows smoking and lung cancer rates in the UK.

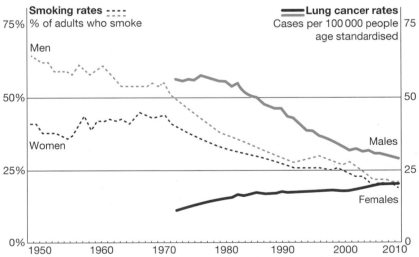

Describe the trends in the data and evaluate the evidence for a link between smoking and lung cancer.

6 Marks

Total: 40 Marks

COORDINATION AND CONTROL

ORGANS WORK TOGETHER AS SYSTEMS.

- Organs are aggregations of tissues.
- Organ systems work together to form organisms.
- Glands in the digestive system produce digestive enzymes.

METABOLISM INVOLVES CHEMICAL SYNTHESIS AND BREAKDOWN OF SUBSTANCES.

- Products of digestion are used to build carbohydrates, lipids and proteins.
- In animals, carbohydrate is stored as glycogen.
- Glucose is required by all cells for respiration; carbon dioxide and water are waste products.
- Carbon dioxide is excreted by the lungs.
- Excess protein is converted to urea.
- Other waste products from cells are transported in the blood and excreted by the kidneys.

HOW HUMANS REPRODUCE.

- The male and female reproductive systems are structured differently and adapted to their specialised functions.
- Male and female gametes join together in the process known as fertilisation.
- The fertilised cell develops to form an embryo during pregnancy.
- Some diseases are transmitted sexually and this can be prevented by some forms of contraception.

IN THIS CHAPTER YOU WILL FIND OUT ABOUT:

CONDITIONS IN THE BODY, AND HOW PROCESSES AND ORGAN SYSTEMS ARE COORDINATED AND CONTROLLED.

- Regulation of the internal conditions in the body is called homeostasis.
- The nervous and endocrine systems are involved in this coordination and control.
- The nervous system works using electrical impulses, transmitted using nerves; the endocrine system uses chemicals called hormones, which are secreted by endocrine glands.
- In the nervous system, receptors can be grouped into sense organs, such as the eye.
- Different regions of the brain coordinate our responses, though spinal reflexes can by-pass it.

CONTROL OF METABOLISM AND LEVELS OF CHEMICALS IN THE BODY.

- The concentrations of glucose, water and salts must be kept within strict limits.
- Glucose concentration in the blood is controlled by hormones.
- Lack of insulin, or a loss of sensitivity to it, causes a condition called diabetes, which must be controlled.
- The control of hormone secretion by many glands is by negative feedback.

CONTROL OF SEXUAL DEVELOPMENT AND HUMAN REPRODUCTION.

- Reproductive hormones cause secondary sexual characteristics to develop.
- Pituitary gland hormones regulate egg development and release, and along with reproductive hormones, prepare the body for a possible pregnancy.
- Different methods of contraception help to prevent unwanted births.
- Fertility drugs and *in-vitro* fertilisation are possible solutions to infertility.

Homeostasis

Learning objectives:

- explain the importance of homeostasis in regulating internal conditions in the body
- recall that these control systems involve nervous or chemical responses
- describe how control systems involve receptors, coordination centres and effectors.

KEY WORDS

endocrine system
homeostasis
hormone
nervous system
target organ

Eve is running a marathon. While she is running, mechanisms in her body will try to keep internal conditions as constant as possible.

What changes in Eve's body?

As Eve is running, the rate at which her body cells respire increases. Her heart rate, breathing rate and breath volume increase during exercise to supply her muscles with more oxygenated blood. Her muscle cells break down glucose to release the energy she needs. Thermal energy is also released.

The thermal energy is carried around Eve's body by her blood. Normal body temperature is 37 °C, the optimum temperature for enzyme action and other cell functions. The human brain, for instance, is very sensitive to changes in temperature.

Eve must control her body temperature within strict limits.

One way she does this, as she runs, is to sweat. But sweating will also affect the water level in her body. She takes in extra water from sports drinks during the race. The drinks also contain some glucose. Her stores of glycogen will decrease during the race and, as she suffers from fatigue at the end of the race, her blood glucose concentration falls.

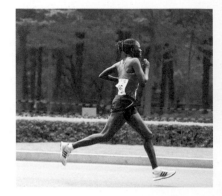

Figure 5.1 Conditions in Eve's body will change during the marathon.

1. **Why does body temperature need to be kept constant?**

2. **Name two other things that have to be controlled by the body.**

Homeostasis

Homeostasis is the regulation of internal conditions in the body. It is necessary to maintain optimal conditions for body functioning. These internal conditions can change as a result of processes within the body and as external conditions change.

The control systems involved in homeostasis are 'automatic' – they happen all the time or if conditions change – we do not have to think about taking any action. The body systems that are responsible for homeostasis are:

- the **nervous system** – uses electrical impulses to communicate
- the **endocrine system** – uses chemical molecules to communicate.

Figure 5.2 A nerve is a bundle of nerve cells enclosed within a sheath of connective tissue.

③ Write down a definition of homeostasis.

④ Which two body systems are responsible for homeostasis?

Control systems

All control systems in the body, whether nervous or endocrine, have the same pattern.

Figure 5.3 The components of the body systems that are responsible for homeostasis

The nervous system and endocrine system are different in nature but, in practice, the two systems interact with and regulate each other.

	Nervous system	Endocrine system
response	rapid and short duration	slower but acts for longer
nature of message	nerve impulse – electrical	a **hormone** – chemical
action	carried in nerves to specific location, e.g. muscle	carried in blood to all organs, but affects the **target organ** only

The nervous and endocrine systems compared

⑤ How are changes detected by the body?

⑥ Compare and contrast the nervous system and the endocrine system.

DID YOU KNOW?

The squid has giant nerve cells, up to 1 mm in diameter. Studying these has been key to our understanding of how nerve impulses are transmitted.

ADVICE

Remember the sequence of receptor → coordination centre → effector.

The nervous system

Learning objectives:

- explain how the nervous system is adapted to its functions
- describe the structure of the central nervous system and nerves.

KEY WORDS

central nervous system
myelin sheath
neurone
receptor

Nerve cells communicate with each other and with muscles, glands and other structures. There are critical periods during our lives when nerve cells are able to make these connections with other nerve cells. That is why we are able to learn different skills at different times – usually early on – in our lives.

The structure of the nervous system

Our nervous system enables us to detect our surroundings, and coordinate our behaviour.

The structure of the nervous system is well adapted to these functions.

1 **What is the function of the nervous system?**

2 **What are the two parts of the nervous system?**

Nerves

The nervous system consists of nerve cells or **neurones**. Neurones are specialised for transmitting messages in the form of an electrical impulse.

The part of the cell containing the nucleus is called the cell body. The cell body of all neurones is found in the CNS. Neurones, however, have an extended shape so that they can carry nerve impulses from one part of the body to another. Neurones also have fine branches at their tips to communicate with other neurones.

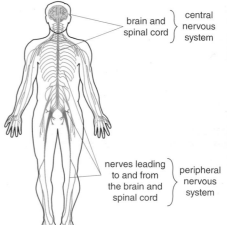

Figure 5.4 The nervous system is made up of the **central nervous system** (CNS) and the peripheral nervous system (PNS).

Figure 5.5 The projections that extend from a nerve cell communicate with other nerve cells.

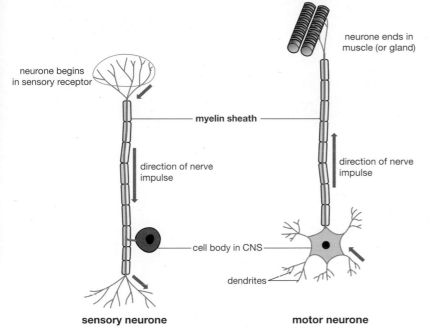

Figure 5.6 Two types of neurones. The long regions of neurones are bundled together as 'nerves'.

Receptors are cells that detect any changes in the environment. Receptors are sometimes grouped to form sense organs; for example, the eyes, ears, nose, tongue and skin contain sensory receptors. Sensory neurones relay nerve impulses from these receptors to the CNS.

The CNS processes the information and coordinates how the body should respond.

Motor neurones relay impulses from the CNS to the effector – for instance, a muscle or gland.

The sequence of events is:

stimulus → receptor → coordinator → effector → response

3 What is the scientific name for a nerve cell?

4 Describe the pathway of a nerve impulse, beginning with the stimulus and ending with the response.

MAKING CONNECTIONS

Link the information given here back to topic 1.7, and how nerve cells are adapted to their functions.

DID YOU KNOW?

Conditions such as multiple sclerosis, and diseases such as leprosy can seriously damage nerves and affect the transmission of nerve impulses.

Reflex actions

Learning objectives:

- explain the importance of reflex actions
- describe the path of a reflex arc
- explain how the structures in the reflex arc relate to their function.

KEY WORDS

reflex action
reflex arc
relay neurone
synapse

Nasim's doctor tests his reflexes by tapping the tendon just below the kneecap. Nasim's leg kicks up.

Reflexes are related to survival

Reflex actions are rapid, automatic responses to a stimulus. We do not have to think about them. Reflex actions form the basis of behaviour in simpler organisms. In humans, they prevent us from getting hurt. In other animals, our human ancestors and babies they are also related to survival.

Some reflex actions include:

- removing our hand from a hot or sharp object
- the grasping reflex, in which a baby grips a finger
- blinking our eyes if an object approaches rapidly
- the pupil reflex, whereby the pupil gets wider in dim light and narrower in bright light.

Figure 5.7 The knee-jerk reflex; a normal reaction time is around 50 ms.

1 What is a reflex action?

2 Why are reflex actions important?

The reflex arc

Our spinal reflexes do not involve the brain. Or, at least, not to begin with. In a reflex action, the nerve impulse follows a pathway called the **reflex arc**.

Figure 5.8 shows the pathway taken by a nerve impulse when a person puts a hand on a hot object.

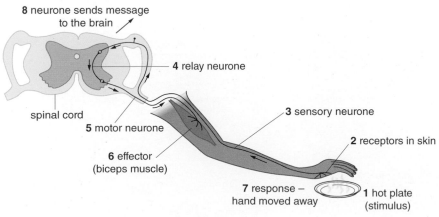

8 neurone sends message to the brain

4 relay neurone

spinal cord

5 motor neurone

6 effector (biceps muscle)

3 sensory neurone

2 receptors in skin

7 response – hand moved away

1 hot plate (stimulus)

Figure 5.8 The reflex arc. Follow the numbers 1–8. The pathway is through the spinal cord.

The pathway includes:

- a sensory neurone – transmits nerve impulses from the receptor to the CNS
- a **relay neurone**, in the spinal cord – transmits the impulses from the sensory to the motor neurone
- a motor neurone – sends impulses from the CNS to the effector.

In this case, the effector is the biceps muscle, which moves the arm. The hand is moved away from the hot object.

Other neurones in the spinal cord link via synapses with those of the reflex arc, so a message is sent to the brain *after* the hand has been removed (number 8 in the figure). It tells us that the plate was hot.

3 **Name the nervous pathway that a nerve impulse takes during a reflex action.**

4 **Explain how the parts of this pathway relate to their function.**

Linking nerves

The three neurones in the reflex arc do not link *physically*. There is a gap – called a **synapse** – between each pair. This means that *many* neurones can connect with one another. In the brain, neurones can link with up to 10 000 others.

Nerve impulses pass across a synapse with the help of chemical transmitter molecules.

MAKING CONNECTIONS

Be able to transfer your knowledge and describe the pathway taken by the reflex arc in another type of reflex action.

Chemical transmitter molecules are released into the synapse.

Transmitter molecules diffuse across the synapse.

Chemical transmitter molecules bind to receptors.

Channels in the next neurone open.

The nerve impulse is initiated in the next neurone.

Figure 5.9 Chemical transmitter molecules cause an impulse to move from one neurone to the next.

5 **What is the gap between neurones called?**

6 **How does a nerve impulse travel from one nerve to the next?**

7 **Compose a flow diagram to describe and explain the sequence of events in a reflex arc.**

Investigating reaction time

KEY WORDS

dominant hand
reaction time
valid

Learning objectives:

- select appropriate apparatus and techniques for the measurement of biological processes
- carry out physiological experiments safely
- use appropriate techniques in problem-solving contexts.

Our reflex actions protect us from harm. Quick reactions are also important in sport.

Measuring reaction time

A group of students worked in pairs to find their **reaction times** using the ruler drop test.

One student dropped a 30 cm ruler while another student caught it between their outstretched thumb and index finger of their **dominant hand**.

In the test, the release of the ruler is detected by our eyes and a message is sent to the sensory region of our brain. A message is then sent to another part, the motor region, which instructs muscles in our hand to contract.

After the student has carried out the test ten times, they rest their hand and then drink a cup of coffee. The student takes the test again to investigate the effect of coffee on their performance.

These pages are designed ❗ to help you think about aspects of the investigation rather than to guide you through it step by step.

Figure 5.10 In cricket, fielders need fast reaction times

Test number	Experiment 1: Normal student	Experiment 2: Student after drinking coffee
	Distance the ruler dropped (mm)	
1	119	98
2	116	98
3	117	92
4	113	91
5	150	92
6	113	93
7	108	92
8	109	92
9	108	91
10	107	91

The student's results for the ruler drop test

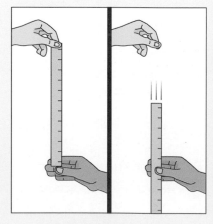

Figure 5.11 The ruler drop test

1. Write a risk assessment for this experiment.

2. Identify any anomalous results.

3. Calculate the average distance fallen by the ruler before and after drinking coffee.

Calculating reaction time

The distance travelled by the ruler before it is caught gives an indication of a student's reaction time, but not the reaction time itself.

Another group of students finds a formula on the Internet that is used to calculate reaction time:

where t = time in seconds

d = distance in metres,

a = acceleration as a result of gravity = 9.81 m/s²

They use this formula to calculate their reaction times.

$$t = \sqrt{\frac{2d}{a}}$$

4. Calculate the mean reaction time for the student before and after coffee.

5. The ingredient in coffee that affects our nervous system is caffeine. When testing its effect on other students, explain why the experiment must be carefully controlled to produce **valid** results.

Pooling class results

All the students in the year group measured their minimum reaction time. They used an alternative test on the computer. They had to click on the mouse when the screen changed colour. The reaction time was measured by the computer timer.

The students produced a tally of those falling into different ranges of reaction time.

Mean reaction time (ms)	101–200	201–250	251–275	276–300	301–325	326–350	351–375	376–400	401–500
Number of students within range	1	3	16	24	33	14	6	2	1

The tally of student reaction times across the year group

6. What type of chart would be best suited to displaying the data shown above? Draw a chart of the results.

7. Determine the median and modal reaction time categories.

8. Suggest why the computer method for measuring reaction time may be better than the ruler drop method.

DID YOU KNOW?

Caffeine works by affecting chemical transmitter molecules. It binds to one type that makes us sleepy. Fewer receptors are, therefore, available and nervous activity speeds up.

KEY SKILL

Selecting equipment, carrying out a risk assessment and processing data appropriately are important skills.

The endocrine system

Learning objectives:

- recall that the endocrine system is made up of glands that secrete hormones into the blood
- know the location of the major endocrine glands
- understand why the pituitary gland is the 'master gland'.

The world's tallest man was Robert Pershing Wadlow (1918–1940). He was 2.72 m when he died at the age of 22.

His height was caused by an excess of growth hormone, produced by the pituitary gland.

The endocrine system

Hormones are produced by glands of the **endocrine system**. **Endocrine glands** secrete hormones directly into the blood.

Hormones are often described as *chemical messengers*. They circulate in the blood and produce an effect on target organs. Many hormones are large molecules.

Like the nervous system, hormones work on effectors. But, unlike the nervous system, the effects they produce do not take milliseconds. With the exception of a hormone called adrenaline, effects of hormones take minutes or hours to occur, and in the case of hormones involved in our development, they can act for years.

Figure 5.12 We all produce growth hormone. Maximum production is during our youth.

1 What is the function of the endocrine system?

2 On what does the endocrine system act?

Location of the endocrine glands

There are a number of endocrine glands situated in different parts of the body. Some of these are gender specific and some produce enzymes as well as hormones.

3 Which organ secretes hormones and also digestive enzymes?

4 Which endocrine glands are found in the female only?

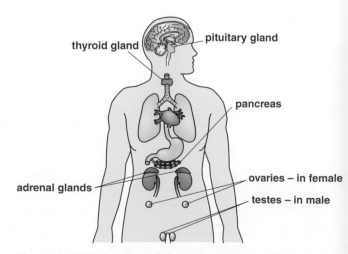

Figure 5.13 The location of the major endocrine glands in the body

The master gland

The pituitary gland is an outgrowth from the base of the brain.

Some hormones that the pituitary gland secretes, such as growth hormone, have a direct effect on their target organs. Other hormones have an indirect effect; they cause other glands to secrete hormones. Therefore, it is called the master gland, as it regulates the secretion of other endocrine glands.

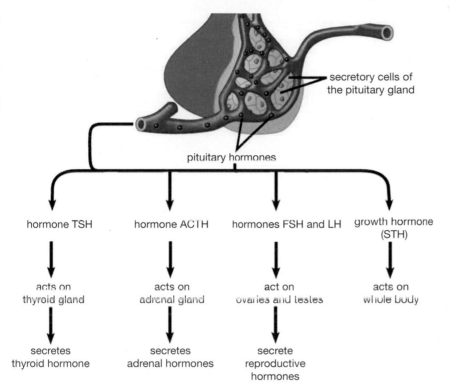

Figure 5.14 Some of the hormones secreted by the pituitary gland

DID YOU KNOW?

Some people do not produce enough growth hormone. In the 1960s, 27 000 people worldwide were given growth hormone extracted from the pituitary glands of dead people. A small number ended up with the brain disease, CJD, from infected brain tissue. Growth hormone is now produced by genetically modified organisms.

5 **Explain why the pituitary gland is called the master gland.**

6 **Name one hormone that exerts its effects over the whole body.**

Controlling blood glucose

Learning objectives:

- recall that blood glucose is monitored and controlled by the pancreas
- understand how insulin controls the blood glucose level
- understand how insulin works with another hormone – glucagon – to control blood sugar level.

Pao cannot produce enough of the hormone insulin to control her blood sugar level. She has diabetes. She needs injections of insulin to stay alive.

Controlling blood sugar

The pancreas secretes enzymes that digest carbohydrates, proteins and lipids.

The pancreas also has another function. It produces hormones that control the concentration of our blood glucose. Glucose is needed by all cells for respiration to release energy. It is carried to cells in our blood. But its concentration must be strictly controlled within certain limits.

After a meal, the concentration of glucose in our blood increases. The hormone **insulin** causes glucose in the blood to move into our body's cells. Here, this glucose can be used for respiration. In cells of the liver and muscle, the glucose is also converted into glycogen so that it can be stored.

Figure 5.15 Insulin secreted into the bloodstream causes our body cells to take up glucose.

1 **Name a hormone that controls blood glucose.**

2 **What effect does this hormone have on body cells?**

Blood glucose concentration

Insulin restores the blood glucose concentration to its normal level. A little insulin is produced as you first smell or chew food. As you eat food and it is digested, the blood glucose level rises, which causes a surge in insulin. The insulin level reaches a peak, then gradually falls.

Figure 5.16 shows what happens to blood glucose on eating a meal and then with the effect of insulin.

3 Describe how a person's blood glucose concentration changes after a meal.

4 How long after having a meal did this person's blood glucose level start to fall?

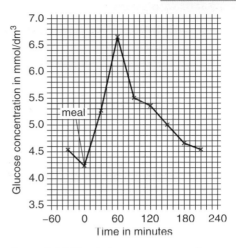

Figure 5.16 Blood glucose concentrations can rise to up to 8 mmol/dm³ after a meal or snack, before falling as insulin is secreted.

HIGHER TIER ONLY

Glucagon

Blood glucose is normally regulated at between 4.5–7.5 mmol per dm³ of blood. To obtain this fine control, another hormone that is produced by the pancreas is also involved – **glucagon**.

Insulin and glucagon achieve this fine control by balancing glucose with carbohydrate stored as glycogen. This balance is maintained via a negative feedback cycle.

Insulin promotes the uptake of glucose by cells, and its conversion into glycogen in the liver and muscles.

Glucagon, which is secreted in response to low blood glucose concentration, promotes the conversion of stored glycogen into glucose, which is released into the bloodstream.

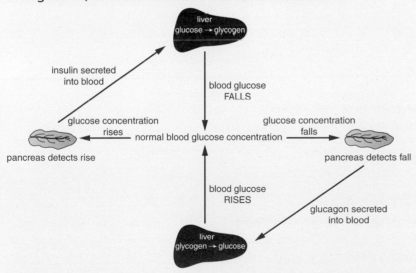

Figure 5.17 The control of blood glucose concentration by insulin and glucagon

5 What is the normal concentration of blood glucose? Why is it important to maintain this level of blood glucose?

6 Explain how a constant level of blood glucose concentration is maintained.

DID YOU KNOW?

Until the discovery of insulin in 1921 by Frederick Banting and Charles Best, diabetes was not treatable. Banting and Best carried out experiments on dogs and, later, themselves, before testing purified insulin on a teenager with diabetes in 1922.

ADVICE

Remember: don't confuse the storage compound glycogen with the hormone glucagon.

Diabetes

Learning objectives:

- understand the causes of Type 1 and Type 2 diabetes
- compare Type 1 and Type 2 diabetes
- evaluate information on the relationship between obesity and diabetes, and make appropriate recommendations.

KEY WORDS

body mass index
glucose tolerance
  test
Type 1 diabetes
Type 2 diabetes

Diabetes, if poorly controlled, can damage circulation, nerves, and muscles in the feet and legs, which may then need to be amputated.

Type 1 diabetes

In **Type 1 diabetes**, the pancreas is unable to produce enough, or any, insulin.

Without insulin, the body's cells are unable to take up glucose. The blood glucose level becomes uncontrollably high, and glucose is excreted in the urine.

Without glucose, cells must use alternative energy sources. Fat and protein are used. The person will lose weight. If the condition is not controlled, kidney failure and death will result.

Figure 5.18 Diabetes causes damage to the retina of the eye. If left untreated, it may lead to blindness.

1. What is the cause of Type 1 diabetes?

2. Describe the sequence of events that will occur if a person has diabetes that isn't controlled.

Type 2 diabetes

The main cause of **Type 2 diabetes** is that the body's cells lose their sensitivity – they no longer respond, or respond as effectively – to the insulin being produced.

One test for diabetes is the **glucose tolerance test**. After 8–12 hours of no eating or drinking, blood glucose is measured. The person is then given glucose and their blood retested 2 hours later. If the person's tolerance to glucose is lowered, the glucose will be above a certain level when retested.

3. What is the cause of Type 2 diabetes?

4. Describe how the glucose tolerance test can help to diagnose Type 2 diabetes.

5. Use Figure 5.19 to describe the effects of insulin secretion in the three examples of people shown on the graph.

What causes diabetes?

Only 10% of people with diabetes have Type 1. The cells that produce insulin have been destroyed. This can be an autoimmune condition – in which the immune system attacks the person's own body.

Figure 5.19 Blood glucose increases after a meal in a person with Type 2 diabetes, and is not brought back to normal if left untreated.

Type 2 diabetes tends to cluster in families. But it is also associated with a Western lifestyle – one that includes high-energy 'fast' foods and an inactive life. There is a clear link with obesity.

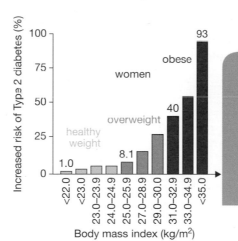

Figure 5.20 There is a correlation between increased risk of diabetes and obesity, as indicated by **body mass index** (BMI)

Type 2 diabetes is now emerging in young people. The first cases were in the year 2000, in children aged 9–16. Around three in ten children are now obese.

6 Discuss links between genetics and the environment with Type 2 diabetes.

7 Compare the correlation between obesity and Type 2 diabetes in men and women.

DID YOU KNOW?

These types of diabetes are called diabetes *mellitus.*
Diabetes *insipidus* is completely unrelated, but one symptom is the same – the production of very large volumes of urine.

ADVICE

Remember the consequences of lack of insulin by working out the sequence of events if the body's cells are unable to take up glucose.

KEY INFORMATION

Body Mass Index (BMI) is a measure of body fat based on height and weight.

Diabetes recommendations

Learning objectives:

- understand the causes of Type 1 and Type 2 diabetes
- compare Type 1 and Type 2 diabetes
- evaluate information on the relationship between obesity and diabetes, and make appropriate recommendations.

In 2014, 3.3 million people in the UK had been diagnosed with diabetes. Diabetic patients are currently costing the NHS about £10 billion a year. *That's £1 million per hour.*

Treatment

There is currently no cure for diabetes. **Type 1 diabetes** cannot be prevented. Patients with Type 1 diabetes *control* it with insulin injections.

For **Type 2 diabetes**, obesity accounts for 80–85% of the risk of developing it; so, it is preventable. The most important way of managing the condition is by modification of lifestyle. This involves exercise and diet. Carbohydrate-controlled diets are important for all diabetics. Foods that rapidly affect blood sugar level should be avoided.

Figure 5.21 It's within our hands to control Type 2 diabetes.

1 How can Type 1 diabetics control the condition?

2 What recommendations should be given to Type 2 diabetics?

Ethical considerations

Public guidelines and national programmes of weight management have been designed to help to prevent Type 2 diabetes.

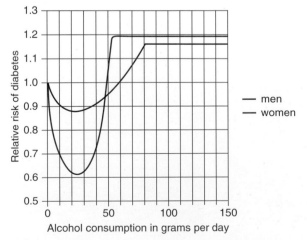

Figure 5.22 The intake of alcohol is one factor that affects the risk of developing diabetes. The risk is relative to that for people who have never drunk alcohol.

It is clear that a change in the lifestyle of many people would reduce the incidence of Type 2 diabetes. However, we cannot *insist* that people do this. In any case, do we have a right to? Factors such as a person's ethnicity also affect the prevalence of the condition. Is it ethical for the authorities to make this type of distinction when giving guidance or making policy?

The sugary drinks and snacks produced by food manufacturers contribute to obesity. Do they have an ethical responsibility to produce healthier foods? Must restaurants and school canteens be responsible for providing healthy foods?

3 What measures could be taken to reduce Type 2 diabetes?

4 What advice should be given to anyone who drinks alcohol about the risk of developing diabetes?

Figure 5.23 A 'traffic light system' on food labels informs consumers of its nutritional content.

Social considerations

A professor of food policy thinks that some snacks, which are just sugar and flavouring, should not be termed 'foods' at all.

One possible solution is a 'sugar tax' on the cost of sugary foods, or on food companies that continue to produce foods that contribute to poor health. However, a tax might affect most the people who could least afford it. A Health Survey for England report found that the risk of diabetes was highest among the most deprived of the population.

> **ADVICE**
>
> Be prepared to make recommendations for the control of diabetes, considering social and ethical issues and consequences.

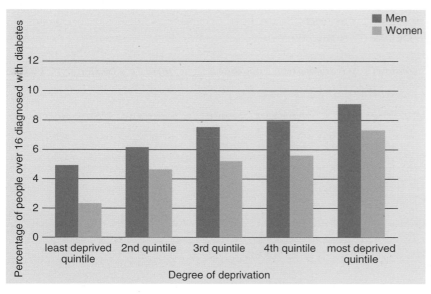

Figure 5.24 The effect of deprivation on the risk of Type 2 diabetes

5 Discuss what food manufacturers and caterers could do to reduce diabetes.

6 Suggest explanations for the trend in the graph in Figure 5.24.

> **KEY INFORMATION**
>
> Quintiles refer to any of five equal groups into which a population can be divided, according to the distribution of values; in this case, according to how deprived they were.

Negative feedback

Learning objectives:

- explain the role of thyroxine in the body
- understand the principles of negative feedback, as applied to thyroxine.

Priya is tired and sluggish and is putting on weight. Her heart rate feels slow. She also feels the cold. Priya could have a problem with her thyroid gland.

HIGHER TIER ONLY

The thyroid gland

The thyroid gland affects our activity by producing the hormone **thyroxine**. Thyroxine stimulates the body's **basal metabolic rate** – it increases the metabolism of all the body cells. Priya has an underactive thyroid. That explains her symptoms.

Under- or over-active thyroid glands are common. As adults, these conditions are fairly easily treated. But thyroxine also controls our growth and development – starting in the uterus. In the embryo, infant or child, mental and physical development is severely retarded by insufficient levels of thyroxine.

Figure 5.25 This 6-year-old's finger shows stunted development owing to lack of thyroxine. Children in the UK are tested at birth using a drop of blood from their heel.

1 **Suggest a symptom of an *over*active thyroid gland.**

2 **What is the function of thyroxine?**

Control of thyroxine secretion

The **pituitary gland** controls secretions from other glands. One such gland is the thyroid gland.

Levels of thyroxine in the blood are increased when the pituitary gland secretes thyroid-stimulating hormone (TSH). The thyroid gland responds by secreting thyroxine. If levels of thyroxine become too high, TSH secretion is blocked.

Thyroxine increases the respiration rate of cells. In the process, thermal energy is released. The body will secrete thyroxine when its temperature falls. The same is true of adrenaline, the hormone that is released when we are frightened or excited. Both hormones raise our body temperature, particularly with thermal energy released by the liver. If our body temperature becomes too high, the thermoregulatory centre in the brain detects the temperature rise, and the hormones' secretion is blocked.

Figure 5.26 A simplified version of the negative-feedback system that controls thyroxine secretion

3 Which hormone regulates thyroxine production?

4 When is thyroxine secreted?

The principles of negative feedback

The endocrine system keeps the conditions in the body constant using feedback systems.

A simple *negative*-feedback system is the central-heating system in your home. If the temperature falls in your living room, the thermostat detects this and switches on the heating. The room warms up.

When the thermostat temperature is reached, it detects this, and turns off the heating. This is **negative feedback** because when the desired effect is reached, the system is switched off.

Negative feedback within the endocrine system prevents a system from becoming overactive. The system is inhibited by its own products.

5 Give a definition of a negative-feedback system.

6 Figure 5.27 illustrates a *simple* negative-feedback system, but it is not a perfect comparison with thyroid secretion. Explain why.

Figure 5.27 Negative feedback in a central-heating system

Human reproduction

Learning objectives:

- describe the roles of hormones in sexual reproduction
- explain how hormones interact in the menstrual cycle.

KEY WORDS

follicle
FSH
LH
oestrogen
progesterone

secondary
sex
characteristics
testosterone

Our first exposure to sex hormones is not at puberty, but as a foetus. In the presence of male sex hormones (which needs a Y chromosome), male characteristics develop; in their absence, the foetus becomes female.

Reproductive hormones

Secondary sex characteristics develop as our bodies produce reproductive hormones at puberty.

Oestrogen is the main female reproductive hormone that is produced at this time. It is produced by the ovaries. Eggs start to mature in the ovaries and are released, at approximately one every 28 days. This process is called ovulation.

In the male, **testosterone** is the main reproductive hormone. It is produced by the testes. It stimulates sperm production.

DID YOU KNOW?

Oestrogen, progesterone and testosterone are steroid hormones. Steroid hormones also help to control glucose and protein metabolism, and water balance.

1 **Give the main reproductive hormones in males and females.**

2 **What happens in males and females under the influence of these hormones?**

The menstrual cycle

The menstrual cycle is the reproductive cycle in women, which – by convention – starts with a period (menstruation), if the woman is not pregnant.

Four hormones control the menstrual cycle:

- follicle stimulating hormone (**FSH**) causes eggs to mature in the ovaries
- luteinising hormone (**LH**) stimulates the release of an egg from an ovary
- oestrogen and **progesterone** maintain the lining of the uterus.

3 **Which four hormones control the menstrual cycle?**

4 **Which hormones maintain the lining of the uterus?**

Figure 5.28 The menstrual cycle lasts approximately 28 days, but this is highly variable.

Menstrual cycle hormones

The menstrual cycle is concerned with the maturation of an egg every month and preparing the uterus to receive that egg if it is fertilised. This could result in pregnancy.

These hormones interact with each other during the menstrual cycle.

Figure 5.29 The menstrual cycle is controlled by four main hormones.

Figure 5.30 The roles of the hormones as the cycle progresses are:

1 FSH is secreted by the pituitary gland.

2 FSH causes the eggs to mature in the ovaries.

3 FSH stimulates the ovaries to produce oestrogen.

4 & 5 Oestrogen inhibits further release of FSH and stimulates release of LH.

6 LH triggers ovulation – the release of the mature egg from the ovary – and …

7 … leads to the secretion of progesterone by the empty **follicle** that contained the egg.

8 Progesterone inhibits the release of LH and FSH.

9 Progesterone maintains the lining of the uterus during the second half of the menstrual cycle, in readiness for receiving a fertilised egg.

5 Which two hormones repair the uterus after menstruation and encourage its growth?

6 Suggest which hormones are involved in negative feedback.

IVF

Learning objectives:

- explain the use of hormones in technologies to treat infertility
- describe the technique of *in-vitro* fertilisation
- evaluate the scientific, emotional, social and ethical issues of *in-vitro* fertilisation.

KEY WORDS

fertility drug
in-vitro
 fertilisation
IVF cycle

Louise Joy Brown was born on 25 July 1978 at Oldham General Hospital. She was the first 'test tube baby'.

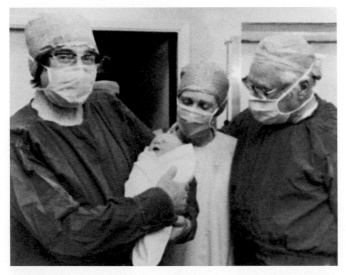

Figure 5.31 Louise was born following the pioneering technique of physiologist Dr Robert Edwards and gynaecologist Dr Patrick Steptoe.

HIGHER TIER ONLY

Treating infertility

The NHS recommends that if a couple has been trying to conceive for a year – 6 months if the woman is over 35 – but with no success, it may be time to investigate.

For women whose levels of FSH are too low to conceive, combined hormones can be given as a **'fertility drug'**.

After treatment with a fertility drug, many women ovulate and become pregnant. They are warned of the possibility of multiple births.

If treatment is successful, it's usually within the first 3 months.

Figure 5.32 The women's ovaries are monitored with ultrasound to look at the number and size of developing follicles.

1 **Explain why FSH and LH are given as fertility treatments.**

2 **Why are the ovaries monitored after treatment?**

In-vitro fertilisation

In-vitro fertilisation (IVF) may be an option to treat infertility. Here, eggs are fertilised outside the body. '*In vitro*' means, literally, 'in glass'. Eggs are removed from the mother and are fertilised, in the laboratory, with sperm collected from the father.

The technique is more successful if the woman:

- is younger
- has previously been pregnant
- has a BMI within the range of 19–30
- has low alcohol and caffeine intake, and does not smoke.

Counselling is important at this stage. The couple must be optimistic, yet prepared for failure.

3 **What is *in-vitro* fertilisation?**

4 **Give two criteria that increase the possibility of successful IVF.**

Stages of the process

The stages of IVF:

- The woman is given FSH and LH to stimulate the production of more eggs than normal in her ovaries.
- Eggs are then collected. The woman is sedated but conscious.
- Eggs are mixed with the father's sperm in the laboratory for 16–20 hours. They are monitored microscopically for fertilisation.
- Any embryos are allowed to develop for 5 days. They will contain around 100 cells.
- One or two embryos are selected and placed in the mother's uterus.

A number of **IVF cycles** – from stimulation of the ovaries to implantation – can be attempted. If a cycle is unsuccessful, a gap of 2 months is usually left as the treatment is emotionally and physically stressful.

5 **If the father's sperm count is low, explain how the procedure is sometimes modified.**

6 **What is a cycle of IVF treatment?**

7 **Compare and contrast fertility treatment with IVF.**

DID YOU KNOW?

Cryopreservation – or freezing – of eggs can be an option for someone who is undergoing a harmful cancer therapy and yet wants to be able to conceive later on.

Figure 5.33 If the man's sperm count is low, a *single* sperm is sometimes selected and injected into the egg. The procedure is carried out microscopically.

COMMON MISCONCEPTION

Don't confuse *fertility treatment* and *IVF*. IVF is just one type of fertility treatment.

IVF evaluation

Learning objectives:

- describe the technique of *in-vitro* fertilisation
- evaluate the scientific, emotional, social and ethical issues of *in-vitro* fertilisation.

KEY WORDS

eugenics
IVF

Scientists in Oxford have devised a test that could improve the success rate of IVF. A clinical trial resulted in a pregnancy rate of 80%.

HIGHER TIER ONLY

The couple's perspective

IVF has been available on the NHS – provided certain criteria are fulfilled. The National Institute for Health and Care Excellence (NICE) produces guidelines, and the final decision is made by the woman's local NHS.

The process begins with counselling. This prepares the couple for the success, or the chance of failure. Emotional support is continuous through the process.

1 Who determines the selection procedure for IVF on the NHS?

2 Why is counselling important for potential IVF couples?

Figure 5.34 The test is based on mitochondrial DNA. Many IVF embryos had unusually high levels that prevented their implantation.

Medical and scientific evaluation

Around half the embryos produced by IVF have an incorrect number of chromosomes. One-third of the normal embryos actually selected will not implant in the uterus.

Age of woman in years	Proportion of live births in %
Under 35	32.2
35–37	27.7
38–39	20.8
40–42	13.6
43–44	5.0
Over 44	1.9

The woman's age is one factor affecting success.

Figure 5.35 Eggs or embryos are stored cryogenically. That way, they can be used later on. But does freezing and then thawing affect them?

The success rate is not high, but it *is* rising – by 1% per year. There are reports of higher incidences, among IVF babies, of premature births, stillbirths, low birth-weights and infant deaths. But rates are higher still in babies born to couples with infertility problems who eventually manage to conceive naturally.

One possible drawback of successful IVF is an increased possibility of multiple births, as more than one embryo is implanted. This increases the risk to the mother and babies.

3 The data in the table are based on NHS 2010 statistics. Estimate the *current* success rate for a woman under 35.

4 Describe three medical issues of IVF.

Ethical issues

Many people object to the technique and the treatment of embryos:

- One argument says that fertility treatments are just removing natural obstacles to fertility, but IVF is not natural. It is replacing the physical and emotional relationship of conceiving with a laboratory technique.
- Embryos that are not transplanted are eventually destroyed. Is a human embryo a mass of cells to be used, selected and discarded? Should we accept these losses as the price for success? Or does an embryo demand the *unconditional* moral respect given to any human being?

Modern microscopical and genetic techniques have enabled embryos to be screened for abnormalities. One serious concern is that couples with no fertility problems may use IVF as a technique to select a child, possibly using dubious selection criteria – a form of **eugenics.**

5 Discuss one ethical issue of IVF.

6 How could the screening of embryos be misused?

DID YOU KNOW?

Nobel Prize winner Professor, later Sir, Robert Edwards was aware that his work was controversial. After publication of a paper on producing embryos, he stopped research for 2 years while considering whether it was right to continue.

REMEMBER!

Use this topic to help you to evaluate the range of issues associated with IVF.

Systems working together

KEY WORDS

adrenaline
adrenal medulla

Learning objectives:

- describe the effects of adrenaline
- understand that automatic control systems may involve nervous responses and chemical responses
- understand that combinations of hormones work to produce a response.

Harry is frightened of having of having a flu vaccination. He screams. His heart begins to race. His skin goes pale.

Figure 5.36 These effects are the result of the release of a hormone called adrenaline.

HIGHER TIER ONLY

Adrenaline

Adrenaline prepares us – very quickly when we get a fright – for emergency action. It has a number of effects on the body.

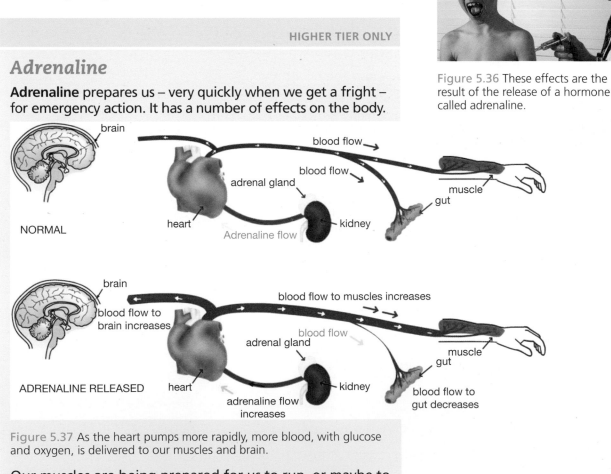

Figure 5.37 As the heart pumps more rapidly, more blood, with glucose and oxygen, is delivered to our muscles and brain.

Our muscles are being prepared for us to run, or maybe to fight. Adrenaline is called the 'flight-or-fight' hormone.

1 **Which hormone is released when we become frightened?**

2 **There is only a set volume of blood in the body. Suggest how more blood can be pumped to the brain and muscles.**

The nervous and endocrine systems interact

The release of adrenaline is a good example of how the nervous and endocrine systems interact.

Connections to and in the brain and to the adrenal glands are *nervous*. The part of the adrenal gland called the **adrenal medulla** responds to nervous stimulation by releasing the hormone adrenaline.

The adrenaline that is released – as you have seen previously – acts on various parts of the body, including the liver cells. In the liver, it promotes the breakdown of glycogen into glucose, and its release into the bloodstream.

Most of us don't use the flight-or-fight response on a regular basis. But it is there if we need it.

Figure 5.38 The nervous and endocrine systems produce our reaction to a fright.

3 Explain how the nervous and endocrine systems work together in times of stress.

4 Which other hormone stimulates the breakdown of glycogen in the liver?

Hormones working together

You will now have realised that *several* hormones are involved in glucose metabolism – insulin and glucagon topic 5.6, thyroxine topic 5.9, and now adrenaline (and also cortisol).

Likewise, several hormones, act together to control water balance.

And a number of hormones work together to control our development and reproduction.

These hormones and many others work together in our bodies to ensure that our bodies *do* work as a coordinated whole.

5 Describe the action of three hormones on glucose metabolism.

6 Describe how two hormones affect our development.

7 Use your knowledge of the endocrine system to create a concept map, which links keys words that are covered in the topic, and explains how the words are linked.

DID YOU KNOW?

The brain's response to fear also leads to the release of a hormone by the pituitary gland. This hormone acts on a different part of the adrenal gland. A hormone called cortisol is released. Its release is not as quick as adrenaline – it sustains our response to possible danger.

ADVICE

This topic provides an illustration of how the body systems work together to produce a coordinated response.

Contraception

Learning objectives:

- understand that fertility can be controlled by different hormonal and non-hormonal methods of contraception
- evaluate the different methods of contraception.

KEY WORDS

cervix
combined
  contraceptive pill
progesterone
progestogen-
  only pill

If the population continues to increase at the current rate, human life on Earth will not be sustainable. Efforts to bring down the birth rate need to continue.

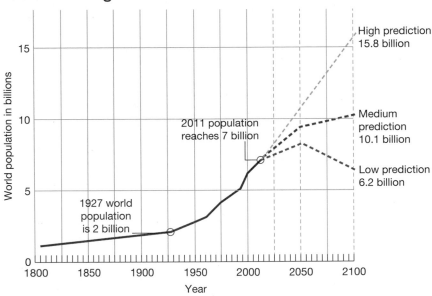

Figure 5.39 One set of predictions for world population growth

Contraceptive methods

Most contraceptive methods fall into one of two types:

- methods that use hormones
- non-hormonal methods, or barrier methods.

Some people choose *natural* planning methods. A woman's time of ovulation is linked with:

- her menstrual cycle, occurring at around 14 days
- a *slight* increase in body temperature
- thinning of mucus secreted from the **cervix**.

By estimating when ovulation occurs, it is possible to avoid having sexual intercourse when an egg might be in the oviduct. But eggs and sperm can live for several days, and women's cycles can be irregular.

Some people choose to have surgery. In the woman, the oviducts are cut, sealed or blocked by an operation. In the man, the sperm ducts are cut, sealed or tied. Surgical methods are designed to be permanent.

DID YOU KNOW?

Oral contraceptives were first approved for use in Britain in 1961. The hormone content was equivalent to seven of today's pills.

KEY SKILL

You may be provided with new information or data on contraceptives that you have to analyse and interpret.

1. How can contraceptives be divided into broad categories?
2. List three indicators of ovulation.

Barrier methods

Barrier methods prevent sperm from reaching an egg.

Injection: an injection of a progestogen is given.

Condom (male)		a rubber or polyurethane sheath that is rolled over the erect penis
Diaphragm (cap; female)		latex or silicone device that is put into the vagina to cover the cervix

Two commonly used barrier methods

A spermicidal cream is toxic to sperm. It can help with the effectiveness of other contraceptives such as diaphragms. It should not be used on its own, or with condoms.

3. Give two examples of barrier methods of contraception.
4. When should a spermicidal cream be used?

Hormonal methods

Hormonal methods of contraception use reproductive hormones to prevent pregnancy. The **combined contraceptive pill** contains a synthetic oestrogen and **progesterone**.

For women for whom the combined pill isn't suitable, for example, if they are older or have high blood pressure, there is also a **progestogen-only pill** (POP, mini pill). This contains a synthetic version of progesterone.

These contraceptives inhibit the release of the pituitary hormones that control egg maturation and release. They also thicken cervical mucus, which helps to prevent sperm reaching an egg. The combined pill is taken for 21 days, allowing periods to occur. The POP is taken every day.

Some other types of contraceptive can include hormones. Intrauterine devices (IUDs) are placed in the uterus. They prevent a fertilised egg from implanting in the uterus.

Plastic IUDs also release progestogen. Copper versions have copper wound around plastic. Copper is toxic to sperm.

5. How do oral contraceptives work?
6. What is an IUD?

Implant: a small flexible rod is implanted under skin of the upper arm. Progestogen is released slowly.

Patch: A sticky patch is put on the skin. It releases a synthetic oestrogen and progestogen slowly.

Figure 5.40 Hormonal contraceptives can also be used as injections, implants or patches.

Figure 5.41 An IUD

Which contraceptive?

Learning objectives:

- understand that fertility can be controlled by different hormonal and non-hormonal methods of contraception
- evaluate the different methods of contraception.

KEY WORDS

condom
IUD

A microchip implant has been developed that can store and release regular, controlled doses of a contraceptive for up to 16 years.

The chip can be controlled wirelessly. It could be turned off at any time to start a family.

Reliability

People who are considering using contraceptives should look at their success rate.

Successful surgery is 100% effective but irreversible. Natural family planning methods *can* be effective if used correctly, with guidance and teaching. Computerised devices that monitor hormone changes improve reliability of natural methods.

1. How can the reliability of natural family planning methods be improved?

2. Which method(s) is, or are, the most effective contraceptive?

Advantages and disadvantages of different methods

With surgery, couples no longer need to think about contraception at all. But the decision should be carefully considered.

Hormonal contraceptives are convenient, although POPs do need to be taken at the same time every day to be effective. Implants last for 3 years, injections 12–13 weeks and patches 1 week. With injections, fertility may not immediately return to normal.

With the combined pill, implant and patch, periods may be more regular, lighter and less painful. Oral contraceptives also reduce the risk of certain cancers, though those containing oestrogen slightly increase the risk of blood clots, and breast and cervical cancer.

Type of contraception	Percentage of pregnancies prevented
condoms	98
diaphragm	92–96
implants	99
IUD	>99
oral contraceptives	>99

The effectiveness of contraceptives when used *perfectly*

Method	Advantages	Disadvantages
condoms	• widely available • can protect against transmitted infections, e.g. HIV	• may slip off • must withdraw after ejaculation and not spill semen
diaphragm	• put in just before sex • no health risks	• needs to be left in for several hours after sex • some people are sensitive to spermicide
IUD	• works immediately • can stay in place for 10 years (copper); 3–5 years (hormonal)	• insertion may be uncomfortable periods may be longer or more painful

Advantages and disadvantages of other methods

3 **Suggest why oral contraceptives are affected by vomiting or diarrhoea, but injections, implants and patches are not.**

4 **Give one advantage and one disadvantage of using an IUD.**

Wider issues

People must decide whether to use contraception or not. This could be influenced by religious factors.

If people do use contraception, they must choose a method.

Health factors are important in family planning, but for many people the decision to use contraception is *economic*, or it can be a *lifestyle* choice:

• Can a couple afford to start a family?
• Is contraception likely to be needed every day?
• How soon would the woman like to become pregnant *after* using contraception?

A wider issue associated with contraception is one of world population and sustainability, although there are ethical issues with its use in population control. It can be seen as interfering with human rights and reproductive freedom.

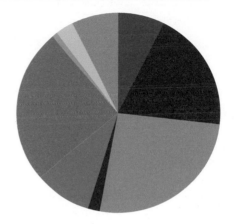

■ sterilisation: female
■ sterilisation: male
■ contraceptive pill
■ other methods, including emergency pill
■ intrauterine devices (IUDs)
■ male condom
■ vaginal barrier, including spermicides
■ hormonal injections and implants
■ traditional methods, e.g. abstaining and withdrawal

Figure 5.42 Contraceptive use in the UK, 2008–9

5 **Name the most widely used contraceptive method in the UK.**

6 **Discuss non-scientific questions around a need for contraception.**

7 **Some governments have considered compulsory sterilisation to control population growth. Evaluate the advantages and disadvantages of sterilisation.**

DID YOU KNOW?

Fifteen types of contraceptive are used in the UK. Two are designed *specifically* for men; 13 for women.

KEY SKILL

Be prepared to evaluate data on the use of different types of contraception.

MATHS SKILLS

The spread of scientific data

Learning objectives:

- be able to calculate means and ranges of data
- understand how to estimate uncertainty from a set of measurements.

KEY WORDS
....

estimate
mean
range
repeatability
uncertainty

When results are collected, how they are spread out is important. It helps us to make judgements about the quality of the data we have collected. This is important when attempting to identify trends in data.

The spread of data

A person's blood glucose level was measured. The measurement was repeated three times on the same blood sample. The following values were obtained:

6.2 mmol/dm³   6.1 mmol/dm³   6.0 mmol/dm³

If you carry out *any* experiment and then do it again, you often get a slightly different result. This may not be because you've used the equipment wrongly. In any measurement there are always random errors that cause measurements to be spread around the true value. This is why it's best to repeat measurements and find the mean.

A **mean** reduces the effect of random errors and gives you the best **estimate** of the true value.

The mean value of a set of measurements is the sum of the values divided by the number of values:

$$\text{mean} = \frac{6.2 + 6.1 + 6.0}{3} = 6.1 \text{ mmol glucose/dm}^3$$

The **range** is a measure of spread. It is calculated as the difference between the largest and smallest values:

6.2 − 6.0 mmol/dm³, or 0.2 mmol/dm³.

The spread of data on graphs

Data that are consistent are said to be repeatable; the narrower the range of a set of data, the higher the degree of **repeatability**. Vertical range bars are sometimes added to points on a graph to show the spread of the measured data about the mean.

1 Another set of readings, using a blood sample from a different person, were:

9.6 mmol/dm³
9.5 mmol/dm³
9.8 mmol/dm³

What is the mean of these values?

2 What is the range of this set of values?

Estimating uncertainty in data

The best estimate of the true value of a quantity is the mean of repeated measurements. When calculating a mean, include all the values for data you have collected, unless you have any anomalous results (measurements that do not fit into the pattern of the other results). You could check if a result was an anomaly by repeating it. The more repeated readings you take, the better the estimate you'll get of the true value. Three to five repeats are often suggested.

The table shows some data collected on the effect of the hormone thyroxine on heart muscle tissue:

Time in minutes	Oxygen uptake, in cm³ oxygen/g of heart muscle tissue					
	Experiment 1	Experiment 2	Experiment 3	Experiment 4	Experiment 5	Mean
10	3.3	3.9	3.6	3.8	3.9	3.7
20	7.8	8.3	8.0	7.8	8.1	8.0
30	11.7	11.2	11.5	11.6	11.5	11.5
40	14.6	14.8	15.1	14.9	14.6	14.8
50	17.7	17.2	17.5	17.6	17.5	17.5
60	26.7	26.0	26.5	27.4	26.9	

The effect of thyroxine on heart muscle was measured by the oxygen uptake by the cell.

For the data collected after 10 minutes:

The mean is 3.7 cm³ oxygen/g of heart muscle.

The *range about the mean* gives an estimate of the level of **uncertainty** in the data collected

For this set of data, the upper limit is 3.9 cm³/g; the lower limit 3.3 cm³/g.

The range is 0.6 cm³/g. So, according to our data, the true value could be up to 0.3 cm³/g above the mean, or 0.3 cm³/g below the mean.

Uncertainty is therefore calculated by:

$$\text{uncertainty} = \frac{\text{upper limit of range} - \text{lower limit of range}}{2}$$

So, as we have seen above, uncertainty $= \frac{3.9 - 3.3}{2} = \frac{0.6}{2} = 0.3$

Uncertainty is written next to the mean. In this instance, it is:

3.7 cm³/g ± 0.3 cm³/g

Note that the units are written after *both* the mean and the value of uncertainty. The value of uncertainty has the same units and number of decimal places as the measurements.

③ Calculate the mean for the set of data collected at 60 minutes.

④ Calculate the uncertainty in these measurements.

Check your progress

You should be able to:

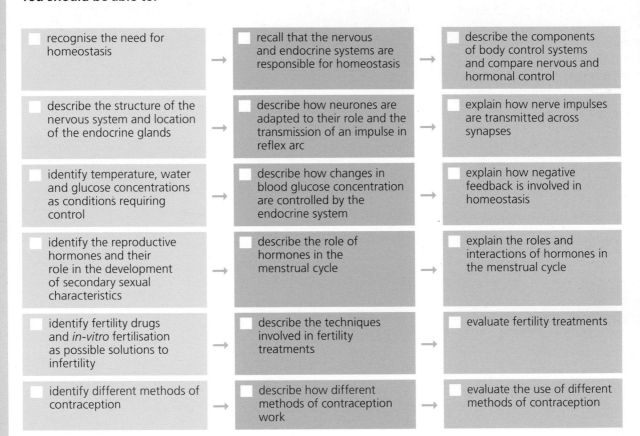

recognise the need for homeostasis → recall that the nervous and endocrine systems are responsible for homeostasis → describe the components of body control systems and compare nervous and hormonal control

describe the structure of the nervous system and location of the endocrine glands → describe how neurones are adapted to their role and the transmission of an impulse in reflex arc → explain how nerve impulses are transmitted across synapses

identify temperature, water and glucose concentrations as conditions requiring control → describe how changes in blood glucose concentration are controlled by the endocrine system → explain how negative feedback is involved in homeostasis

identify the reproductive hormones and their role in the development of secondary sexual characteristics → describe the role of hormones in the menstrual cycle → explain the roles and interactions of hormones in the menstrual cycle

identify fertility drugs and *in-vitro* fertilisation as possible solutions to infertility → describe the techniques involved in fertility treatments → evaluate fertility treatments

identify different methods of contraception → describe how different methods of contraception work → evaluate the use of different methods of contraception

Worked example

1 **Priya has an underactive thyroid gland. She does not secrete enough of the hormone thyroxine.**

Describe how secretion of thyroxine is controlled.

Secretion of thyroxine is controlled by the release of the hormone thyroid-stimulating hormone (TSH) by the pituitary gland. It is secreted when levels fall. If levels increase to above normal levels, secretion of TSH is shut down.

> This is a good answer. The student has been careful to say that TSH is released by the pituitary gland, as it is not produced there.
>
> The student has, however, omitted a key term to describe the process – negative feedback. An annotated diagram could have been used to illustrate the principle (see section 5.9).

2 **Priya is given several injections of thyroxine over six days of treatment.**

The graph shows the effect of the hormone on her Basal Metabolic Rate (BMR).

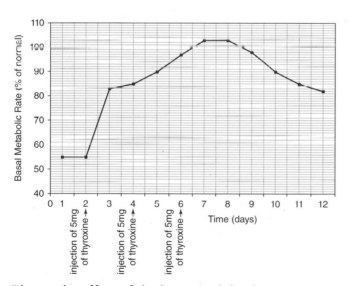

Discuss the effect of the hormone injections.

The injection of the hormone after 2 days produces a sharp increase in Priya's metabolic rate. The next two injections only produce slight increases. After 8 days, her BMR starts to fall.

> This is a part answer to the question.
>
> The student has described the trend but could have illustrated the answer using data from the graph, e.g. after 2 days Priya's BMR increases from 55 to 83, after 4 days, … etc.
>
> The student should have made clear that Priya's BMR attained its normal value after 6½ days, increased to slightly above normal (113%), and then, after eight days, decreased steadily.
>
> The student's answer is a description, but not really a discussion. It should have been stated that it is the role of thyroxine to act on the body's cells to increase their metabolism.
>
> On the basis of the fall in BMR after 8 days, the student could have suggested that the treatment would be unlikely to be effective without repeated injections.

End of chapter questions

Getting started

1 **a** What is the ruler-drop test used to measure? `1 Mark`

b How should the person being tested hold the ruler at the beginning of the test? `1 Mark`

c The table below shows some results from the ruler-drop test:

Test number	Distance ruler dropped in cm
1	8
2	4
3	3
4	6
5	5
6	7
7	4
Mean	

Calculate the mean distance dropped by the ruler. `1 Mark`

2 The following diagram shows the location of the major endocrine glands.

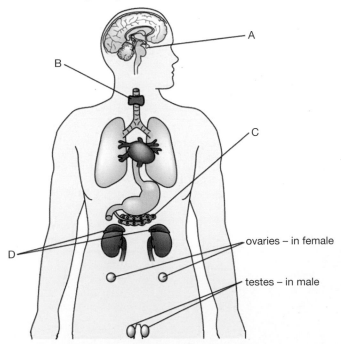

a   Which letter labels the thyroid gland? `1 Mark`

b   Which letter represents the gland, where, if it produces insufficient hormone, diabetes results? `1 Mark`

3 Describe the recommendations a doctor would make to a patient diagnosed with Type 2 diabetes.

2 Marks

4 The bar chart below records the success rate of *in-vitro fertilisation (IVF)* in Australia in 2013.

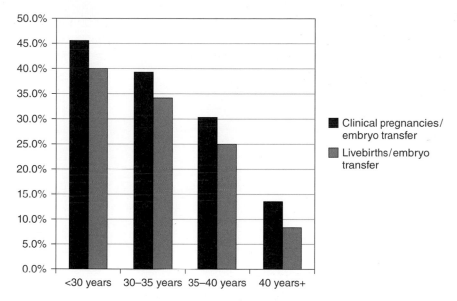

Describe the effect of the mother's age on the success rate of *IVF*.

2 Marks

Going further

5 Compare the nervous and endocrine systems according to their:

- type of message
- speed of response.

2 Marks

6 Which hormone leads to oestrogen production by the ovaries?

1 Mark

7 Scientists have researched the relationship between the number of sugar-sweetened soft drinks consumed by a group of women and the relative risk of diabetes.

Their results are shown in the graph on the next page.

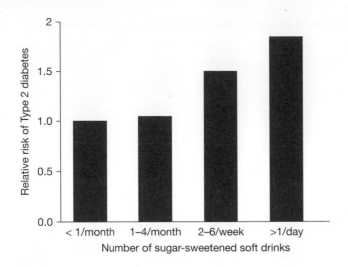

Describe the pattern shown by the graph and explain what this suggests about the cause of Type 2 diabetes.

2 Marks

8 Describe how hormonal methods of contraception work.

2 Marks

More challenging

9 Describe the role of glucagon in the control of blood glucose.

2 Marks

10 The botulinum neurotoxin – used in Botox injections – affects the functioning of a chemical transmitter in the nervous system.

Suggest how blocking a chemical transmitter can be used to paralyse facial muscles.

4 Marks

Most demanding

11 Explain how thyroxine levels affect body temperature.

2 Marks

12 A mother places her finger on her baby daughter's palm. The baby grasps it. It is a reflex action.

Describe the process by which this reflex action occurs. You can use a diagram to help with your description.

6 Marks

13 This graph shows data relating to glucose concentration in the bloodstream. 4 Marks

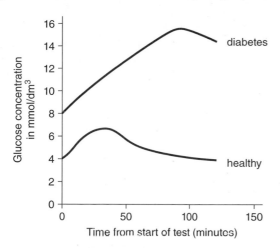

Explain what the graph shows about the difference in response of healthy and diabetic patients to increasing glucose levels.

14 Endometriosis is a condition where the type of cells that normally line the uterus are found 'trapped' in the pelvic area and lower tummy.

During the menstrual cycle the cells that have moved can react in the normal way to the hormones controlling menstruation.

This can cause a number of problems including abdominal pain and painful periods.

Using the information from the graph below, as well as your own knowledge, explain what happens to the cells that have moved and how doctors could treat the condition using sex hormones. 6 Marks

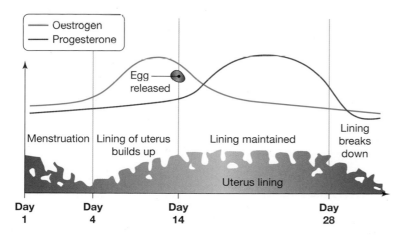

Total: 40 Marks

GENETICS

OUR CELLS CONTAIN GENETIC INFORMATION.

- Genetic information is contained within genes on our chromosomes.
- Our chromosomes and genes are found in the nucleus of our cells.
- Our knowledge of the structure of DNA comes from the work of Crick, Watson, Franklin and Wilkins.
- A change to our DNA, called a mutation, can lead to cancer.

IN MULTICELLULAR ORGANISMS, CELLS HAVE TO DIVIDE.

- Cells divide as we're growing, and to replace cells that are injured, worn out or have died.
- This type of cell division is called mitosis.
- When a cell divides by mitosis, two daughter cells are produced, each with an identical number of chromosomes and identical DNA.

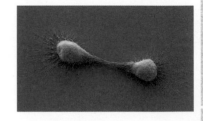

OUR CHARACTERISTICS ARE INHERITED AND PASSED ON.

- Passing on genetic information is called heredity.
- Sexual reproduction in humans leads to similarities and variation between individuals.

OUR UNDERSTANDING OF DNA AND THE WAY GENES WORK.

- DNA is a polymer made up of units called nucleotides.
- A gene is a short section of DNA that codes for the production of a particular protein.
- Proteins are synthesised from the DNA template.
- The unique structure of each protein enables it to do a particular job.
- The Human Genome Project (HGP) is increasing our understanding of DNA which will lead, in the future, to personalised medicine.
- Because of the HGP, we now know that not all genes that are present control protein synthesis.

PRODUCTION OF SEX CELLS FOR REPRODUCTION.

- In asexual reproduction, only one parent is involved. *No* sex cells are produced and cells divide by mitosis.
- During sexual reproduction, a cell divides by meiosis to produce four gametes, each with half the number of chromosomes.
- Meiosis ensures that we keep our chromosome number constant – 46, or 23 pairs – in each generation.
- Meiosis also produces gametes that are genetically unique, leading to variation between individuals.
- Our sex is determined by the 23rd pair of chromosomes.
- The way chromosomes are inherited means that the number of boys who are born is roughly same as the number of girls.

CHARACTERISTICS ARE INHERITED FROM ONE GENERATION TO THE NEXT.

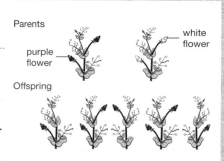

Parents

purple flower

white flower

Offspring

- The science of genetics was established by the work of an Austrian monk, Gregor Mendel.
- Genetics allows us to understand the inheritance of certain characteristics in humans and in many other organisms.
- We can use genetic terms and predict the outcome of crosses.
- Genetics enables us to track the inheritance of certain human diseases, although the inheritance of most is more complex.

DNA and genes

Learning objectives:

- describe the structure of DNA
- describe a gene as a small section of DNA that codes for a protein.

DNA, deoxyribonucleic acid, the molecule that carries our inheritance, was first isolated by the Swiss scientist, Friedrich Miescher, from white blood cells in 1869. He called it nuclein, as it was from the cells' nuclei.

The genome of an organism

The **genome** of an organism is the entire genetic material of that organism.

The genetic information is carried by a chemical called deoxyribonucleic acid (DNA). DNA is a polymer of nucleotides made up of two strands that form a double helix. The DNA is found within structures called **chromosomes**.

DNA is a polymer made up of two strands. Its structure is like a twisted ladder.

A **gene** is a short section of DNA that contains the instructions for one characteristic of an organism. Genes control all our inherited characteristics. These characteristics range from things like our blood group, hair colour and eye colour, down to the minutest detail of our cells.

Figure 6.1 You may have extracted DNA in the lab from fruit or vegetables, such as kiwi, strawberries or peas.

Figure 6.2 The shape of DNA is called a double helix.

1. What is the name given to the structure of the DNA molecule?

2. Describe the shape of the DNA molecule.

Genes work by providing the code for the production of amino acids that make specific proteins.

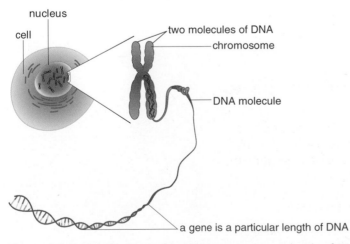

Figure 6.3 Each half of a double chromosome is a molecule of DNA.

DID YOU KNOW?

The work of other scientists also helped Crick and Watson to work out the structure of DNA.

This included data from Rosalind Franklin and Maurice Wilkins in London and from Erwin Chargaff in the USA.

③ What is the chemical called that makes up our chromosomes?

④ What is a gene?

Genes

Our genes are distributed along our chromosomes.

The chromosomes in a chromosome pair have the same types of genes, in the same order, along their length.

the genes controlling a certain characteristic are at the same location on each chromosome of the pair

Figure 6.4 The chromosomes of an organism contain our genes. One gene pair per chromosome is shown here. In reality, there are thousands on each chromosome.

Every person has two copies of each gene – one inherited from each parent.

⑤ Where are genes located on a chromosome pair?

⑥ How many copies of a gene does an organism have?

DNA, genes and chromosomes

Human cells have 46 chromosomes. This number varies from one organism to another. It's the chromosomes contained within a cell and their genetic make-up that determine the type of organism.

The DNA has proteins associated with it that help it to condense into chromosomes. Certain other parts of the cell also contain DNA – for example, mitochondria.

The plasmids of bacteria are made from DNA. They are not part of the chromosome, so do not contribute to the running of the cell, but they have genes that help the survival of the organism, for instance, in antibiotic resistance.

⑦ Name two structures of human cells that contain DNA.

⑧ Give an advantage to a bacterium of having one or more plasmids.

⑨ What is the difference between a gene, DNA and a chromosome?

Figure 6.5 The female jumper ant has just one pair of chromosomes; the male just one chromosome. One species of fern has over a thousand.

COMMON MISCONCEPTIONS

Do not think that the amount of DNA or number of genes in a cell is linked with the complexity of an organism.

DID YOU KNOW?

The marbled lungfish has more than 40 times the amount of DNA per cell as humans. And the number of protein-coding genes of a chicken is similar to that of a human.

The human genome

Learning objectives:

- describe a gene as a small section of DNA that codes for a protein
- explain the importance of understanding the human genome.

The Human Genome Project (HGP) was a study to map all the genetic information on the chromosomes of a human being. The work began in 1990 and the research was published in 2003.

Work is continuing. Now a new science – *genomics* – has developed with the aim of increasing our understanding of human DNA.

Figure 6.6 Sequencing of the human genome in the early days of the project

Increasing our understanding of genes

The HGP has helped scientists to understand more about human diseases, such as diabetes, cancer and heart disease. So far, around 4000 genes have been shown to be involved in human diseases.

The HGP has also helped scientists to understand more about inherited disorders. Some of these, such as cystic fibrosis, are linked with just a single gene. One way to develop effective treatments is to target and correct defective genes. **Gene therapy** and **genome editing** are techniques being developed to do this.

1. How might the HGP help in the way we deal with human diseases?

2. Name one condition resulting from a defective single gene.

Is personalised medicine possible?

Most conditions and diseases are associated, not with single genes, but with many genes that interact in complex ways. These genes also interact with the environment. Understanding these genes, and the regions of DNA that vary from person to person, is key to effective medicine.

In future, by understanding a person's **genome**, doctors may be able to:

- recommend better preventative medicine
- identify the targets of drugs more effectively
- tailor healthcare to the individual.

3. How might an understanding of genes lead to personalised medicine?

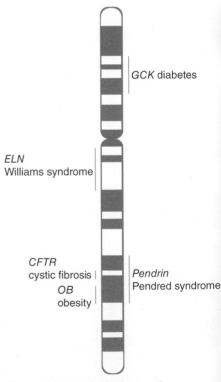

Figure 6.7 A simplified map of chromosome 7. Five genes that are linked with diseases are shown. Note that the chromosome actually has 1800 genes in total.

Understanding more about the human genome

Late in the 20th century, before the work of the HGP, it had been estimated that there were around 100 000 genes in the human genome. We now know that there are many fewer. The HGP and ongoing research have revealed that there are 20 000–25 000 genes that code for proteins; this is only around 1.5% of the human genome.

Scientists used to think that the remainder of the DNA – the part that *did not* code for proteins – was simply 'junk'. We now know that it is teeming with biological activity. Much of this DNA – we are not yet sure how much – is responsible for switching genes on and off.

Figure 6.8 DNA base sequencing

4 What percentage of our genome is made up of genes that code for proteins?

5 All cells carry the same genes. Suggest how those in a muscle cell work.

6 The Human Genome Project was estimated to have cost about 2.7 billion US dollars. Evaluate whether it was worth the money.

DID YOU KNOW?

The 100 000 Genome Project has been set up by the Department of Health. It will analyse complete genomes of people suffering from rare diseases, cancer and infectious disease.

COMMON MISCONCEPTIONS

It is convenient to think that genes just code for production of proteins – that's what we used to think – but far more is involved in gene regulation.

Tracing human migration

KEY WORDS

genome
genomic
migration pattern
Y-chromosome

Learning objectives:

- explain the importance of understanding the human genome
- discuss the use of the human genome in understanding human migration patterns.

The study and comparison of current human *genomes* is also helping to trace human *migration patterns* across history.

One of the largest studies of its kind – the Genographic Project – was launched in 2005 by the National Geographic Society and computer giant IBM.

Figure 6.9 Volunteers in the project take a swab of DNA from their mouth and send it for analysis.

The Genographic Project

Regional centres from around the world have collected DNA samples from local human populations. The project has also sought samples from volunteers from the public.

Unlike the HGP, the Genographic Project has not focused on the *whole* human genome. The first phase of the project focused on analysing data from people's **Y-chromosomes** – inherited down the male line – and from DNA in mitochondria. Mitochondrial DNA is inherited through our mothers.

REMEMBER!

You do not need to know details about the Genographic Project, but it is important to understand the processes and principles that are involved.

1️⃣ **Suggest why the Genographic Project does not investigate the whole human genome.**

2️⃣ **What were the sources of DNA analysed in the first phase of the project?**

Representative sampling of the world's populations

Representative sampling of world populations is critical. Little information would be gained if whole populations were excluded from the study.

By 2015, data from 700 000 people in 1000 populations and 130 countries has been sampled.

3️⃣ **Why is representative sampling important in this type of project?**

4️⃣ **What evidence supports the suggestion that sampling *has* been representative?**

Figure 6.10 The first findings of the project support the 'Out-of-Africa' hypothesis. So, it is likely that humans *did* originate in Africa.

The second phase of the study

Many additional research organisations are now involved in the study. The current phase is also focusing on many thousands of additional regions of DNA across the non-sex (autosomal) chromosomes.

There were ethical concerns with this project. Could the data collected find its way into the hands of medical or pharmaceutical companies and be exploited?

Steps have been taken to ensure regions of DNA were selected for analysis that did not code for proteins and that had no known function. The data, therefore, *cannot* be exploited.

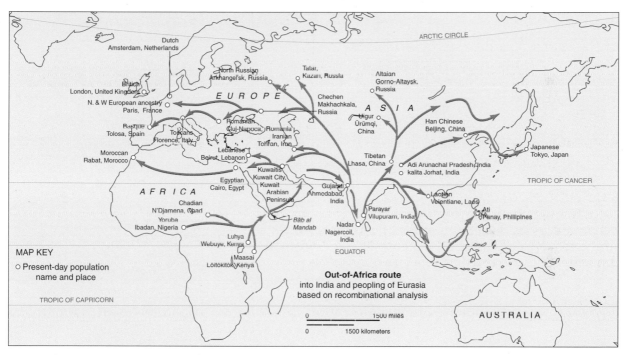

Figure 6.11 The **genomic** evidence to date suggests that early humans migrated out of Africa 60 000 years ago, through Arabia.

5 What ethical concerns were there about collection of DNA data from populations across the world?

6 How were these ethical concerns addressed?

7 Give three applications of the mapping of the human genome.

8 According to the Genographic Project, humans began to migrate away from Africa about 60 000 years ago. Suggest a reason for this.

DID YOU KNOW?

Forensic scientists also look at specific regions of DNA to make comparisons in the technique of genetic fingerprinting. In the UK, DNA 17 analysis was introduced in July 2014. It makes comparisons across 16 regions (also called loci or markers) of our DNA, where there are different numbers of repeating sequences of bases in different people, plus the gender identifier.

Meiosis

Learning objectives:

- explain how meiosis halves the number of chromosomes for gamete production
- explain how fertilisation restores the chromosome number
- understand that the four gametes produced by meiosis are genetically different.

KEY WORDS

gamete
genetic variation
meiosis
sex determination
X-chromosome
Y-chromosome

You already know that each cell in the human body has 46 chromosomes. How is this number kept at 46 during sex-cell production and fertilisation?

Meiosis is a reduction division

Mitosis is the type of cell division used during growth, or when old or damaged cells need replacing.

But another form of cell division takes place when sex cells are produced in the ovaries and testes in animals, and in the carpels and stamens of plants.

During **meiosis**:

- four **gametes** are produced from one parent cell
- each gamete has half the number of chromosomes of the parent cell (in humans, that's 23 chromosomes instead of 23 pairs).

1 How many gametes are produced from one cell during meiosis?

2 How many chromosomes does a gamete have?

	Female gametes	Male gametes
animals	egg cells	sperm
plants	egg cells	pollen grains

DID YOU KNOW?

In mammals, Y-chromosomes house the gene that controls gender. Both the X- and Y-chromosomes arose from autosomes around 200 million years ago. During evolution, the Y-chromosome has lost most of its genes.

What happens during meiosis?

In meiosis, the DNA of each chromosome is copied, just as in mitosis. But it then divides *twice*, so the chromosome number is *halved*.

So, in mitosis, there is one replication of DNA and one division, but in meiosis, there is one replication of DNA and two divisions.

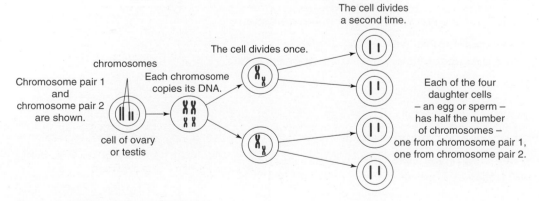

Figure 6.12 An overview of meiosis

When the gametes fuse at fertilisation, the normal number of chromosomes is restored.

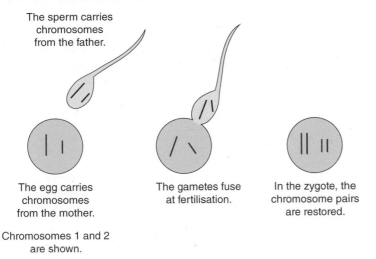

The sperm carries chromosomes from the father.

The egg carries chromosomes from the mother.

The gametes fuse at fertilisation.

In the zygote, the chromosome pairs are restored.

Chromosomes 1 and 2 are shown.

Figure 6.13 Fertilisation restores the chromosome number.

One of each chromosome pair is inherited from our mother; the other from our father. But for each chromosome pair, it is a completely random event as to which of these goes into the egg or sperm.

3 How many replications of DNA occur in meiosis?

4 How many divisions occur in meiosis?

> **REMEMBER!**
>
> You should aim to be able to recognise or describe differences and similarities between meiosis and mitosis.

All gametes are genetically different

Another thing that makes each gamete unique is that there's some exchange of genetic material during meiosis. This contributes to **genetic variation**. When an egg or sperm is produced, it does not *just* receive *unchanged* chromosomes from the parent.

What determines our sex?

Each gamete also contains one of the two sex chromosomes – from pair 23. These carry the genes for **sex determination**. Female humans have two X-shaped chromosomes (XX). Males have an X- and a Y-shaped chromosome (XY).

All the eggs produced by the mother contain **X-chromosomes**. Half of the father's sperm contain the X-chromosome; the other half contain the **Y-chromosome**.

5 Explain how meiosis leads to genetic veriation.

6 In the UK, the proportion of live births was in the proportion of 1.05 males:1.00 females. Suggest why it is not exactly 1:1.

		Mother (XX) gametes	
		X	X
Father (XY) gametes	X	XX female	XX female
	Y	XY male	XY male

Figure 6.14 In theory, 50% of live-born children are female; 50% male.

Asexual and sexual reproduction

Learning objectives:

- understand that asexual reproduction involves just one parent and produces genetically identical offspring
- understand that sexual reproduction leads to variety in the offspring.

Some organisms, such as the malaria parasite, use both asexual and sexual reproduction during their life cycle.

One parent or two?

Asexual reproduction involves just one parent. The offspring are identical to the parent. They are **clones**. New cells are produced by mitosis.

Most organisms reproduce sexually. Two parents are involved. The parents produce sex cells or gametes by meiosis.

Sexual reproduction provides advantages:

- Genetic material comes from both parents, producing **variation**. Offspring are different from each other, and from their parents.
- If the environment changes, because of their genetic differences, some offspring are more likely to survive than others. This gives a survival advantage through **natural selection**.

Sexual reproduction of animals and plants can be manipulated by humans. Selection processes can be changed to produce new varieties of plant and breeds of animal for food.

Figure 6.15 The parasite is transferred to and from humans as the *Anopheles* mosquito feeds on blood.

1 **Give two advantages of sexual reproduction.**

Using both forms of reproduction

Flowering plants reproduce sexually by seeds. But many also reproduce asexually. New plants can be produced quickly, without the need for sexual reproduction.

Reproducing asexually gives lots of identical plants quickly, but, if affected by disease, they may *all* die out.

Many fungi, such as moulds, grow asexually most of the time, but sometimes reproduce sexually if different strains meet.

Figure 6.16 Mature strawberry plants produce stems that run along the ground, called runners. The new plants on a runner can root and grow. Daffodils produce new bulbs after they have flowered.

2 Name three organisms that reproduce both sexually and asexually.

Adapting to circumstances

It is thought that organisms reproduce asexually to produce large numbers quickly when the conditions are favourable.

Sexual reproduction is an adaption to increase the chances of survival if circumstances change. With greater variation, at least *some* individuals will survive a change.

The disease malaria is caused by a protist called *Plasmodium*. *Plasmodium* is transferred to and from humans by mosquitoes.

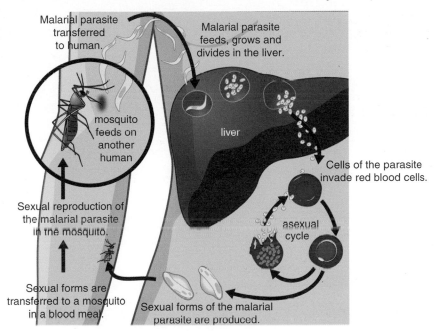

Malarial parasite transferred to human.

Malarial parasite feeds, grows and divides in the liver.

liver

mosquito feeds on another human

Cells of the parasite invade red blood cells.

Sexual reproduction of the malarial parasite in the mosquito.

asexual cycle

Sexual forms are transferred to a mosquito in a blood meal.

Sexual forms of the malarial parasite are produced.

Figure 6.17 *Plasmodium* has a complex life cycle that includes asexual phases in humans, then sexual reproduction in a mosquito.

In the human, the organism has a plentiful supply of food and warm conditions. Scientists believe that the sexual phase may be triggered as the human immune system, or perhaps antimalarial drugs, start to challenge the parasite.

3 Where do the asexual and sexual phases of the malarial parasite occur?

4 Why is it an advantage for the parasite to reproduce sexually?

5 Describe the conditions in the liver that favour asexual reproduction.

DID YOU KNOW?

Bees, ants and wasps reproduce partheno-genetically. This means that if the female lays a fertilised egg, a female is produced. If she lays an egg that has not been fertilised, a male emerges.

Genetics

Learning objectives:

- understand and be able to use genetics terms, such as gamete, chromosome, gene, dominant, recessive, genotype, phenotype, homozygous and heterozygous
- know that some human conditions are caused by a recessive allele.

KEY WORDS

allele
carrier
dominant
recessive
genotype
phenotype
homozygous
heterozygous

Jenny has cystic fibrosis. She needs physiotherapy to keep her lungs working. Fifty years ago, children with cystic fibrosis rarely lived beyond the age of 5. Today, life expectancy is over 40.

Cystic fibrosis is *a gene disorder*

Cystic fibrosis is an example of an inherited disorder. Sufferers produce mucus that is thicker and stickier than normal, making it difficult to breathe.

Figure 6.18 Researchers are working with gene and stem-cell therapies to find a possible cure for cystic fibrosis.

Cystic fibrosis is linked to a gene on chromosome 7. It codes for a protein called CFTR. The protein controls the movement of water and ions in and out of certain cells, including those of the tissue that lines the lungs.

Each gene can have more than one form, called **alleles**. Cystic fibrosis occurs when alleles of the CFTR gene are defective.

A CFTR allele is present on each of the chromosomes of chromosome pair 7.

(a) two normal alleles   (b) one normal allele one defective allele   (c) two defective alleles

Figure 6.19 Three combinations of alleles of the CFTR gene are possible.

If a person has one normal and one defective allele, the presence of the normal allele means that they still produce CFTR protein. They do not *have* cystic fibrosis. But they are a **carrier**; they could pass on the allele to their children. A person with two defective alleles has cystic fibrosis.

1. What are different forms of a gene called?

2. In Figure 6.19, explain why a person with each combination that is shown has, or does not have, cystic fibrosis.

An organism's genetics

Many characteristics are controlled by a single gene. Examples are red-green colour blindness in humans and fur colour in mice. Each gene has different forms called **alleles**. Alleles can be **dominant** or **recessive**. In Figure 6.19b, the person does not have cystic fibrosis. Both alleles are present in the gene pair; the dominant allele is expressed. The recessive characteristic is only shown if there are two recessive alleles.

When describing the genetics of an organism, we give the alleles letters. A dominant allele is given a capital letter; a recessive allele is written in lower case. If we use the letter 'C' for the CFTR gene, the combinations of alleles in Figure 6.19 are CC, Cc and cc.

The alleles present for a particular gene make up the organism's **genotype**. How the gene is expressed (the appearance or characteristics of an organism) is the **phenotype**.

When an organism has two alleles of the same type – either dominant or recessive – they are said to be **homozygous** for that characteristic. If the alleles are different, they are described as **heterozygous**.

Figure 6.20 Eye colour is controlled by many genes. While we can write down the phenotype, it's not possible to write a genotype.

> **REMEMBER!**
>
> It is important that you know, understand and can use the genetics terms on these pages.

> **DID YOU KNOW?**
>
> Height and skin colour are polygenic – they are controlled by several genes. These characteristics show a continuous gradation across populations.

3. What is meant by a dominant allele?

4. What is the difference between an organism's genotype and phenotype?

5. 'A dominant trait is the most likely to be found in the population.' Discuss this statement. Do you agree with it? Justify your answer.

Genetic crosses

KEY WORD

Punnett square

Learning outcomes:

- use the terms dominant, recessive, genotype, phenotype, homozygous and heterozygous
- know that some human conditions, such as cystic fibrosis, are caused by a recessive allele
- complete or construct a Punnett square to predict the outcome of a genetic cross.

Cystic fibrosis has been recorded since the sixteenth century. One symptom is production of sweat with an increased salt content.

In the 1980s, the gene for cystic fibrosis was mapped to chromosome 7. We can now diagnose cystic fibrosis quickly and predict its inheritance.

Genetic crosses

Let's take an example where a mother with cystic fibrosis has children with a father who does not.

The mother's genotype must be cc, as she has the condition. The father could be CC or Cc. Let's start by assuming he's CC.

All the sperm produced by the father will be C. The eggs produced by the mother will be c. So at fertilisation, *all* the children will be Cc. Their phenotypes will be normal.

1 What is the genotype of a person who is homozygous dominant for a gene, B?

2 What types of gametes will the person produce?

Genetic diagrams

Let's now assume the father is Cc – he's normal but a carrier. This time, the cross is a little more complicated. It's best to display the cross in a diagram called a **Punnett square** to show the possible outcomes. See Figure 6.22.

Figure 6.23 shows the possibilities when a mother and father are *both* carriers of the cystic fibrosis allele. We know that as carriers, they both have Cc genotypes. They will produce both C- and c-carrying gametes.

Figure 6.21 This X-ray shows a there is a widening of the airways and a build-up of mucus in the lungs.

	Mother (cc) gametes	
	c	c
Father (Cc) gametes C	Cc unaffected (but a carrier)	Cc unaffected (but a carrier)
c	cc cystic fibrosis	cc cystic fibrosis

Figure 6.22 There is a 50%, or 1 in 2, chance that a child will be born with cystic fibrosis.

	Mother (Cc) gametes	
	C	c
Father (Cc) gametes C	CC unaffected	Cc unaffected (but a carrier)
c	Cc unaffected (but a carrier)	cc cystic fibrosis

Figure 6.23 The probability of the couple having a child with cystic fibrosis is 1 in 4.

The ratio of children without cystic fibrosis to children with it would be 3:1. The ratio gives an *overall* probability, but of course which allele is in the sperm and which allele is in the egg will be completely random.

HIGHER TIER ONLY

3 The ability to taste a chemical called PTC is controlled by a single gene that codes for a taste receptor on the tongue. A man who is heterozygous for gene T has children with a woman who is homozygous recessive for the gene. Draw a Punnett square, showing the possible genotypes of the children.

4 For an eye colour gene in parrots, the brown allele is dominant to red.

Draw a Punnett square to show the genotypes and phenotypes of a mating between two heterozygous parrots.

DID YOU KNOW?

Reginald Crundall Punnett was a Professor of Biology, and later Genetics, at the University of Cambridge. With William Bateson, he helped to establish genetics as a science.

REMEMBER!

You need to be able to interpret Punnett square diagrams, and to construct them if working at a higher level. For most of the questions you will encounter, you will find a 1:1 ratio, a 3:1 ratio, or – if crossing a homozygous dominant individual with a homozygous recessive – the offspring will all have the dominant phenotype.

Tracking gene disorders

Learning objectives:

- understand the use of a family tree to show the inheritance of a characteristic
- explain economic, social and ethical issues concerned with embryo screening.

KEY WORDS

embryo screening
family tree
in-vitro
  fertilisation

We can predict the possibility of a child being born with some gene disorders. A simple test, using cheek cells or blood, identifies if potential parents are carriers of a disease-causing allele.

Gene disorders caused by dominant alleles

Most, but not all, inherited conditions are caused by recessive alleles. Some are the result of a defective dominant allele.

In these instances, the presence of one allele will cause the characteristic to be seen in the phenotype.

1 Write down the three possible genotypes and phenotypes for the polydactyly gene.

2 Draw a Punnett square between a father who is heterozygous for polydactyly and a homozygous recessive mother.

Family tree diagrams

In genetics, we can use a genetic **family tree** to show how a condition is passed down through a family.

Figure 6.24 A genetic counsellor can advise on the risks of passing on a genetic disorder.

Figure 6.25 Polydactyly – having extra fingers or toes – is caused by a dominant allele.

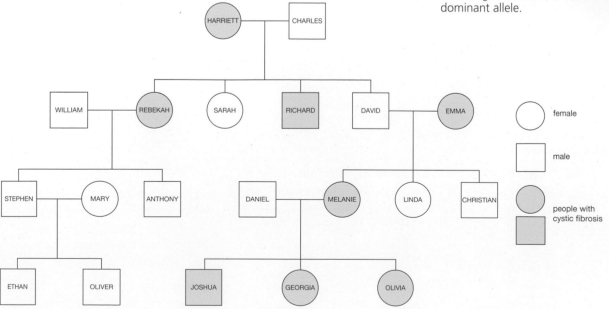

Figure 6.26 An example of the inheritance of cystic fibrosis in a family

Some of the genotypes of the family in Figure 6.26 can be worked out.

We know that Harriett, and the other members of the family affected by cystic fibrosis, *must* be cc. Anyone unaffected will be either CC or Cc. Charles *must* be Cc, because both Rebekah and Richard have cystic fibrosis. If Charles were CC, none of his children could possibly have the condition.

3 **What can we say about William's genotype?**

4 **Identify the people in the family tree who are *certain* to be carriers.**

Embryo screening

When a couple use *in-vitro* **fertilisation** (see Chapter 5), a number of embryos is usually produced. A few cells can be removed from an embryo and tested for a defective allele. This is **embryo screening**.

In families where there is a known history of a genetic disorder, embryos can be screened. A decision can then be made whether or not to implant an embryo into the mother. Embryo screening raises ethical, social and economic issues.

Embryos that are not chosen for implantation can be frozen for possible future use, or used for research. Eventually, if they are not used, they are destroyed.

One worry about embryo screening is the potential selection of embryos for social reasons, for instance, to have a baby of a particular sex.

Embryo screening is carefully monitored in the UK. Guidelines on how embryos are used are provided by the Human Fertilisation and Embryology Authority (HFEA).

A defective gene may not have immediate life-threatening consequences. It could suggest an increased risk of a particular disease or decreased life expectancy. So, what if the information from screening was obtained by insurance companies? Or a potential employer?

5 **Give one possible medical, social and economic consequence of embryo screening.**

6 **The HFEA was asked to rule on couples who wanted their embryos screened for gene mutations that gave an increased risk of breast cancer. Not all people with these mutations go on to develop breast cancer. What would *your* ruling have been? Give reasons to justify your choice.**

DID YOU KNOW?

In the case of many gene disorders, a person may be infertile and so not able to pass the allele on. Most women with cystic fibrosis can become pregnant without difficulty, but only 2–3% of affected men are fertile.

REMEMBER!

Include all the stages when working through a genetic cross. When constructing a Punnett square, write down the genotypes of the parents and the gametes before you work out the cross. Be careful with letters where upper and lower case could be confused.

KEY CONCEPT

Genetics is simple – or is it?

Learning objectives:

- explain how certain characteristics are controlled by a single gene
- understand that many characteristics are the result of multiple genes interacting
- describe the search for genes linked to disease.

KEY WORDS

complex diseases
Mendelian
inheritance

Huw is one of the 1 in 12 males in the UK who is colour blind. The condition affects just 1 in 200 females.

Colour blindness

Huw suffers from red-green colour blindness. This is the most common form. He confuses colours that have some red and green in them.

A single gene determines whether a person has normal colour vision or is red-green colour blind. A defective allele of this gene means that the cells in Huw's eyes (called cones) that detect red and green don't function properly.

The gene is on the X-chromosome.

normal colour vision

red-green colour blind

Figure 6.27 The lower image shows how this set of pencil crayons might appear to someone with red-green colour blindness.

1 **What is red-green colour blindness?**

2 **Where is the gene for red-green colour blindness located?**

3 **How many alleles will a male and a female have for this characteristic?**

Genomics and inherited disease

Observations of populations, and more recently, investigations using genomics have confirmed that most of our characteristics are controlled by not just one gene, but usually by many.

The same is true of genetic diseases. Single-gene disorders, such as cystic fibrosis, follow what is known as **Mendelian inheritance**. But these single-gene disorders are rare.

Most diseases are referred to as **complex diseases**. These include heart disease, diabetes and obesity. They result from the interaction of many genes, non-coding regions of the genome and environmental factors.

Complex diseases do cluster in families but they have no clear pattern of inheritance, because multiple genes are involved.

Figure 6.28 Research does not just focus on the *human* genome; 84% of the genes known to cause human disease have a zebrafish equivalent.

4. **Give two examples of a single-gene disorder.**

5. **Give two examples of a disease linked to multiple genes.**

Studying pathogen genomes

Scientists are also analysing the genomes of human pathogens, to help us understand and control infectious disease. We now have complete genomes of many, including MRSA. MRSA is a type of bacterium that is resistant to a wide range of antibiotics.

One day, it will be possible to analyse the genomes of pathogens and quickly select the best treatment, according to genomics of the strain of bacterium.

Figure 6.29 A nurse with an MRSA patient

6. **Describe how MRSA has arisen.**

7. **How could analysis of the MRSA genome help in the control of an outbreak?**

8. **Write a scientific argument to say why it is important for our government to invest money into researching pathogen genomes.**

DID YOU KNOW?

Recent excavations in London unearthed the graves of medieval plague victims. Scientists analysed DNA of the plague bacterium isolated from victims' teeth. The genomes of the 1349 bacterium, and the one that caused an outbreak in Madagascar in 2014, are *identical*.

KEY INFORMATION

Remember that most of our characteristics are controlled by multiple genes. Those controlled by a single gene are rare.

MATHS SKILLS

Fractions, ratio, proportion and probability

Learning objectives:

- understand and use fractions and percentages
- understand and use ratio and proportion
- understand and use probability when predicting the outcomes of genetic crosses.

KEY WORDS

fraction
percentage
probability
proportion
ratio

Predicting the outcome of genetic crosses quantitatively matters in understanding the inheritance of human characteristics, or of genetic diseases.

Fractions and percentages

In sections 6.6 to 6.8, you looked at the inheritance of cystic fibrosis.

The fraction of affected children =

$$\frac{\text{the number of affected children}}{\text{the total number of children shown}} = \frac{1}{4}$$

A quarter are born with cystic fibrosis.

When comparing fractions with different denominators it is helpful to convert them to a **percentage**.

The percentage of affected children =
$$\frac{1}{4} \times 100 = 25\%$$

If we know the total number in a population, we can calculate the number in a fraction (or percentage) of that population.

In the UK, 48%, or 48/100 people, in a 2014 survey, had blue eyes. So, in the UK population of 63 500 000 in 2014:

The number of people in the UK with blue eyes =
$$\frac{48}{100} \times 63\ 500\ 000 = 30\ 480\ 000$$

			mother	
			Cc	
			C	c
father	Cc	C	CC unaffected	Cc carrier
		c	Cc carrier	cc cystic fibrosis

Figure 6.30 Punnett square showing the cross between two carriers of cystic fibrosis

DID YOU KNOW?

In the early 1900s, a mathematical law for calculating the frequency of a genotype in a population of organisms was developed by Godfrey H. Hardy.

1. In a cross between a heterozygous and a homozygous recessive individual for a recessive disorder, what fraction of the offspring would be expected to have the condition?

2. Three alleles of the MC1R gene are involved in the inheritance of red hair. One of them, R160W, is found in 9% of the UK population. What number of people in the UK have this allele?

KEY INFORMATION

Remember that geneticists can only work with probabilities and not certainties.

Ratio and proportion

In the Punnett square in Figure 6.30, there are three normal children to every one child with cystic fibrosis: a **ratio** of 3:1.

In other words: For every 4 people, 1 will probably have cystic fibrosis and 3 will not. These are often described as the **proportions** of a given population.

If we have a ratio of 3:1 in a population, we would *expect* that as the number of normal children increases, so will the number of those with cystic fibrosis.

In genetics crosses, expected numbers will follow a certain multiplication factor, known as 'the constant of proportionality', so are said to be directly proportional.

3 **The allele for Huntington's disease is dominant. What ratio of offspring would you expect if a heterozygous couple had a family?**

4 **In a town with a population of 100 000, 40 people are affected with cystic fibrosis. Assuming direct proportionality, how many affected people would you expect in the population of a city with 1½ million people?**

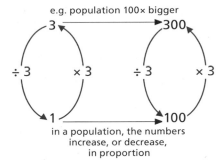

Figure 6.31 Numbers of normal children, and those with cystic fibrosis, increase by a multiplication factor of 3.

Probability

A couple with a history of cystic fibrosis in the family visit a genetic counsellor to assess the **probability** – or likelihood – of their children being born with cystic fibrosis.

Probabilities can be expressed as a fraction, percentage or ratio, or on a scale of 0 to 1, where 1 represents certainty. If an event happens once for every four trials, then the probability of this happening is ¼ or 0.25 or 25%. In biology, we often work with the decimal representation.

The genetic counsellor draws up a Punnett square.

The *probability* of producing a child with cystic fibrosis will *never change* for this couple – It is always ¼.

In reality, probability will not be exact because fertilisation is random.

5 **The first child of a couple who are carriers of cystic fibrosis does not have the condition. They think the chances of having an affected child will be increased next time. Explain to them why it is not.**

6 **Suggest why, when working with plants, the ratio of the outcomes were very close to those expected, while those in a family might not be.**

		mother	
		Cc	
		C	c
father Cc	C	CC child ①	Cc child ②
	c	Cc child ③	cc child ④

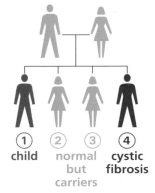

There is a probability that one child with cystic fibrosis will be born in every four children.
Two in every four will be carriers.
This is the case in the sequence of children in this family.

Figure 6.32 Predicting the probability of children from two carriers of cystic fibrosis

Check your progress

You should be able to:

recall the definition of the genome → describe a gene as a section of DNA that controls a particular characteristic → understand that genes work by coding for the production of a particular protein, and non-coding genes switch genes on and off

recall that the entire human genome has been mapped → describe the importance of the mapping of the human genome → explain the mapping of the human genome in understanding historical human migration

identify that organisms reproduce by asexual and sexual reproduction → explain that the method of reproduction may depend on circumstances

identify meiosis as the cell division used to produce gametes → explain the need for meiosis in producing gametes → explain that the gametes produced by meiosis are genetically unique

recall that genes exist in different forms called alleles, and know key genetic terms → complete Punnett squares to show the inheritance of characteristics controlled by single genes → construct Punnett squares to predict the outcome of genetic crosses

recall that some disorders are inherited → describe the inheritance of polydactyly and cystic fibrosis → make judgements about embryo screening

Worked example

A couple's second child was born with a condition called phenylketonuria (PKU). The condition is caused by a recessive allele.

The family tree shows that there is a history of PKU in the mother's (8) family. The father (7) was unaware of the condition in his family.

The couple would like another child. A genetic counsellor draws a family tree.

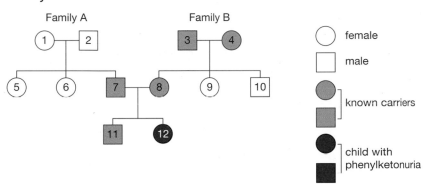

The student has identified the genotype correctly.

1. **The genetic counsellor talks about the father's family's medical history.**

   a **What is the genotype of the father (7)?**

   Pp

   b **What can be deduced about the genotype of the father's parents, 1 and 2? Explain your answer.**

   One is a carrier.

   The answer would have been better with more explanation. One parent (or both) must be carriers. For 7 to be a carrier, he must have inherited one recessive allele. So, one parent must have passed on a recessive allele. The other parent would have passed on a dominant allele (otherwise 7 would have PKU). Their other allele *could* have been the recessive allele, which was not passed down to any of the three children.

   c **Draw a genetic diagram to show how 12 came to have PKU.**

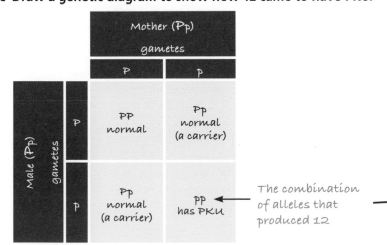

   The combination of alleles that produced 12

   The student has included the parental genotypes, the gametes produced, the possible genotypes and phenotypes produced, and has highlighted the combination of alleles that must have produced 12.

End of chapter questions

Getting started

1 The genetic term used to describe the entire DNA of an organism is:

1 Mark

    a phenotype   b genome   c double helix   d allele

2 The process of cell devision that results in the formation of gametes is:

1 Mark

    a natural selection   b mitosis   c meiosis   d cloning

3 Use the words provided to complete the sentences.

alleles	bases	chromosomes	different positions
DNA	each chromosome	identical positions	one chromosome

Alleles for a particular characteristic are located at _____ on _____ of the chromosome pair.

1 Mark

The structure of _____ is like a twisted ladder. The rungs of the ladder are chemicals called _____ .

1 Mark

4 Explain how scientists can use information from the mapping of the human genome.

2 Marks

5 People can either roll their tongue into a U-shape, or are unable to roll their tongue.

    a The diagram shows a pair of chromosomes.

      Is the allele for tongue-rolling dominant or recessive? Explain your answer.

2 Marks

    b Give the other possible genotypes related to tongue rolling.

1 Mark

    c Give the phenotypes for these genotypes.

1 Mark

genotype TT
can roll tongue

Going further

6 Draw two lines to match the types of cell division with where they occur. `1 Mark`

Cell division   Where it occurs

| Asexual reproduction in bacteria |

Meiosis

| Growth of a human embryo |

Mitosis

| Sperm production |

7 Describe the process of sex determination in human offspring. `2 Marks`

8 In a species of mouse, black coat colour is dominant to white.

Two black mice mate.

a Complete the Punnett square below to show the genotypes and phenotypes of the offspring. `2 Marks`

b Calculate the probability of producing a white mouse. Express your answer as a fraction. `2 marks`

c The chromosome containing the genes for coat colour was found to have 220 million base pairs. Write this number in standard form. `1 Mark`

9 Scientists have investigated how the mutation rate of certain organisms is affected by the size of their genome.

Figure 6.47 has some data from various groups of organism.

  a What conclusion can be drawn from the data?

  1 Mark

  b Suggest how the confidence in your conclusion could be increased.

  1 Mark

More challenging

10 Explain how a mutation can affect the production of a protein.

2 Marks

11 When investigating the migration patterns of humans, what type of DNA samples should be taken from current world populations?

1 Mark

12 Give one example of a human characteristic that is controlled by a single gene.

1 Mark

13 Mutations can occur in genes. Mutations can cause genetic disorders in humans. Phenylketonuria (PKU) is a genetic disorder caused by a gene mutation. People with PKU produce an inactive enzyme.

6 Marks

The normal base sequence and the mutated base sequence which can cause PKU are shown below.

normal base sequence .... C T C G G C C C T............

mutated base sequence .... C T T G G C C C T............

Describe and explain how the changes that have occurred in the mutated base sequence can result in an inactive enzyme being produced.

Most demanding

14 Why is meiosis important in an organism that reproduces sexually?

2 Marks

15 A bacterial cell divides using binary fission, and produces 128 cells in 175 minutes. Calculate the time between each division.

1 Mark

16 In Estonia, a large percentage of the population have blue eyes. In an Estonian town with a population of 14 000, a survey reveals that 12 600 have blue eyes. Assuming direct proportionality, how many people would you expect to have blue eyes in another Estonian town with a population of 20 000?

1 Mark

17 A team of scientists analysed the amount of DNA bases in the cells of 32 species of bacteria.

6 Marks

They used their data to plot a graph of the proportion of bases in the bacterial cells that were T (thymine) over the proportion of bases that were A (adenine).

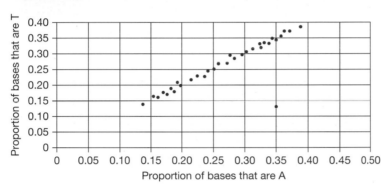

What can you conclude from the graph?

Evaluate the data obtained. In this evaluation, comment on:

- any anomalous results
- why the proportions of A and T do not add up to 1
- any additional investigations that could be carried out.

Total: 40 Marks

VARIATION AND EVOLUTION

IDEAS YOU HAVE MET BEFORE:

THERE ARE DIFFERENCES BETWEEN AND WITHIN SPECIES.

- Variation between individuals is continuous or discontinuous.
- Variation can be measured and the data represented graphically.
- Hereditary material is passed from one generation to the next through the genetic material, DNA.

VARIATION BETWEEN SPECIES CAN DRIVE NATURAL SELECTION.

- Variation between individuals of the same species means that some organisms compete more successfully than others.
- When an animal or plant is more successful it passes more of its genes to the next generation. Less successful organisms will not pass on as many genes. This is natural selection.
- The science of genetics was established by the work of an Austrian monk, Gregor Mendel.
- Genetics allows us to understand the inheritance of certain characteristics in humans and many other organisms.

CHANGES IN THE ENVIRONMENT CAN LEAD TO EXTINCTIONS.

- Some individuals within a species, and some species, are less well adapted than others.
- Changes in the environment can lead to the extinction of those individuals that are less well adapted.
- Gene banks can be used to preserve hereditary material.

IN THIS CHAPTER YOU WILL FIND OUT ABOUT:

WHAT CAUSES VARIATION AND WHAT ARE ITS EFFECTS ON THE INDIVIDUAL?

- Variation has genetic and environmental causes.
- Mutation, sexual reproduction and meiosis are processes that lead to variation.
- Variation results in differences in phenotypes and genotypes in a population.

HOW DO VARIATION, A STRUGGLE FOR EXISTENCE AND NATURAL SELECTION LEAD TO THE EVOLUTION OF NEW SPECIES?

- In any population, there is a struggle for existence.
- Because of variation, some individuals are better suited to the environment, so they reproduce and pass on their genes to the next generation, a process called natural selection.
- Natural selection acts on populations, and if the environment changes a new species may result, by the processes of evolution and speciation.
- In 1858, Charles Darwin and Alfred Russel Wallace separately proposed the theory of evolution.
- The evidence for natural selection and evolution comes from observations of current organisms, the fossil record and biochemistry, including DNA.
- During the 100 years that followed the theory, many scientists pieced together the connection between inheritance, genetics, evolution, genes and the genetic code.
- Humans can also change the genetic make-up of organisms by selective breeding and genetic engineering.
- Fossils are used to create evolutionary trees to help understand the relationships between groups of organisms.

WHAT ARE THE CAUSES OF EXTINCTIONS?

- Extinction arises from changes in the environment, diseases and the introduction of new species that are predators or out-compete existing species.
- The five mass extinctions to date are thought to have been caused by climate change, or a catastrophic event such as a volcanic eruption or a collision with an asteroid.

Variation

Learning objectives:

- recall that differences in the characteristics of individuals in a population is called variation
- understand the genetic and environmental differences leading to variation.

KEY WORDS

environmental variation
evolution
genetic variation

Harriett and Imogen are sisters. Their differences in appearance are the result of genetic and environmental variation.

Genetic and environmental variation

The sisters inherited genes from their parents. They are similar to, but not identical to, their parents. They also resemble each other.

Individuals of every organism that have been produced by sexual reproduction are different. With the exception of identical twins, we all have different genomes. Our genome gives us a unique set of characteristics.

Some of the sisters' features have nothing to do with genetics. Harriett wears non-prescription spectacles and has braided hair. Differences that arise during development are part of **environmental variation**. Some environmental causes of variation are under our control, but others are not.

Figure 7.1 The two sisters have features in common, but they also have differences.

Some human characteristics – the person's phenotype – are the result of the interaction of the genome with the environment.

Some characteristics in humans affected by:

Our genetics	The environment	A combination of both
blood group	hair colour and length	height
eye colour	language	skin colour
natural colour of hair	scars	weight
shape of earlobe	tattoos	sporting achievements

1. Give two characteristics in humans that result from:
   - **genetic variation**
   - **environmental variation.**

2. Give two characteristics in humans that result from a *combination* of genetic and environmental influences.

Variation and survival

Variation is essential to survival. There is usually a large amount of genetic variation within a population. This is essential to survival. Scientists studying populations of organisms can see how variation has led to changes. Variation is crucial to **evolution**. Each species in a stable environment is there because it has adapted to survive in that habitat.

Figure 7.2 Brown bears are adapted to life in the forest; polar bears to life on Arctic ice. Polar bears evolved from brown bears more than 350 000 years ago.

3 How is an organism able to live in a specific habitat?

4 Suggest two characteristics that enable polar bears to live on the Arctic ice.

The mechanism of genetic variation

Genetic variation is the product of three processes that lead to differences in genomes: mutations, sexual reproduction and meiosis.

Mutations occur continuously. They happen spontaneously, by accident. Most mutations have no effect, but a few are harmful. Rarely, mutations give rise to new phenotypes where the new characteristics are advantageous. When this occurs, the change in an organism can be quite rapid – over generations, rather than millions of years. Examples include the peppered moth and antibiotic resistance in bacteria.

Figure 7.3 A series of mutations in rats and mice have made some populations resistant to warfarin poison.

5 List three processes leading to genetic variation.

6 Give an example of where a mutation has been beneficial to an organism.

> **REMEMBER!**
>
> There are three processes that lead to genetic variation. Remember also that some mutations are not expressed in an organism, but where they are, most are harmful.

> **DID YOU KNOW?**
>
> Warfarin disrupts the blood-clotting mechanism. It is used as a drug to help control strokes and heart attacks. When used as a rat poison, the animals bleed to death. As a result of mutations, and the fact that rats reproduce rapidly, many rat populations are now resistant to the poison.

The theory of evolution

KEY WORDS

evolution
natural selection

Learning objectives:

- recall that all species of living things have evolved from simple life forms
- explain how evolution occurs through natural selection.

Around 1¾ million species of eukaryotes have been named and described. But the real number of species alive today may be more like 9 million.

The theory of *evolution* states that the species alive today have descended from simpler organisms.

Developing the theory of evolution

In the early 19th century, several scientists began to think that the species of animals and plants on the planet could actually change over time. At that time, almost everyone believed that God had created each species that lived. And this was in a single creation event.

One early theory of evolution suggested that organisms survived by adapting during their lifetime. The theory suggested that body parts developed during the organism's lifetime would be passed on to the next generation.

Later theories realised that the changes in populations of animals and plants over time were the result of changes in *inherited characteristics*.

1 Describe how early scientists thought living organisms develop.

2 Why was the theory wrong?

How does evolution happen?

Differences in a population will give some individuals in that particular environment advantages, compared with others.

In animals, these advantages might make an organism better able to catch food, resist disease or attract a mate.

Organisms best suited to the conditions would survive and breed. If the desirable characteristics were genetic, they would be passed on to their offspring. These inherited characteristics are the result of genes and alleles.

This is called **natural selection**. Nature is, effectively, selecting the organism with the most useful genes. Evolution happens through natural selection.

3 Suggest characteristics that might help plants to survive.

4 What is natural selection?

Figure 7.4 Insect species outnumber all others.

REMEMBER!

You do not need to know all about the theory of evolution.

Environmental change

Environmental change accelerates the rate of evolution. This could be a change in the climate. Or it could be through geographical isolation. Organisms can become isolated by a mountain range, valley or water. Each population will develop differently, dependent upon the demands of the unique habitat.

The animals – or plants – with the characteristics that are most suited to the new environment will survive to produce offspring.

Figure 7.5 The mechanism of evolution, and how polar bears may have evolved from brown bears that were isolated by ice.

5 **What changes in an organism's environment might lead to different selective pressures?**

DID YOU KNOW?

Early thoughts about evolution were wrong. But it is now clear that our genome *is* influenced by the environment. Addition of a chemical group – a methyl group – to our DNA is key to its regulation.

KEY INFORMATION

Evolution explains the diversity of life on Earth and how organisms evolved from their ancestors.

The origin of species by natural selection

KEY WORDS

evolution
natural selection

Learning objectives:

- explain the evidence that led Darwin to propose the theory of evolution by natural selection
- describe the process of natural selection.

Charles Darwin, along with Alfred Russel Wallace, proposed the theory of evolution by natural selection.

Evidence for Darwin's theory

From 1831 to 1836, Charles Darwin travelled around the world on board the H.M.S. *Beagle*.

A short period of the voyage, in 1835, was spent on the Galápagos Islands. Those 19 days were to shape the ideas for his theory.

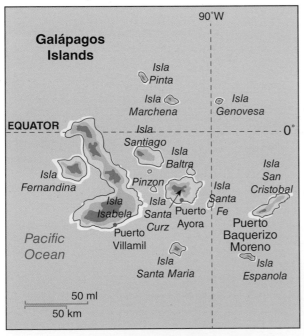

Figure 7.6 The Galápagos Islands are 600 miles off the coast of South America. They arose from the sea by volcanic action.

On the Tendency of Species to form Varieties; and on the Perpetuation of Varieties and Species by Natural Means of Selection. By CHARLES DARWIN, Esq., F.R.S., F.L.S., & F.G.S., and ALFRED WALLACE, Esq. Communicated by Sir CHARLES LYELL, F.R.S., F.L.S., and J. D. HOOKER, Esq., M.D., V.P.R.S., F.L.S., &c.

[Read July 1st, 1858.]

London, June 30th, 1858.

MY DEAR SIR,—The accompanying papers, which we have the honour of communicating to the Linnean Society, and which all relate to the same subject, viz. the Laws which affect the Production of Varieties, Races, and Species, contain the results of the investigations of two indefatigable naturalists, Mr. Charles Darwin and Mr. Alfred Wallace.

Figure 7.7 Short papers by Darwin and Wallace were read together to the Linnean Society in London 1858.

Darwin realised that animals and plants that lived there must have originated from mainland South America.

Some species on the islands were similar to those on the mainland, but *not* the same. Others were very different. The giant tortoises were all different from island to island. Darwin also noted three species of mockingbird, each living on a different island.

DID YOU KNOW?

Darwin applied Thomas Malthus' work on human populations to other living organisms.

He realised that species were not fixed: they can change.

Darwin recorded his observations and collected specimens of the animals and plants from the islands.

1 What part of the *Beagle's* voyage was critical to Darwin's theory?

2 What observations were key to Darwin's theory of evolution?

Artificial selection

On his return to England, Darwin spent time breeding domestic pigeons. Darwin was convinced that the different breeds must be descended from the rock dove, or 'pigeon' (on the right in Figure 7.9).

These changes had been produced in a short space of time. Could a similar process be at work in nature?

3 Name the process humans use to produce new breeds of animal.

4 Which animal did Darwin think was the ancestor of all pigeon breeds?

A struggle for existence

Darwin knew that organisms produced more offspring than they needed to maintain their numbers. But numbers in populations of organisms were reasonably stable. The death rate must therefore be high.

There was, Darwin said, a 'struggle for existence'. Because of variation in a species, some individuals survived better than others. Darwin called this **natural selection**.

When populations of organisms become separated and isolated, natural selection operates differently on the populations. This is what must have happened to animals and plants arriving on the Galápagos Islands.

Key to Darwin's thinking about **evolution** was that species change. This was contrary to the thinking of the time, which was that all the species on Earth were created. The domestication of animals and plants by humans was clear evidence that species can be changed.

5 What did Darwin think produced a 'struggle for existence'?

6 What processes led to the development of new species on the Galápagos Islands?

giant Pinta tortoise   marine iguana

flightless cormorant   Galápagos penguin

Figure 7.8 Animals of the Galápagos are very unusual.

Figure 7.9 Darwin's pigeons – on the left – are at the Natural History Museum.

KEY INFORMATION

Ideas that led Darwin to formulate his ideas on evolution came from three sources:

- his observations, notes and specimens
- his realisation that selective breeding could change species
- knowledge of geology and fossils.

Fossil evidence

Learning objectives:

- understand how, and the situations in which, fossils are formed
- understand how fossils are used as evidence for evolution of species from simpler life forms.

Darwin's work in geology was important. He formulated a theory on how volcanic islands had formed.

Fossils are the remains of organisms that lived millions, or hundreds of thousands, of years ago.

How are fossils formed?

If an organism dies in water, or is washed into water, conditions may be right for it to be fossilised.

Most **fossils** are formed as a dead animal or plant becomes buried in mud, silt or sand. Oxygen must be excluded. Otherwise, microorganisms would feed on the body and it would quickly decay.

During the process of fossilisation, the hard parts of an animal (bones, shell or teeth) or hard woody parts of a plant become replaced by minerals.

Figure 7.10 Fossils were well known in Darwin's time. *Ichthyosaurus* – featured here in a commemorative stamp – was found in 1811 by fossil hunter Mary Anning.

An organism dies.
It sinks to the bottom of the water.

The organism becomes covered in sediment.
The soft parts of the body decay.
The sediment begins to turn to rock.

More sediments settle. Other organisms die. If conditions are right, they begin to fossilise.
The sediments are compressed as further layers are added.
An exchange of minerals occurs between the skeleton and the water.
The skeleton is turned to rock - it has become a fossil.

The rock layers become lifted up.
They are eroded by wind and rain.

Faults in rocks and erosion expose the fossils.

Figure 7.11 How organisms become fossilised; fossils may later become exposed by erosion and earth movements.

1. **Describe how mineralised fossils are formed.**

2. **Which parts of an animal or plant are usually fossilised?**

Other remains of organisms

As well as mineralised remains, fossils can be formed in other ways.

Sometimes traces of organisms are left, such as footprints, burrows or spaces left by plant roots. Occasionally, whole organisms are found. Whole insects or plant parts have been found trapped in amber, a hardened form of tree sap. Occasionally, trunks of trees have been found after being buried in mud containing volcanic ash.

The conditions must be just right for fossil formation. It is actually a very rare occurrence.

3 What fossil traces of organisms have been found?

4 Where have whole fossilised organisms been found?

Evidence from the fossil record

As layer upon layer of rock is added, each must be younger than the one beneath it. We can tell the relative ages of the rock layers. Nowadays, with **radiometric dating**, it is also possible to find the absolute age of rocks.

The fossil record shows us how organisms that lived in the past differ from those around today. It also shows how long a species existed, by when it enters and leaves the fossil record. It shows us extinction, and the slow and successive appearance of new species

younger fossils and rocks

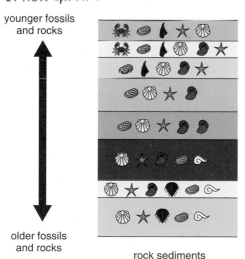

older fossils and rocks

rock sediments

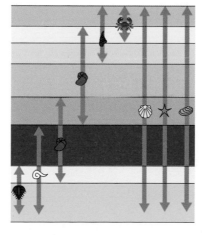

the succession of animal species through geological time

Figure 7.12 Palaeontologists record the fossils found in rock sediments. Rocks are dated and a picture is built up of the organisms that we know were present at the time.

5 How are the relative ages of fossil species worked out?

6 How can scientists find the actual age of fossils?

How much have organisms changed?

Learning objectives:

- understand why the fossil record is incomplete
- use the fossil record to understand how much, or how little, organisms have changed as life developed on Earth.

KEY WORDS

fossil record
missing link
palaeontologist

About 250 000 fossil species have been discovered, but one estimate suggests that this represents less than 1 in 20 000 of the species that ever lived. There must, of course, also be large numbers that remain undiscovered.

Fossils are missing from the record

The **fossil record** is incomplete. Conditions must be just right for fossil formation. The chances of this are small. In addition, geological activity over many years will have destroyed most fossils. And the older a fossil is, the more likely it is to have been lost.

Many early life forms were microorganisms or they were soft bodied. So fewer traces of them exist. Sometimes, however, conditions have enabled soft-bodied animals to be found.

Figure 7.13 **Palaeontologists**, working with scientists using medical techniques, created these three-dimensional models of an early type of green alga.

Figure 7.14 Darwin was delighted when an *Archaeopteryx* was found in Bavaria in 1861. It was reptile-like but had feathers. It was a critical piece of evidence showing that birds have evolved from reptiles.

And some of the Archaea and Bacteria have left traces of the unique chemicals that they have produced. There is now clear evidence of life going back 3.5 billion years.

Nevertheless, the fossil record is very incomplete. And Darwin appreciated that if life evolved, then there must be intermediate forms, or '**missing links**', between different organisms, as they evolved.

1. Why do we have few fossils of early life forms?

2. Which early organisms have left traces?

Fossil horses

Often, we can learn from the fossil record how much, or how little, life on Earth has changed.

When you look at the horse, for example, there is an extensive fossil record of horse-like animals. And new ones are still being found. We can trace the evolution of the modern horse, *Equus*, from an animal the size of a small dog, called *Hyracotherium*, which had toes. These toes have been lost during evolution and hooves developed.

3. From which animal are horses thought to have evolved?

4. Describe the trends in the evolution of the horse.

Some life has changed very little

In contrast, other organisms, such as certain bacteria, have changed little in billions of years. It can also be easy to distinguish fossil archaeans from fossil bacteria because of traces of the unique chemicals in their cell membranes.

5. Give an example of a type of organism that has changed very little in billions of years.

6. Explain how we know this.

DID YOU KNOW?

Modern analysis of fossils has revealed features of the animals that lived. Analyses of *Archaeopteryx* fossils suggest that it had white feathers with black edges and tips.

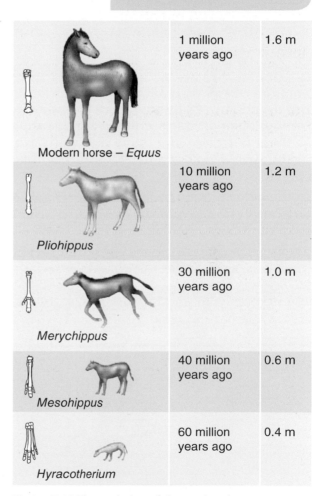

Modern horse – *Equus*	1 million years ago	1.6 m
Pliohippus	10 million years ago	1.2 m
Merychippus	30 million years ago	1.0 m
Mesohippus	40 million years ago	0.6 m
Hyracotherium	60 million years ago	0.4 m

Figure 7.15 The evolution of the modern horse; we now know that this evolution is not a simple straight line – their evolutionary tree branches and has offshoots – with some intermediate stages actually being smaller.

REMEMBER!

Fossils are rare, so any 'missing links' will be even rarer.

Evidence of natural selection and evolution?

Learning objectives:

- understand how scientific theories develop over time
- plan experiments to test hypotheses.

The peppered moth is white, 'peppered' with black spots. In 1848, in Manchester, the first mutant black, or melanic, peppered moth was recorded. By 1898, 95% of the moths were melanic.

The hypothesis

Lepidopterist James W. Tutt suggested an explanation. Polluted city air was laden with sulfur dioxide and soot, killing **lichens** and blackening the bark of trees. Dark moths were well camouflaged on tree trunks and less likely to be eaten by birds. In the countryside, the opposite would have been true: pale-coloured moths were camouflaged, but melanic forms were quickly seen and eaten.

In the heavily polluted Britain of the 1950s, the melanic moths appeared to have a selective advantage over the pale form.

Figure 7.16 In Victorian times urban areas such as Manchester became heavily polluted.

○ 0–30% melanic
◐ 30–60% melanic
● 60–80% melanic
● 80–100% melanic
■ Industrial city

Figure 7.17 In the 1950s, the melanic form was spreading, in particular downwind from industrial areas.

DID YOU KNOW?

A lepidopterist is someone who specialises in the study of moths and butterflies.

1 What caused the dark form of the moth to be produced?

2 What was Tutt's hypothesis?

Testing Tutt's hypothesis

Amateur lepidopterist Bernard Kettlewell carried out a series of experiments.

His first experiment was in heavily industrialised woodland near Birmingham, with around 90% melanic moths.

Kettlewell released a large number of peppered moths, marking the underside of the wings with a spot of paint. He then caught 770 peppered moths. Recaptured moths from the first part of the experiment were identified by the spot of paint. Others were wild.

	Number of melanic moths	Number of pale moths
No. of moths released initially	447	137
No. of marked moths recaptured	149	20

In 1955, Kettlewell carried out a similar study in unpolluted woodland in Dorset. Here, none of the local moths were melanic.

	Number of melanic moths	Number of pale moths
No. of moths released initially	473	496
No. of marked moths recaptured	30	62

Figure 7.18 Kettlewell's photographs of peppered moths, on a lichen-covered tree and a green leaf

Kettlewell demonstrated that the distribution of peppered moths was correlated with the level of pollution.

3 Suggest how Kettlewell might have improved the way he controlled variables.

4 Discuss possible difficulties that Kettlewell might have had with carrying out this experiment.

Support of Kettlewell's study

Since then, anti-pollution measures of the 1950s and 1960s have taken effect. The dark form has decreased in abundance, just as predicted by the hypothesis. **Melanism** has also been observed in other species, such as ladybirds.

Although there has been some criticism of Kettlewell's work in the past 15 years, Professor Mike Majerus concluded in one of the most recent studies that the moth is 'the proof of evolution'.

5 Why did air quality improve in the UK in the 1950s and 1960s?

6 What other evidence supported Kettlewell's findings?

COMMON MISCONCEPTION

Do not think that pollution affects the moths. Melanic moths arise anyway, by random mutations, and they survive if they have a selective advantage.

DID YOU KNOW?

Scientists have used molecular genetics to show that one mutation of a single gene leads to moths becoming melanic.

Antimicrobial resistance

Learning objectives:

- recall that bacteria develop that are resistant to antibiotics, which is evidence of evolution
- understand the mechanism by which antibiotic resistance develops
- understand the effects of the development of antibiotic resistance on the treatment of disease.

Antibiotics saved countless lives during the Second World War and after. In 1947, however, within 4 years of the first antibiotic – a type of penicillin – being introduced, the resistance of some bacteria to the antibiotic was observed.

Developing resistance

Bacteria and other microorganisms are becoming resistant to the drugs that have been designed to kill them.

The mutation of genes in pathogenic bacteria produces new strains of the bacteria. Some of these strains may be resistant to an antibiotic used on a patient. So the bacteria will not be killed.

As they reproduce, the genes that give the bacteria resistance spread throughout the population. Antibiotic resistance is an example of natural selection. Bacteria can evolve quickly because of their rapid reproductive rate.

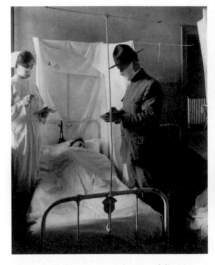

Figure 7.19 An American soldier is given a dose of penicillin. Penicillin significantly reduced the deaths of soldiers from infection.

A population of bacteria. A mutation occurs. One or more bacteria in the population are resistant to the antibiotic.

A bacterium with the resistant gene(s) survives.

The whole population of the bacterium is now resistant to the antibiotic.

Figure 7.20 A simplified diagram of how resistance to antibiotics spreads throughout a population of bacteria. In reality, more than one mutation is required.

Certain bacteria, such as *Staphylococcus aureus*, are building resistance to antibiotics very quickly. *Staphylococcus* that are resistant to the antibiotic methicillin are called MRSA.

1. Describe how antibiotic resistance develops.

2. Explain how this resistance is evidence for Darwin's theory of evolution.

Antimicrobial resistance

An antibiotic will not work against a resistant bacterium. An alternative antibiotic must be used. Gradually, bacteria become resistant to more and more antibiotics.

For serious infections, certain antibiotics are kept in reserve, the so-called 'last-resort' antibiotics.

Many scientists consider antibiotic resistance – or, more correctly, **antimicrobial resistance** (AMR), because resistance is also developing against antivirals, antiprotozoals and antifungals – to be the worst public health problem facing us today.

Dame Sally Davies, the UK's Chief Medical Officer, says Britain faces 'returning to a 19th century world where the smallest infection or operation could kill' us. Major advances in organ transplants and cancer treatment would be wiped out.

3 How do we currently treat bacteria that are resistant to common antibiotics?

4 Why is it suggested that we are returning to a medical world of the nineteenth century?

Growing resistance

AMR would occur anyway, but it is happening at a quicker rate than it should because of the over-prescription of antibiotics.

Antibiotics are often prescribed, inappropriately, for minor viral infections such as colds or respiratory infections. Doctors are also often persuaded by patients to prescribe them.

Key
AT = Austria
BE = Belgium
CZ = Czech Republic
D = Germany
DK = Denmark
ES = Spain
FI = Finland
FR = France
HR = Croatia
HU = Hungary
IE = Ireland
IT = Italy
LU = Luxembourg
NL = The Netherlands
PL = Poland
PT = Portugal
SI = Slovenia
SW = Sweden
UK = UK (England only)

Figure 7.21 Antibiotic use and penicillin-resistant bacteria across Europe. In some countries antibiotics are available 'over the counter' without a prescription.

5 What is the cause of growing resistance to antibiotics?

6 Describe trends in resistance of pneumonia bacteria to penicillin in the European countries.

Combatting antimicrobial resistance

KEY WORD

....

AMR

Learning objectives:

* describe how to reduce the rate of development of antibiotic resistance
* understand the requirement for, and the impact of, new antibiotics.

In 2015, a new method for growing bacteria enabled scientists to isolate 25 new antibiotics. One of them – teixobactin – is described as a 'game-changer'. Researchers could not find any mutations of *Staphylococcus aureus* or *Mycobacterium tuberculosis* that were resistant.

Slowing down antimicrobial resistance (AMR)

Many people, when prescribed antibiotics, do not complete the course. But completing the prescribed course is essential – all bacteria must be killed. Any bacteria left by not completing the course will be more resistant to antibiotics than the least resistant bacteria that were killed first.

Patients must never share antibiotics or skip doses, or save some for later on. Doctors must limit the prescription of antibiotics and not prescribe antibiotics inappropriately, such as for non-serious or viral infections.

The widespread use of antibiotics, for example in agriculture, should also be restricted.

1 Why must a course of antibiotics always be completed?

2 What advice is given to doctors to reduce the problem?

ANTIBIOTIC **GUARDIAN**

EUROPEAN ANTIBIOTIC AWARENESS DAY

A European Health Initiative

Figure 7.22 People can pledge their support to cut unnecessary use of antibiotics with the *Antibiotic Guardian*. November 18 is European Antibiotic Awareness Day.

ADVICE

....

Remember the ways of reducing AMR.

Modelling the future

The British government commissioned three reports on **AMR**, published in 2014 and 2015.

In one of the reports, scientists had modelled the projected numbers of deaths from AMR in the future. These numbers were based on current estimated death rates and the rate of developing resistance.

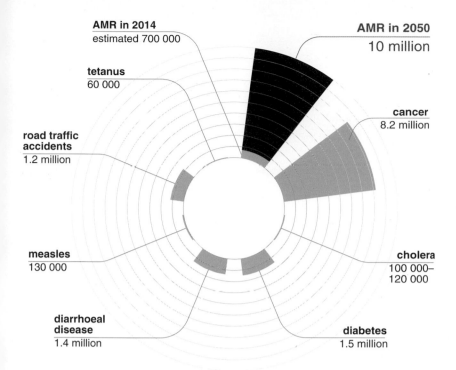

AMR in 2014
estimated 700 000

tetanus
60 000

road traffic accidents
1.2 million

measles
130 000

diarrhoeal disease
1.4 million

AMR in 2050
10 million

cancer
8.2 million

cholera
100 000–120 000

diabetes
1.5 million

Figure 7.23 The global death rates from various diseases and road traffic accidents, and current and projected death rates from AMR

3 Compare current death rates from different diseases and road traffic accidents with current and projected death rates from AMR.

4 What assumptions are made when modelling the number of deaths from AMR in 2050?

5 The report also suggested that AMR would cost the world up to $100 trillion by 2050. Suggest why.

Can we solve the problem?

AMR is a global concern, and reducing the problem cannot be achieved by action in the UK alone. Governments across the world are encouraging pharmaceutical companies to develop new antibiotics.

The problem for drugs companies is partly economic. The testing, development and trialling of new antibiotics is slow and costly. And, any new antibiotic is likely to be used sparingly, or as a last resort. So pharmaceutical companies will not sell much of their new antibiotic. They will lose money.

Another problem is that, as new resistant strains emerge, an antibiotic may not be effective for long.

But there is also cause for optimism. Advances in genetics and genomics will change the way that infection by resistant pathogens is detected, reported and treated.

6 Discuss the scientific and economic development of new antibiotics.

7 Should governments finance pharmaceutical companies to develop new antibiotics?

DID YOU KNOW?

Most current antibiotics work by affecting cell wall production, or protein or DNA synthesis in bacteria.

Scientists have tricked tuberculosis bacteria into becoming suicidal. They have blocked synthesis of an enzyme, which leads to the lethal build-up of a sugar.

Selective breeding

Learning objectives:

- describe the process of selective breeding
- recall how selective breeding enables humans to choose desirable characteristics in animals
- explain how selective breeding can lead to inbreeding.

Humans have been domesticating animals and plants for thousands of years. DNA evidence suggests that dogs were the first animals to be domesticated, perhaps as early as 33 000 years ago.

Selective breeding

Among the first animals to be domesticated were goats, then sheep. They would have been kept and bred for their meat, milk and hides or skins, which were used for clothes and shelter.

Animals in a population show genetic variation. Humans would have selected those with the characteristics required – the ones that produced the most meat or milk, for instance – and allowed them to breed.

From the offspring of those animals, the humans would then have selected those animals producing the largest yields and bred those. This was repeated over many generations.

① The animal breeder selects the sheep with the most muscle.

② Offspring are produced from the sheep selected.

③ Some offspring are more muscular than others.

④ The most muscular sheep are selected and bred to produce offspring.

⑤ An increased number of the population will be muscular.

The breeding programme continues until all the flock are muscular.

Figure 7.24 Sheep are bred for their lean meat (muscle) and quick production of meat.

This is called **selective breeding**. Darwin referred to it as artificial selection, in contrast to natural selection.

The outcomes of different selective breeding programmes are different **breeds**. The breed produced will depend on the characteristics required.

Related characteristics are often selected together, such as quality *and* volume of milk produced in cattle.

Figure 7.25 The Belgian blue (top) has been bred for its meat, which is muscle. The Jersey (bottom) has been bred to produce rich, creamy milk.

1. Suggest what other characteristics sheep may be bred for.

2. Describe the technique of selective breeding.

Domesticating dogs

Breeding dogs for hunting, or for their appearance and temperament, has involved selective breeding. The dog breeder selects dogs with characteristics of the breed.

Popular breeds of large dogs look different, but they are all the same species. They can still interbreed.

A person buying a dog looks for its 'pedigree'. This is a record of the animal's parentage, to show how true a dog is to the breed.

3. List some characteristics for which dogs are bred.

4. Explain why, even though they look very different, all dogs belong to the same species.

Problems with inbreeding

Pedigree dogs are bred from individuals of the same breed. This maintains their characteristics. They will have a limited gene pool, or range of genes in the population. They will become inbred. Usually, the incidence of rare disease alleles will increase in inbred animals.

Studies show that **inbreeding** puts dogs at risk of birth defects and genetically inherited health problems, and makes them prone to disease. Unnaturally small or large dogs are particularly prone to problems.

> **REMEMBER!**
>
> It is important to be able to understand and describe, the principles of selective breeding.

> **DID YOU KNOW?**
>
> Analysis of mitochondrial DNA suggests that modern dogs are related to the first dogs – which would have been kept for hunting – which originated in Europe between 19 000 and 32 000 years ago.

Hip dysplasia, where the hip joint is not correctly formed, and size are correlated in large dogs.

Many Dalmations are predisposed to deafness.

In bulldogs the large head and narrow hips mean that sometimes puppies have to be born by Caesarean section.

Figure 7.26 Some problems with inbreeding in certain dog breeds

5. Explain why breeding dogs with other dogs of the same breed causes problems.

6. List some of the problems with this process.

7. Evaluate whether the benefits of breeding pedigree dogs outweigh the health risks to the dog.

Producing new plant varieties

Learning objectives:

- describe the process of selective breeding
- recall how selective breeding enables humans to choose desirable characteristics in plants.

Lack of *genetic variation* in potatoes cultivated in Ireland in the 1850s was a factor that contributed to the potato famine. Many people died of starvation. Most of the potatoes grown were one variety: the Lumper.

Producing new plant varieties

In modern agriculture, new crop varieties are bred for disease resistance. Increased yields and improved quality of food crops are also the main goals of plant breeders. Other beneficial characteristics are that crops:

- grow and mature quickly
- have a distinctive taste, aroma or colour, for example, in strawberries
- have long shelf-life, store well or can be frozen.

Selective breeding enables crop growers to plant large areas with identical plants, giving maximum yields. But this does mean that many crops are genetically uniform. The whole crop could be lost if there is **environmental change**.

① Suggest three characteristics that crop plants could be bred for.

② What could happen to a crop made up of just one variety if the environment changed?

Traditional plant breeding

In traditional plant breeding, a plant with a desirable trait is crossed with another plant having the same or another desirable trait. The plants selected would be from a **mixed population**, or existing varieties. Pollen is transferred from the flowers of one plant to the other. The plant is prevented from self-fertilising or being cross-pollinated by another plant.

The process is repeated over several generations until the plants breed true for the required characteristics.

Plants in horticulture are developed, for instance, for the size and colour of their flowers and scent.

Clematis is a wild flower that grows in hedgerows and climbs trees. In the nineteenth century, plant breeders in Britain, France, Belgium and Germany raced to produce varieties with the largest, most colourful flowers.

Figure 7.27 In a plant-breeding programme, plants of one variety or species are crossed with another.

REMEMBER!

You should aim to be able to explain the benefits of and risks of selective breeding.

Figure 7.28 Wild clematis (top left) and two flowers of modern clematis varieties. Plant breeders still use wild clematis because it is tolerant of clematis wilt disease.

3 How does the plant breeder control which pollen is transferred to which female flower?

4 Explain why it is still useful to use wild versions of a cultivated plant in breeding programmes.

Producing a new variety

It can be very difficult to combine several desirable characteristics in a plant, for example, yield, disease resistance and perhaps other characteristics. And it is expensive.

A traditional plant-breeding programme will commonly take 12–15 years. It will involve the selection and crossing of suitable individual plants, various selection processes and a series of trials.

DID YOU KNOW?

Many plant scientists are now using marker-assisted techniques in plant breeding. We can identify genetic markers in a plant's DNA linked to key important characteristics, such as nutritional qualities, disease resistance, yield, etc.

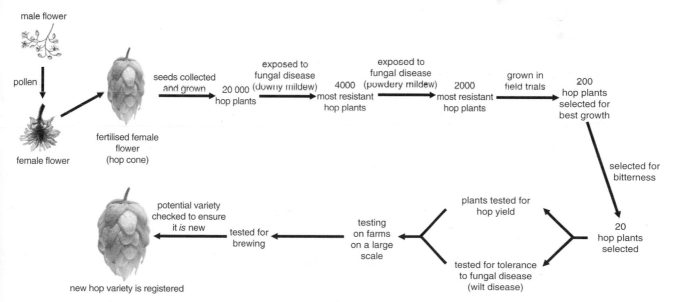

Figure 7.29 A hop-breeding programme uses traditional plant-breeding techniques.

5 Explain why a plant-breeding programme can take up to 15 years.

6 What three characteristics are hops bred for?

Genetic engineering

Learning objectives:

- give examples of how plant crops have been genetically engineered to improve products and describe how fungus cells are engineered to produce human insulin.
- describe the process of genetic engineering

KEY WORDS

genetic engineering
GM crops
vector

Genetic engineering **involves taking specific genes from one organism and introducing them into the genome of another. Scientists can now, more or less, transfer genes from any organism, including plants, animals, bacteria or viruses.**

Producing human insulin

Patients with Type 1 diabetes need regular injections of the hormone insulin. Since the early 1920s, insulin was extracted from the pancreas of pigs or cattle. But these types of insulin differ *slightly* from human insulin in the amino acids they contain. They had some side effects.

With **genetic engineering** it became possible to genetically engineer the bacterium, *Escherichia coli*, and the fungus, yeast, to produce 'human' insulin. This is *identical* to the insulin produced by the human body.

Yeast produces a more complete version of the insulin molecule. Less processing is required, so this method is often preferred.

Figure 7.30 Human insulin production in India. This photograph shows the purification process.

1 What is genetic engineering?

2 Name two organisms that can be genetically engineered to produce insulin.

Genetically engineered plants

Genetic engineering has transformed crop production. Genes from many organisms, often not even plants, are cut out of their chromosomes and inserted into the cells of crop plants. Such crop plants and other organisms are called genetically modified, **GM crops** or GM organisms (GMOs).

Plants have been engineered to be resistant to disease, and to increase yields, such as producing bigger, better fruit. Several types of crop plant have been produced that are resistant to diseases caused by viruses.

In the wet summer of 2012, potato plants became exposed to the potato blight fungus. In 2014 British scientists produced a GM potato that is resistant to potato blight. Genes from two wild relatives of the potato were inserted into the Desiree potato variety.

Figure 7.31 Pesticides are sprayed over crops to protect them from diseases. Disease resistant GM plants do not need the pesticides.

3 Give two reasons for the genetic modification of plant crops.

4 What types of organisms cause diseases in plants?

HIGHER TIER ONLY

The genetic engineering technique

Enzymes are used to remove the required gene, or genes, from the organism that carries the gene(s).

The gene is transferred, using a **vector**, to the organism that is to be modified. The vector is often a plasmid. The gene is inserted and sealed into the plasmid DNA using another enzyme. Bacteria have plasmids, and so do some eukaryotes, such as yeast. Viruses may also be used as vectors, including tobacco mosaic virus. Viruses that have had other genes modified, so that they are not infective, have been used in vaccine production.

DNA is extracted from pancreas cells.

the Insulin gene in a fragment of the pancreatic DNA.

bacterial cell
plasmid
bacterial chromosome

An enzyme is used to isolate the gene that codes for insulin production.

A plasmid is cut open using the same enzyme.

The insulin gene is inserted into the plasmid.

The plasmid is put back into the bacterial cell.

The genetically modified bacteria are cultured.

The genetically modified bacteria are grown in fermenters; the product is removed and processed into human insulin.

Figure 7.32 Insulin production using *Escherichia coli*

5 How is the required gene removed from the donor organism?

6 How is the gene transferred to the organism that is to be genetically modified?

DID YOU KNOW?

Genes for human insulin were cloned and transferred to *E. coli* in 1978. The first drug produced using genetic engineering was human insulin.

KEY INFORMATION

If genes are transferred to plants, this needs to be done at an early stage of their development. Older organisms have too many cells that would need to be modified.

Genetically modified crops: the science

KEY WORDS
....
food security
GM crops
larva
order

Learning objectives:

- explain the benefits of, and concerns about, genetic modification
- explain the ethical concerns of genetic engineering.

Biotechnologists in Britain aim to increase wheat yields to 20 tonnes per hectare by 2035.

Feeding the world

Many people think that we have the ability, and a moral obligation, to achieve global **food security** by growing GM organisms. **GM crops** have increased yields and will grow in poor soil and harsh environments. Scientists have also fortified plant crops with extra nutrients.

1 How might GM crops help to achieve global food security?

2 What characteristics are being introduced into GM crops?

Herbicide- and insecticide-resistant crops

Weeds reduce crop-plant yields and encourage fungal disease. GM crops have had genes inserted that make them resistant to a particular herbicide. As the crop grows, the field is sprayed with herbicide. The crop is unaffected, but the weeds are killed.

Another key area is the development of GM crops that resist insect attack. *Bacillus thuringiensis* (Bt) is a soil bacterium that produces a natural insecticide. The gene for this has been inserted into crops.

Figure 7.33 After a few bites of the leaves of this Bt peanut, the caterpillar died.

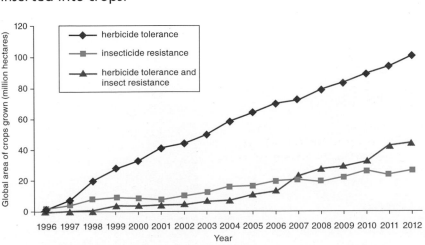

Figure 7.34 Global production of herbicide-tolerant and insect-resistant plants

Bt insecticide is a protein that kills the caterpillar, or **larva**, that eats the crop plant. It only works on some **orders** of insects, such as butterflies and moths, which are the most serious pests.

3 Why are herbicide-tolerant genes inserted into crops?

4 The reproductive rate in insects is very fast. Suggest why some populations are becoming resistant to the Bt gene.

Ecological effects

GM crops growing in the wild have been reported in many countries. 'Escaped' populations usually die out. GM crops may also cross-pollinate a wild or cultivated relative of the crop. GM oilseed rape is genetically capable of cross-pollinating with eight wild relatives.

GM crops have been reported to be swapping genes with other GM crops. A study of 288 oilseed rape plants in America showed that two had 'man-made' genes for multiple pesticides.

Of concern is the Bt gene's effect on non-target organisms. Only insects that eat the crop should be affected. However, pollen of some GM crops is carried in the wind. The pollen could be toxic to other insects that are essential pollinators of crops and other plants.

The monarch butterfly

A monarch butterfly larva, feeding on milkweed

Figure 7.35 One study in 1999 showed that the growth of monarch butterfly caterpillars was affected when its foodplants were dusted with Bt pollen.

Studies suggest, however, that the density of pollen in the wild would rarely come close to the levels needed to harm the caterpillars. The monarch butterfly is in decline, and research is ongoing to find out why.

5 Explain the possible spread of GM plants.

6 What are the concerns about Bt plants?

7 Do you consider GM products to be safe? Justify your answer.

ADVICE

Be critical when you read about genetic modification. Newspapers report scientific information second hand. Look for the original source of the information.

DID YOU KNOW?

Researchers aim to start growing a vitamin-enhanced 'super-banana' in Uganda. The bananas are genetically engineered to have increased levels of β-carotene, which is converted to vitamin A by the body. A deficiency in vitamin A can be fatal.

Is genetic modification safe?

Learning objectives:

- explain the concerns that people have about genetic modification
- explain the possible safety issues of genetic engineering in agriculture and medicine.

KEY WORDS

genetic marker gene

GM food crops and production of hormones by GM have had beneficial effects. But are GM products safe?

Safety concerns of GMOs

Insulin can be produced by yeast or by *Escherichia coli* bacteria. *E. coli* lives in our large intestines. Yeast, in the wild, lives on the surface of fruit. If they escaped from biotechnology production facilities might they be dangerous?

Genetic modification of viruses that are used to transfer genes causes real concern. Viruses can only reproduce in the cells of other organisms, so their genetic manipulation is worrying. The solution is to inactivate genes related to infection.

1 Why are people concerned about GMOs escaping from fermenters?

2 How are viruses used to transfer genes made safe?

Figure 7.36 The Ebola outbreak in 2014. Development of a vaccine has involved inserting genes from the ebola virus into a respiratory virus. The benefits need to be weighed against risks.

Antibiotic-resistance genes

When organisms or cells are modified, not all cells take up the foreign gene. The cells that have not, need to be screened out. When the cells are modified, a **genetic marker gene** is inserted into the organism's genome as well as the required gene. This marker gene is usually one giving antibiotic resistance. When the culture of cells is treated with antibiotic, any cells that have not taken up the required gene successfully will be killed. Resistance is created to the antibiotic kanamycin, which is rarely used today.

3 Why is a genetic marker gene used when genetically modifying organisms?

4 Why has the gene for resistance to the antibiotic kanamycin been chosen as the genetic marker?

Assessing the safety of GM products

The EU's approach to GM crop development is the most stringent in the world.

One significant concern is whether a GM food might cause allergic reactions. No GM products to date have been found to produce new allergies, or are any more or less allergenic than their non-GM versions. GM foods, modified appropriately, could become the solution to, rather than the cause of, food allergies.

Most scientists have found no differences that are statistically significant between other health impacts of GM crops and non-GM versions.

Recent studies have suggested that some GM products may cause cancer. But these studies are controversial.

GM plants are commonly made resistant to a herbicide called glyphosate, or Roundup®. Some harmful effects could be caused by the herbicide, not the genetic modification itself.

Glyphosate is described as harmless to humans and other animals, and is said to break down quickly in the environment. But now some scientists have identified correlations between glyphosate use and an increase in conditions ranging from autism to cancer.

Figure 7.37 A GM field of maize sprayed with glyphosate. Use of this herbicide has increased in the USA since the introduction of GM crops.

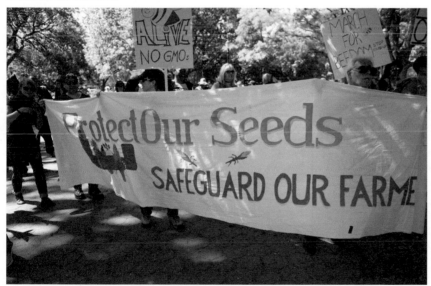

Figure 7.38 Environmental activists protesting against Monsanto's GMO programmes and demanding that foods be labelled

5 Discuss the evidence for GM crops being harmful.

6 Suggest why crop treatments, and not the crops themselves, might be harmful.

REMEMBER!

It may be helpful to be prepared to analyse and discuss negative and positive aspects of genetic modification from information that you are given.

DID YOU KNOW?

US scientists have engineered a bacterium that, to live, needs an amino acid that does not occur in nature. If any organisms escape the culture vessel, they cannot survive.

Ethically wrong, or essential?

Learning objectives:

- explain the benefits of, and concerns about, genetic modification
- explain the ethical issues of genetic engineering in agriculture and medicine.

KEY WORDS

gene therapy
genome editing
vector

Glowing GM fish were created during attempts to produce a fish that would glow in polluted water. Unfortunately, these GM fish glowed all the time.

The ethics of genetic modification

Was the sale of the Glofish® ethical? Or its development in the first place?

Should we be inserting genes from one organism into another? Very often these species are not even closely related. And should we be inserting human genes into other organisms?

Some religious teachings suggest that it is wrong to change natural organisms that God has created. What right do we have to change the genome of another organism? Is it acceptable to do this for the benefit of the human race? Is genetic engineering *ever* justified?

Figure 7.39 Glofish® didn't work as a pollution indicator, but quickly went on sale in pet shops and then on the Internet.

1 Give one ethical reason in favour of genetic modification.

2 Give one ethical reason against genetic modification.

Producing and marketing GM foods

Farmers cannot collect and sow the seed from GM crops because they will not breed true. They have to buy more for the next growing season. The seed companies are perceived as exploiting poor farmers.

Food producers are required to label GM foods, making it clear when a food is genetically modified. Customers can decide whether or not to buy them.

GM food must be clearly labelled. And food manufacturers must ensure that no other food is contaminated with GM ingredients. Unscrupulous food manufacturers might substitute cheaper GM ingredients for more expensive conventional ones.

3 Explain why farmers should not collect seed from a GM crop to sow the following year.

4 Why should GM foods be labelled?

5 How could GM contaminants be detected in food?

Gene therapies

Introducing genes from other organisms into humans would be unethical. But modern medicine has been investigating **gene therapy** in humans to overcome inherited disorders.

Most gene therapy is in its experimental stages. It would largely centre on inserting a normal version of an allele into cells that carry a defective version of that allele.

A deactivated virus is normally used as a **vector** to transfer the gene into the cell. But a major difficulty is how to deliver the replacement gene effectively.

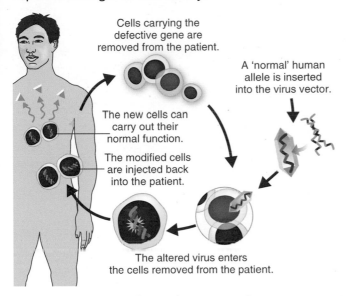

Cells carrying the defective gene are removed from the patient.

A 'normal' human allele is inserted into the virus vector.

The new cells can carry out their normal function.

The modified cells are injected back into the patient.

The altered virus enters the cells removed from the patient.

Figure 7.40 One type of gene therapy procedure

In the early days of gene therapy trials, there were many failures. Some patients died from a massive immune response or developed leukaemia, probably because of the viral vector.

Currently there are thousands of gene therapy trials. In the meantime, another gene technology is showing great potential for improving human health. **Genome editing** involves replacing or removing sections of the DNA of the genome using 'molecular scissors'. Although not new, recent developments have improved the precision and efficiency of the DNA editing process.

Any successful gene therapy would not prevent the person from passing on an inherited condition to their children. It is the patient's body cells that are being modified. Any modification of reproductive cells would be both technically and ethically difficult. This type of therapy involving reproductive cells is currently not permitted by law.

6 Why were early attempts at gene therapy unsuccessful?

7 Explain one of the limitations of gene therapy.

8 What ethical argument could you give against developing gene therapy?

ADVICE

You should aim to be prepared to analyse information and present ethical arguments for and against genetic modification.

Figure 7.41 Many trials have been focused on correcting a severe immune system abnormality called SCID, or 'bubble-boy syndrome'.

DID YOU KNOW?

One of the most publicised applications of gene therapy is for cystic fibrosis. The gene therapy formulation has been based on a plasmid rather than a virus, sprayed into the lungs of patients.

The tree of life

Learning objectives:

- describe how living things have been classified into groups using a system devised by Linnaeus
- describe how new models of classification have developed.

KEY WORDS

binomial system
evolutionary tree

In 2015, scientists discovered a new species of snake in a remote region of Western Australia. When a new species is discovered, scientists try to classify it.

Classifying organisms

All species are classified using the system developed by Swedish scientist Carl Linnaeus. Linnaeus divided all organisms into large groups called kingdoms. These were sub-divided into smaller groups, and these groups into smaller groups still: kingdom, phylum, class, order, family, genus, species. The smallest group is the species.

Linnaeus named species using the **binomial system**. Each organism has two names – a generic name and a species name.

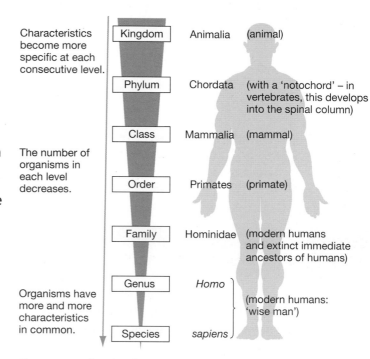

Figure 7.42 The classification of humans. Our scientific name is *Homo sapiens*. There are at least 10 animals in our genus, but all are extinct except for humans.

1 Who devised the classification system that we use today?

2 What system do we use to name an individual type of organism?

Evolutionary trees

An **evolutionary tree** shows how scientists think organisms evolved as they diverged from common ancestors.

There have been many versions of evolutionary trees, and new models continue to be developed. These developments have occurred because:

- Scientific examination has improved as microscopes have developed and our understanding of the physical characteristics (external and internal structures) of organisms has grown.
- Our understanding of biochemistry and biochemical processes has improved.

3 How have new models of classification developed?

4 Name the three domains that have been proposed. It may help to refer back to section 1.5 in Chapter 1.

Modern evolutionary trees

The information for modern evolutionary trees comes from organisms that are alive today and from the fossil record. But now we also look at base sequences of portions of DNA, or the structures of other chemicals such as proteins.

Scientists look at areas of DNA that show large variations between species. As organisms evolve, differences in their DNA accumulate. So the degree of genetic difference – the number of changes in the base sequences of a group of related organisms – can give us an estimate of the relative times at which these branches occurred.

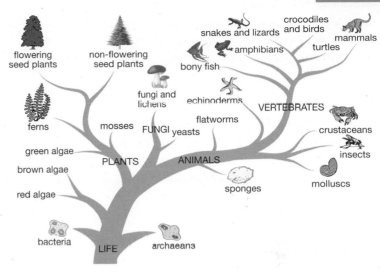

Figure 7.43 One version of an evolutionary tree. Some scientists have now added an extra branch to produce three domains (see Chapter 1).

Computer programs can generate comparisons between the sequences of equivalent lengths of DNA. New evolutionary trees can be built.

DNA evolutionary trees can help to clear up uncertainties in trees that are based on anatomical features. But we cannot be certain of these evolutionary relationships. And obtaining DNA from extinct species is difficult.

5 Explain how modern evolutionary trees are constructed.

DID YOU KNOW?

The 'Barcode of Life' is an international initiative devoted to developing a 'DNA barcode' database of living species, which can be used in identification.

REMEMBER!

You type a scientific name in *italics*, or if it's handwritten, underline it. The genus name has a capital letter but the species name does not. Avoid thinking of some organisms on an evolutionary tree as 'higher' than others. We cannot rank organisms.

Extinction ... or survival?

Learning objectives:

- list the causes of extinction
- explain how new predators, competitors and diseases can lead to extinctions.

KEY WORDS

extinction
invasive species

The Svalbard Global Seed Vault – the 'Doomsday Vault' – is buried deep in the Norwegian permafrost. It was built to safeguard seed varieties from around the world from loss of genetic diversity or famine.

Mass extinctions

The fossil record shows that there have been at least five mass **extinctions** over geological time.

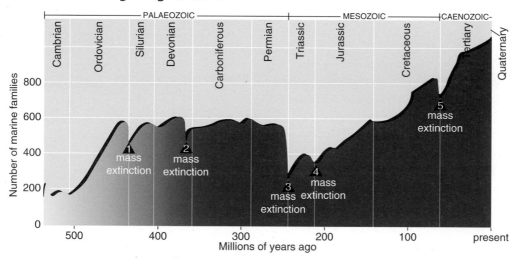

Figure 7.44 The five mass extinctions. The current rate of extinctions is comparable.

Changes to the Earth's environment over geological time must have been a factor. The warming or cooling of the Earth, changes in seasons or ocean currents, and the changing position of the continents would have contributed.

Around 66 million years ago, however, it is thought that a massive asteroid impact killed three-quarters of life on Earth, including the dinosaurs. The dust thrown up would have blocked out sunlight. Plants would have declined, followed by herbivores, and then the carnivores that were dependent on the herbivores. Volcanic eruptions and sea-level change could also have contributed.

The Earth's environment is constantly changing. When the environment changes, organisms either adapt to these changes, or they become extinct. A species is considered to be extinct when there are no remaining individuals of that species still living.

DID YOU KNOW?

According to one estimate in the scientific journal, *Nature*, humans have a century or perhaps two left. Can the sixth mass extinction be stopped?

1. Approximately when were the five mass extinctions?

2. Why can we only estimate the number of extinct species?

Invasive or alien species

Another important cause of extinctions is the introduction of a new species into a location. These may:

- be new predators
- compete for food with native organisms that are present
- introduce new diseases.

On the Galápagos Islands the animals had few natural predators. But then mammals were introduced, including rats, dogs and feral cats. Cats and dogs attacked birds and destroyed the nests of birds, tortoises and turtles. Projects are under way on the islands, or have already been carried out, to eradicate these predators.

In Britain, harlequin ladybirds are a new species. They eat other ladybirds and outcompete them for food. Scientists are worried that our native ladybirds might become extinct.

3 Why are scientists worried that some animals on the Galápagos Islands might become extinct?

4 Suggest one way of preventing these extinctions.

The verge of the sixth extinction?

Some scientists believe we are entering a sixth mass extinction, and that humans are the major contributing factor, through:

- transformation of the landscape
- overexploitation of species
- pollution
- introduction of alien species.

One serious concern in recent years has been the decline of bee populations. It is estimated that bees pollinate over 70% of the 100 crop species that provide 90% of global food supplies. If bees become extinct, the human race will follow soon after.

5 What may contribute to the sixth extinction?

6 How might bees contribute to human extinction?

7 'Humans are responsible for the extinction of species in modern times.' Do you agree with this statement? Justify your answer.

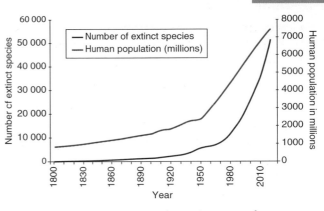

Figure 7.45 Humans are now the main cause of environmental change. This graph shows growth of the human population over time and the estimated numbers of extinctions.

Figure 7.46 The spread of the harlequin ladybird, 2004–14

ADVICE

Remember that while humans have contributed to extinctions, we alone have the ability, although not always the inclination, to prevent many further extinctions.

MATHS SKILLS

Using charts and graphs to display data

Learning objectives:

- understand when and how to use bar charts
- understand how to show sub-groups on bar charts
- understand how to plot histograms.

KEY WORDS

demographic
discrete
grouped bar chart
stacked bar chart

The International Union for Conservation of Nature and Natural Resources (IUCN) monitors species in danger of extinction. It must make this huge amount of data understandable to the public.

Bar charts

Scientists use graphs and charts to display, summarise and analyse data. They can be used to simplify the presentation of complex data and highlight patterns and trends.

Bar charts are used to display data collected for distinct groups. If the data points in the groups can be counted, then this data is known as **discrete** data.

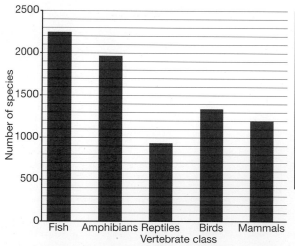

Vertebrate class	Number of species threatened with extinction
Fish	2248
Amphibians	1961
Reptiles	931
Birds	1373
Mammals	1200

Figure 7.47 Data of the number of species in each class threatened with extinction are transferred from a table to a bar chart.

When drawing a bar chart:

- the *height* of the bars is proportional to the measured number of frequency
- the *width* of the bars should be consistent
- the bars do not touch each other; they represent distinct groups
- the bars can be placed in *any* convenient order, although this should not be haphazard.

1 Draw a bar chart for the groups of organisms, shown below, found as fossils in a particular rock type.

Group of organism	Fossils found in %
Algae	14
Arthropods	33
Molluscs	3
Sponges	22
Worms	3

2 What percentage of fossil organisms were unclassified?

DID YOU KNOW?

In his book of 1871, *The Descent of Man*, Darwin discussed the diversity of skull size and shape in different people.

More complex bar charts

Other types of bar charts could be used to provide further information about these endangered species.

From Figure 7.48, we do not know the number of species in each vertebrate class, so we do not have any indication of what proportion of each vertebrate class is endangered.

We can add this information to produce a dual bar chart (also known as a **grouped bar chart**).

A similar type of bar chart is the **stacked bar chart**. We often see these in the media. Here, different sub-groups are stacked on top of each other to produce a single bar for each group included. Note that bar charts can be constructed horizontally as well as vertically.

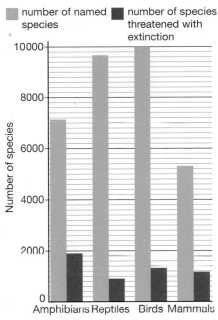

Figure 7.48 A dual bar chart for four of the vertebrate classes

③ **Construct a bar chart to illustrate the proportion of endangered species of fish:**

| Number threatened with extinction | 2248 |
| Number of species | 33100 |

Histograms

A histogram is a statistical diagram, similar to a bar chart. In a histogram, the *area* of each bar is proportional to the frequency of the class interval. The data are continuous instead of being discrete. They're commonly used to show the variation of a characteristic, such as height. Remember:

- the variable on the *x*-axis is continuous, so there are no gaps between bars
- the size of the categories is represented by the area of the bars, although for many of the histograms you will plot the ranges on the *x*-axis have been chosen to be equal.

Histograms can be used to show the range of variation across groups of organisms. One characteristic determined for both living humans and extinct human ancestors is the cephalic index (CI).

$$\text{Cephalic index} = \frac{\text{Maximum head width}}{\text{Maximum head length}} \times 100$$

The CI varies between human populations of different **demographic** groups and over time.

Figure 7.49 The histogram shows the range of the CI for the boys in a group of schoolchildren. Note that the bar for the lowest category is narrower.

④ **Plot a histogram for the range of CIs for the girls in the group.**

⑤ **Plot a histogram for the range of heights in your Biology group.**

Cephalic index (CI)	Boys in %	Girls in %
72.0 ≤ CI < 75.0	7.3	4.8
75.0 ≤ CI < 80.0	28.4	32.8
80.0 ≤ CI < 85.0	30.0	42.6
85.0 ≤ CI < 90.0	34.3	19.6

Check your progress

You should be able to:

distinguish between variation caused by genes and by the environment
→
describe how variation contributes to an organism's survival
→
understand the mechanism of genetic variation

recall early ideas about evolution
→
describe how natural selection leads to a struggle for existence
→
explain how environmental change operating with natural selection leads to the evolution of a new species

recall that the theory of evolution was developed independently by Darwin and Wallace

identify reasons why evolution was not, to begin with, accepted
→
identify the reasons why genetics and evolution were not linked until the twentieth century
→
explain how the scientific work of many scientists contributed to the gene theory

recall and use the classification system developed by Linnaeus
→
explain the features used to develop evolutionary trees
→
explain how microscopic examination, fossils and biochemistry have led to modern evolutionary trees

identify the causes of extinction
→
describe how new species, predators and competitors can lead to extinction
→
evaluate circumstances that may lead to another mass extinction

Worked example

Scientists in Germany have investigated the resistance of rats to two poisons - warfarin and bromadiolone.

They studied populations of rats in four towns where resistance to the poisons had been reported, and one town – Ludwigshafen – where no resistance had been reported to date.

Some of their results are shown below.

Town	Not resistant to either poison (%)	Resistant to warfarin alone (%)	Resistant to both poisons (%)
Dorsten	44	56	0
Drensteinfurt	90	5	5
Ludwigshafen	100	0	0
Olfen	21	21	58
Stadtlohn	5	8	87

1 **Explain why the data collected are evidence for natural selection.**

In a population, some rats will be resistant to the rat poisons, and survive their use. These will pass on their resistant genes. These will spread through the population as the rats breed, until most of the rats become resistant.

2 **Suggest reasons for the differences in the degree of resistance to the poisons.**

Resistance is greatest in Stadtlohn and Olfen. There is no resistance to the poisons in Ludwigshafen.

This could be because of the locations of the towns. If the towns are close together, populations can interbreed so that the resistant gene(s) spread. Ludwigshafen is further away.

This is a concise answer, but one that is not fully detailed. The student should have mentioned that some rats in a population will be resistant to the rat poison because of mutations. It is also important to say that these mutations will spread rapidly through the population because of the rats' rapid reproductive rate.

In this answer the student has overlooked the fact that mutations arise spontaneously in populations, as well as being spread by sexual reproduction.

These could also arise at a greater rate in Stadtlohn and Olfen, perhaps because of the numbers of rats in the different towns, which we do not know from the data given.

The data suggest that resistance arises first to warfarin, followed by bromadiolone. You do not need to know the reason for this, but warfarin was a 'first generation' poison, while bromadiolone was developed because rats became resistant to warfarin.

End of chapter questions

Getting started

1 Draw lines to match the scientists with the scientific work they carried out.

`1 Mark`

Scientist

Scientific work

Charles Darwin

Gregor Mendel

Carried out genetics experiments on peas

Recorded numbers of peppered moths

Wrote *On the Origin of species*

2 Describe how a fossil is formed.

`2 Marks`

3 Why is our fossil record incomplete?

`1 Mark`

4 What is a hybrid?

`1 Mark`

5 Describe what is meant by genetic variation.

`1 Mark`

6 Use the information in this photograph to discuss two of the person's features that have genetic causes, and two features that have environmental causes.

`2 Marks`

7 Draw a bar chart for the groups of organisms shown below, found as fossils in a particular type.

`1 Mark`

Group of organism	Fossils found %
Algae	11
Arthropods	30
Molluscs	4
Sponges	23
Worms	2

8 Calculate what percentage of fossil organisms were unclassified.

`1 Mark`

Going further

9 How can a species new to an area, country or island lead to the extinction of other species?

3 Marks

10 What is meant by the term 'natural selection?'

1 Mark

11 The occurrence of a dark form of the two-spot ladybird was monitored by scientists between the 1960s and the 1980s.

a Some of the scientists' results are shown below.

Year	Frequency of the dark form (%)
1960	47
1965	37
1970	27
1975	19
1980	12
1985	10

The scientists also recorded the yearly amounts of smoke in the air.

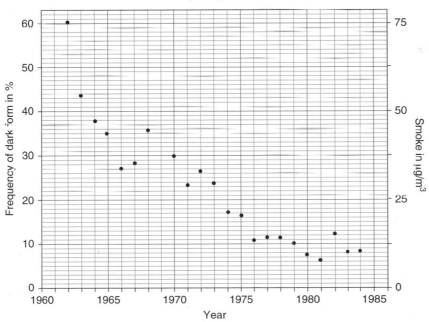

The readings for smoke concentration have already been plotted on the graph.

Plot the frequency of the dark form of the ladybird from 1960 to 1985 on the graph above.

Connect the points with a smooth curve.

4 Marks

b Suggest a reason for the change in frequency of the dark form of the ladybird. Predict what may have happened to the ladybird population after 1984.

2 Marks

More challenging

12 Describe how a human gene that codes for insulin production can be transferred to a bacterium.

2 Marks

13 Give one ethical objection to genetic engineering.

1 Mark

14 Some scientists believe we may be on the verge of entering a sixth mass extinction. Suggest a human action that could be a potential contributing factor.

1 Marks

15 A plant breeder is trying to produce a new variety of wheat that will withstand drought.

Describe how the plant breeder would do this.

6 Marks

Most demanding

16 Scientists have genetically engineered some crops to be resistant to herbicides.

Explain how herbicide resistance is beneficial to genetically modified (GM) crop production.

2 Marks

17 A scientist is investigating variation in bone mineral density measurements between human populations of different demographic groups over time.

The table below shows the data from a sample of people taken from a demographic.

Draw a histogram to show the data below.

Bone mineral density = BMC / W [g/cm^2]	Number of people
81–100	7
101–120	18
121–140	31
141–160	35
161–170	27
171–180	11

2 Marks

18 MRSA is a bacterial infection.

The graph shows the number of cases of hospital patients with MRSA infections from 1993 to 2005.

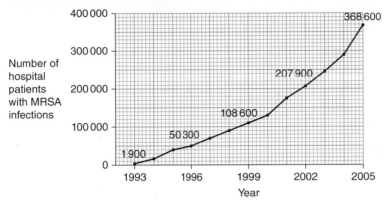

Explain the trend in the graph, even though the patients were treated with antibiotics.

6 Marks

Total: 40 Marks

ECOLOGY IN ACTION

ORGANISMS IN AN ECOSYSTEM DEPEND ON EACH OTHER FOR SURVIVAL.

- Food chains show how energy is transferred between living organisms.
- Food webs are a series of inter-connected food chains.
- A change in the population of one organism affects other organisms in the food chain.
- Insects pollinate crops to provide food for human populations.
- Some organisms survive by living in or on another species.

ORGANISMS AFFECT AND ARE AFFECTED BY THEIR ENVIRONMENT.

- Organisms can affect populations of other plants and animals in their habitat.
- Some animals feed on dead animal and plant matter.
- If one organism is removed from a food web, the whole food web can be affected.
- Adaptations allow organisms to survive in their habitat.

HUMAN ACTIVITIES PRODUCE CARBON DIOXIDE, WHICH IMPACTS ON THE CLIMATE.

- Increased carbon dioxide emissions have caused global temperatures to increase.
- Humans produce toxic substances that can accumulate in food chains.
- Humans frequently destroy ecosystems to use the land for other purposes.

ALL ORGANISMS HAVE TO UNDERTAKE CERTAIN LIFE PROCESSES.

- Plants use carbon dioxide from the atmosphere to photosynthesise and produce simple sugars, such as glucose.
- Plants and animals need to take in water from their habitat; water is needed for chemical reactions.
- Dead plant and animal material is broken down by microbes.
- Plants need mineral nutrients to grow and stay healthy.

IN THIS CHAPTER YOU WILL FIND OUT ABOUT:

WHAT FACTORS AFFECT LIVING ORGANISMS IN A HABITAT?

- Why there is a maximum size to food chains.
- How different groups of decomposers break down dead animal and plant matter.
- How distribution and numbers of species are sampled.

HOW DO PLANTS AND ANIMALS WITHIN A COMMUNITY INTERACT?

- How a change in an abiotic (non-living) factor affects a community.
- How changes in biotic (living) factors affect a community.
- How organisms are adapted to survive in extreme habitats.
- Why animals compete for resources in a habitat.

HOW DO HUMAN ACTIVITIES AFFECT BIODIVERSITY?

- What biodiversity is and why it is important to maintain a good level of biodiversity.
- How human population growth has impacted on the use of land and how this affects biodiversity.
- How waste from human activities has affected the atmosphere and biodiversity.
- How biodiversity can be maintained.

HOW ARE MATERIALS IN A COMMUNITY CYCLED?

- How carbon is cycled from organisms to the atmosphere.
- How water is cycled to provide a constant source of fresh water.

KEY CONCEPT

Learning about ecosystems

Learning objectives:

- describe what an ecosystem is
- explain the importance of high biodiversity
- explain what is meant by a self-supporting ecosystem.

Ecology looks at how organisms survive, how they relate to other organisms and their physical environment, and the features that make them successful in their habitat.

Ecosystems and biodiversity

Living organisms are affected by their environment. For example, if plants cannot absorb enough water for their needs, they wilt and may die. But plants also affect their environment. Plant roots hold soil particles together and stop the wind from blowing the soil away.

An **ecosystem** is defined as the interaction of a community (of living organisms) with the non-living parts of their environment. Ecosystems can be:

- natural, for example, oceans, lakes, puddles and rainforests
- artificial, for example, fish farms and planted forests.

In every ecosystem there are different living organisms. **Biodiversity** is the range of different plant and animal species living in an ecosystem. The living organisms in an ecosystem are described as producers, consumers and decomposers. Decomposers break down dead organisms.

Figure 8.1 A marine ecosystem

1 **What is an ecosystem?**

2 **Describe the biodiversity of the marine ecosystem in Figure 8.1.**

Exploring ecosystems

A **population** is the total number of one species in an ecosystem. A community is all the plants and animals living in an ecosystem. The place where a living organism lives in the ecosystem is its **habitat**.

REMEMBER!

A community is all the different plants and animals in an ecosystem and a population is the total number of one species.

High biodiversity is important in an ecosystem because:

- it allows a wide variation of food sources, reducing the dependence of a species on a particular food source
- it provides us with food, medicines, the atmosphere and water.

Taking more of a species than we need from the environment (for example, by overhunting, deforestation and overfishing), and not replacing them, means that populations are not sustainable. This puts species in danger of extinction.

3 Explain the difference between

   a an ecosystem and a habitat

   b a community and a population.

4 Describe the ecosystems shown in Figures 8.1 and 8.2.

Ecosystem interactions

Some natural ecosystems have high biodiversity, such as the rainforest or shallow tropical coral reefs. They provide a wide variety of food throughout the year and shelter, above and below the ground or water. Other natural ecosystems, such as the Arctic tundra or deep-sea thermal vents, have low diversity, with species adapted to survive those extreme environments.

Figure 8.2 How are these ecosystems similar and different?

Artificial ecosystems have low biodiversity: the variety and number of plants is limited, so only a small number of animal species can survive.

All ecosystems are **self supporting**: all the requirements for living organisms to grow and survive are present. They do need an external energy source, which is usually the Sun.

All animals depend on plants for oxygen and food. Plants depend on animals for carbon dioxide, pollination and seed dispersal. This is called **interdependence**.

5 How is an ecosystem self supporting?

6 Explain how living organisms are interdependent.

7 Construct an argument putting forward reasons for the claim that we should protect areas of high biodiversity such as rainforests.

DID YOU KNOW?

Deserts are advancing and taking over fertile land. In Mali (West Africa) the Sahara advanced about 350 km in approximately 20 years.

Changing abiotic factors

Learning objectives:

- identify factors that affect ecosystems
- explain changes in the distribution of species in an ecosystem
- describe stable and unstable populations.

KEY WORDS

abiotic factor
biotic factor
distribution
competition

Living organisms are affected by many different factors as they grow and try to survive.

What are abiotic factors?

Many factors affect where an organism lives. **Abiotic factors** are physical (that is, non-living) conditions that affect the **distribution** of an organism. These factors include:

- temperature
- light intensity
- oxygen levels for animals that live in water
- carbon dioxide levels for plants
- moisture levels
- soil pH and mineral content for plants
- wind intensity and direction.

Biotic factors are caused by living organisms affecting other populations in their ecosystem. Biotic factors include:

- food availability
- new pathogens
- new predators
- **competition** between species.

Abiotic and biotic factors change over time. For example, temperature varies daily, monthly, seasonally and over many years.

1. Choose one abiotic and one biotic factor. Explain how a lack of each factor would affect a plant and an animal.

2. Apart from blocking light, how else might trees affect the grass that grows beneath them?

Looking at changes

The numbers and types of organisms can gradually change across a habitat. These changes are easy to see on the sea shore, where there are distinct zones of organisms due to changing tides (see Figure 8.4).

Figure 8.3 What abiotic factors affect each of these organisms?

REMEMBER!

Abiotic factors are non-living. Biotic factors are living organisms. Changes in these factors cause changes in the distribution of organisms.

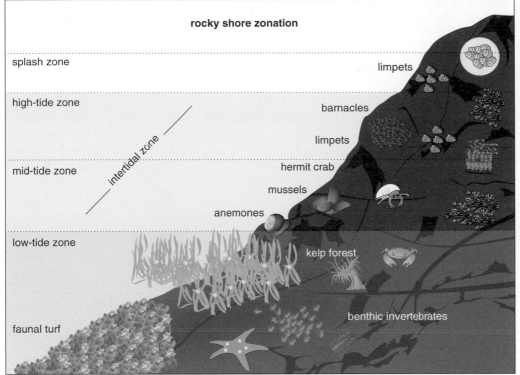

rocky shore zonation

splash zone — limpets — periwinkles

high-tide zone — barnacles — spiral wrack

intertidal zone — limpets

mid-tide zone — hermit crab — bladder wrack

mussels

anemones — saw wrack

low-tide zone — kelp forest

benthic invertebrates

faunal turf

Figure 8.4 Zones on the sea shore

3 Name the abiotic factors that change on the sea shore. How can these factors affect distribution of seaweeds?

4 Suggest why limpets are found higher up the shore than anemones.

Looking at how distribution of species can change

Factors that affect the distribution of organisms do not work alone. Two or more factors can interact to form very different environments within a habitat.

Animals such as rabbits and sheep graze on plants. The amount of grazing affects the numbers of plant species found.

Little grazing allows a few plants to out-compete others. As grazing increases, more plant species grow because dominant plants are controlled by the animals, allowing weaker species to grow. Only specially adapted plants can resist the effect of intensive grazing and survive.

A stable community is where the biotic and abiotic factors are in balance so that population sizes remain fairly constant.

5 What is a stable community?

6 Describe and explain the impact of grazing on plant species as shown in Figure 8.5.

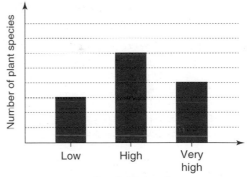

Figure 8.5 How does grazing affect plants?

DID YOU KNOW?

Plants are rare in deserts but after rain the distribution changes. Large numbers grow, flower and make seeds quickly while the water is available.

DID YOU KNOW?

Tropical rainforests and ancient oak woodlands are stable communities.

Investigating predator–prey relationships

Learning objectives:

- describe how changes in one population affect another
- explain interdependent relationships
- explain how predator–prey populations have cyclical changes.

All species in a community depend on each other. This is *interdependence*.

A change in population size

Primary consumers (or herbivores) eat producers (plants). Primary consumers are eaten by secondary consumers (carnivores). Some animals are primary and secondary consumers (they eat plants and animals). They are omnivores, for example, humans.

Consumers that hunt and eat other animals are predators. The animals that they eat are prey. If a predator kills all the prey it will die. In stable communities, the numbers of predators and prey stay in balance.

1 Explain why humans are primary and secondary consumers.

2 Describe what happens to the predator population when:

a prey numbers are high

b prey numbers are low.

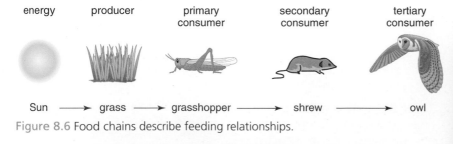

| energy | producer | primary consumer | secondary consumer | tertiary consumer |

Sun ⟶ grass ⟶ grasshopper ⟶ shrew ⟶ owl

Figure 8.6 Food chains describe feeding relationships.

Looking at more relationships

Examples of mutually beneficial relationships are:

- Cleaner fish eat dead skin and parasites off large fish. They get food and avoid being eaten by larger fish.
- Burdock fruits have hooks. They attach to the fur of passing animals for dispersal.

In **parasitism** one organism benefits but the other is harmed by the relationship. If parasites kill their host, they die too.

Figure 8.7 Zooxanthellae live in the golden jellyfish tissues. They have a safe place to live and give the jellyfish some of the energy they need from photosynthesis.

Examples of parasitism are:

- Tapeworms attach themselves to the intestinal wall of their human host and absorb nutrients. The person suffers from malnutrition.
- Head lice live on human scalps. They suck blood for food and make the scalp itch.

3 Explain the relationship between tapeworms and humans.

4 Explain what parasitism is.

Explaining population cycles

In predator–prey relationships the size of each population is dependent on the other. The Canadian lynx was the main predator of snowshoe hares in Canada. Snowshoe hares make up most of its diet. Data from a study between 1845 and 1937 were used to produce the graph showing their relationship (Figure 8.8). The snowshoe hare population rises and falls in a 10-year **cycle**. Because the lynx population is dependent on the snowshoe hare it also rises and falls, but it is **out of phase** (or lags behind) that of the hare population cycle by about 2 years. There is a clear pattern between the populations of the two animals, as shown in the graph.

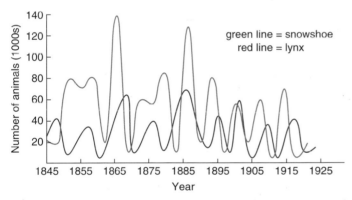

green line = snowshoe
red line = lynx

Figure 8.8 The size of the predator population follows the size of the prey population.

5 Explain how a large and a small predator population will each affect the number of prey.

6 Explain why the predator and prey cycles are out of phase with each other.

REMEMBER!

The population cycle of the predator is out of phase with the cycle of the prey.

DID YOU KNOW?

Scientists study predator–prey cycles to decide if controlling predator populations can help to protect endangered species.

Competing for resources

KEY WORDS

interspecific competition
intraspecific competition

Learning objectives:

- describe how competition impacts on populations
- explain why animals in the same habitat are in competition
- explain interspecific and intraspecific competition.

If plants and animals are to survive, they need certain resources from their habitat. How do living things get what they need?

Why do organisms compete?

Organisms only survive if they have sufficient resources for their needs. They compete for the available resources in their habitat. Plants in a community may compete for:

- light
- space
- water
- mineral ions.

Animals often compete for:

- food and water
- mates
- territory.

Figure 8.9 What are these organisms competing for?

Animals and plants that get more of the resources are more successful than those that get less. Successful organisms are more likely to survive and reproduce so the size of their population is more likely to increase. For example, dolphins feed on several foods and are more likely to survive than dugongs (Figure 8.10) that feed on just seagrass. Animals will travel to where food is available.

1. How does competition affect the distribution and number of organisms?

2. Describe how organisms are competing in Figure 8.9.

Figure 8.10 Dugongs are sometimes called 'sea cows' because they graze on seagrass.

Competition

When species compete, if they are not perfectly matched one will eventually become more successful than the other. A less successful species may:

- do nothing and become extinct
- stay in its habitat but adopt new survival strategies
- move to another area looking for resources.

Humans are very successful organisms. We compete with animals and plants all over the world.

3 **What happens when two organisms compete?**

4 **Explain why organisms in the same habitat are in competition.**

Types of competition

There are two types of competition:

- **Interspecific competition** is competition between different species.
- **Intraspecific competition** is competition within one species. This may result in territorial behaviour.

Intraspecific competition is often more significant than interspecific competition. For example, competition between grey squirrels is likely to affect the population of grey squirrels more than competition with red squirrels. Animals try to avoid competition with other species if they can.

When different species compete with one another for the same resources, it will affect the size and distribution of their populations.

Figure 8.11 How does a farmer compete with other organisms on their farmland?

COMMON MISCONCEPTION

Learn the difference between interspecific and intraspecific competition.

Figure 8.12 What types of competition are these?

5 **Describe examples of interspecific and intraspecific competition.**

6 **Why is intraspecific competition often greater than interspecific competition?**

DID YOU KNOW?

Competition for mates is intense, with many males putting a lot of effort into attracting females, by fighting or by having 'displays' such as the male peacock displaying its feathers.

REQUIRED PRACTICAL

Measure the population size of a common species in a habitat

Learning objectives:

- use scientific ideas to develop a hypothesis
- plan experiments to test a hypothesis
- explain the apparatus and techniques used to sample a population
- explain how a representative sample was taken
- develop a reasoned explanation for some data.

KEY WORDS

hypothesis
meristem
quadrat

It is impossible to count every plant or animal in a habitat, but it can be estimated by taking samples of the organisms from the habitat. The larger the sample, the more accurate your estimate of the population size is likely to be This allows population sizes to be compared between different areas.

Plants can be sampled more easily than animals because they cannot move around.

These pages are designed to help you think about aspects of the investigation rather than to guide you through it step by step.

Developing a hypothesis

It is summer time. Asha and Jalan are going to investigate the population size of daisies in trampled and un-trampled areas of the school field. The centre of the school field is used to play cricket, tennis and train for athletic events. The students run, jump and lie on the grass. Not many students go on the parts of the field away from these areas.

Asha and Jalan need to make a **hypothesis** before they do the investigation. They have made some observations on the field and now know that:

- trampling on soil compacts it
- trampling on plants can destroy the **meristems** as well as crushing delicate leaves and flowers
- daisy leaves are very delicate
- in well-trampled nearly bare ground, plants will have to tolerate large variations in temperature where there is no grass to protect them
- daisy plants have very long fibrous roots and thick leaf cuticles
- plants compete with each other for limited resources.

1. **How do you think compaction may affect**

    a   the soil?

    b   the daisies growing in the soil?

Figure 8.13 A daisy population

Figure 8.14 Leaf, root and flower of a daisy

② If meristems, leaves and flowers can be crushed by trampling, how may this affect the daisies?

③ How can periods of very high temperatures affect the daisies?

④ Suggest a hypothesis for the fieldwork investigation that Asha and Jalan are going to do.

Planning an investigation

The teacher has given Asha and Jalan this equipment. They know that it is important to take random samples, make repeat observations and count whole daisy plants.

transparent plastic

10 cm

100 cm

1 m² quadrat   tape

Figure 8.15 Quadrat and tape

⑤ Suggest how Asha and Jalan can use this equipment to collect representative data to test the hypothesis from question 4.

⑥ Why is it important to count whole daisy plants and not just daisy flowers? How many daisies are in the **quadrat**?

⑦ How can Asha and Jalan calculate the mean number of daisy plants in each area?

⑧ Another student has asked Asha and Jalan for a copy of their results. Suggest why they asked for it.

Developing explanations

Asha and Jalan did their investigation. Look at their data.

Quadrat position on tape (m)	Un-trampled area	Trampled area
0	3	6
5	4	6
10	3	7
15	2	6
20	2	4
25	4	7
30	3	6

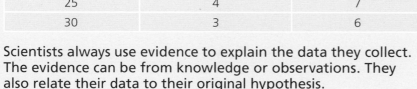

Figure 8.16 Quadrat placed over daisies

> **ADVICE**
>
> Sampling many small sections of an area gives a representative sample of the whole area.

Scientists always use evidence to explain the data they collect. The evidence can be from knowledge or observations. They also relate their data to their original hypothesis.

⑨ Suggest what Asha and Jalan can conclude from their data.

⑩ Explain the data using the information that Asha and Jalan knew before they started the investigation.

⑪ Was the hypothesis in question 4 proved or disproved?

Adapting for survival in animals

Learning objectives:

- recall why animals have adaptations
- explain some adaptations
- use surface area to volume ratio to explain some adaptations.

KEY WORDS

behaviour
camouflage
functional
structural

Abiotic factors vary depending upon where an ecosystem is located. But every ecosystem has living organisms.

Why are adaptations important?

Animals have special features called adaptations that allow them to survive and be successful in their habitat. Animals with more successful adaptations are better able to compete for food, mates and other limited resources.

Figure 8.17 What adaptations do these animals have?

Camouflage is used by predators (so the prey cannot see them) and prey (so they cannot be seen by predators). Many arctic animals have white coats in winter (to blend in against snow) and grey-brown coats in summer (to blend in against plants). Polar bears always have white coats because they have no predators on land.

1 Why are adaptations important?

2 Describe three different adaptations.

Behavioural adaptations

Some ecosystems have extreme conditions. They may have little available water. Animals have to stop body temperatures getting too high or too low. They can do this by changing their **behaviour**.

In hot temperatures many animals:

- are most active during the cooler mornings, and they move to shady areas to keep cool
- remain in burrows during hot days and cold nights, where temperatures are more stable.

In cold temperatures some animals:

- hibernate over winter when food is scarce; their metabolic rate lowers to reduce the need for food
- migrate to warmer countries where there is more food.

Most reptiles struggle to survive in very cold or hot temperatures, because they do not have internal mechanisms to control their body temperature. They need to bask in the sun to increase body temperature or stay in the shade to keep cooler.

3 **Explain how reptiles in the desert control their body temperature.**

4 **Suggest some behavioural adaptations of meerkats.**

Figure 8.18 Meerkats live in the Kalahari desert.

More adaptations

Some adaptations are **structural** (part of the body) and others are **functional** (how the body operates).

In hot temperatures, many animals:

- keep insulating fat and body hair to a minimum to prevent overheating; camels only have fat in their humps
- do not sweat (e.g. camels) to prevent water loss, and need little to drink to cope with water scarcity
- have a large surface area to volume ratio (sometimes called SA:V) to maximise heat loss through the skin
- have special adaptations to increase their SA:V, for example, elephants have large ears to increase their surface area.

> **REMEMBER!**
>
> Animals in cold climates often have smaller surface area to volume ratio, and those in hot climates have large surface area to volume ratio.

Figure 8.19 What adaptations do camels have?

In cold temperatures, many animals have:

- thick fur and blubber for insulation
- a small surface area to volume ratio to reduce heat loss
- small ears to reduce SA:V ratio, to reduce heat loss.

5 **Explain how surface area to volume ratio can be an adaptation to temperature.**

6 **Explain the difference between structural and functional adaptations, using your own example to illustrate your answer.**

> **DID YOU KNOW?**
>
> Predators have adaptations for hunting and prey have adaptations for escaping.

Adapting for survival in plants

KEY WORDS

epiphyte
extremophile

Learning objectives:

- identify adaptations of plants and bacteria
- explain the importance of adaptations
- explain a range of plant adaptations.

Like animals, plants also have many different adaptations that allow them to colonise ecosystems all over the world.

Looking at more adaptations

Plants are adapted in many ways; for example, deciduous trees lose leaves in winter (to protect plants from frost) and flowers die (due to there being fewer pollinators).

Plants in hot climates are adapted by:

- having a reduced surface area (reduces water loss)
- storing water in their tissues (conserves water).

Plants in cold climates are adapted by:

- growing close to the ground (avoids damage by wind)
- having small leaves (conserves water).

Figure 8.20 Suggest the climates where these plants live.

Extremophiles are organisms that can survive in very extreme environments, including:

- very high or low temperatures
- high salt concentrations in water
- high pressures.

Extremophiles survive conditions that would kill most species. Some bacteria live in hot springs or around deep-sea vents. Others live in extreme cold.

1 **Explain adaptations shown by arctic plants.**

2 **What are extremophiles?**

Explaining some adaptations

Organisms with a larger surface area to volume ratio lose more energy and water. Plants are adapted to drier environments by:

- having a reduced surface area
- storing water
- having extensive root systems that are wide (to absorb water quickly when it becomes available) or deep (to find underground water stores).

Cactus plants live in deserts that have:

- hot and dry days
- cold nights
- little rainfall.

Adaptations of cacti include:

- spine-like leaves to reduce surface area, transpiration and damage by primary consumers
- a fleshy stem
- extensive shallow roots
- thick waterproof cuticle
- round shape (reduces surface area to volume ratio).

Bacteria living in deep-sea vents are extremophiles. They are able to survive in temperatures between 40°C and 80°C because their enzymes do not denature.

3 Explain how extremophiles are adapted for survival.

4 Use ideas about surface area to volume ratio to explain why pine trees have needle leaves.

More adaptations

Epiphytes grow in rainforests. They are adapted to live above ground level by:

- growing on other plants, allowing leaves to absorb sunlight through the trees
- having roots that absorb rain and moisture from humidity and minerals from leaf litter
- having upturned leaves to store water.

5 Explain adaptations to temperature using surface area to volume ratio.

6 Explain why there are lots of cacti in the desert but no roses.

7 Studies have shown that tropical and desert plants have different densities of stomata. Suggest and explain why this might be.

> **ADVICE**
>
> Remember that plants open their stomata for photosynthesis and so lose water by evaporation.

Figure 8.21 Marram grass, which lives on sand dunes, has tightly curled leaves to reduce the surface area that is exposed to sunlight and wind. How does this give marram grass an advantage?

Figure 8.22 How are epiphytes adapted?

> **DID YOU KNOW?**
>
> Some plant roots are adapted to grow in sea water.

Cycling materials

KEY WORD

decomposers

Learning objectives:

- recall that many materials are recycled in nature
- explain the stages in the water and carbon cycles
- explain the importance of recycling materials.

All materials in the living world are recycled to provide the building blocks for future organisms.

Natural recycling

Water, carbon, oxygen and nitrogen are some of the materials that are recycled.

The water cycle provides fresh water for plants and animals on land. It describes how water moves on, above or just below the ground. Water molecules move between rivers, oceans and the atmosphere by precipitation, evaporation, transpiration and condensation.

Carbon is found in compounds that make up living organisms. Plants get carbon from air during photosynthesis. Animals get carbon from plants. The carbon in dead plants and animals is released by **decomposers** during the decay process.

1. Give an example of a decomposer that breaks down carbon in dead animals and plants.

2. What is the role of decomposers?

Figure 8.23 Decomposers, such as the fungi shown here, clean up the environment.

Explaining the water cycle

Water is continuously recycled by:

- Precipitation – water droplets in clouds get bigger and heavier; they fall as rain, snow or sleet.
- Evaporation – water evaporates as it is heated by the Sun's energy; water vapour is carried upwards in convection currents.
- Transpiration – water vapour is released into the air through stomata in leaves.
- Condensation – water vapour rises, cools and condenses back into water droplets that form clouds.

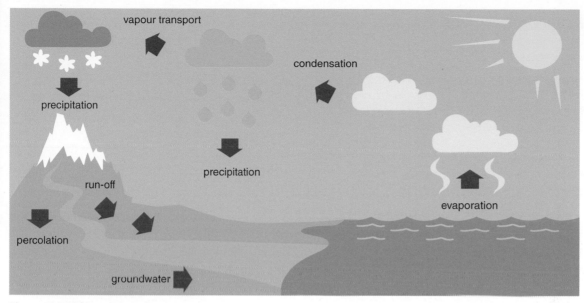

Figure 8.24 The water cycle

The water cycle is important because it circulates water that:

- maintains habitats
- maintains internal fluids and transport systems
- is needed for chemical reactions
- is a reactant in photosynthesis.

3 Explain the stages in the water cycle.

4 In what stage of the water cycle can water be:

a a gas?

b a solid?

Explaining decay

Worms, woodlice and maggots break down waste and dead material into smaller pieces for decomposers to digest.

Decomposers are microorganisms (bacteria and fungi). They break down the smaller pieces of dead material. Decomposers release waste carbon dioxide, water, thermal energy and nutrients (that plants use).

Decomposers decay waste in compost heaps and sewage works.

5 Explain the role of bacteria in decay.

6 Why is the water cycle important?

7 Why are decomposers essential for life? What would happen if they did not exist?'

Figure 8.25 Woodlice live on rotting wood and help to break it down for decomposers.

DID YOU KNOW?

The Body Farm is a research site in the USA where scientists study human decay to support forensic analysis.

ADVICE

Learn the stages of the water cycle and the decay process.

Cycling carbon

KEY WORD

carbon sink

Learning objectives:

- recall that plants take in carbon as carbon dioxide
- explain how carbon is recycled
- interpret a diagram of the carbon cycle.

Materials are recycled through ecosystems continually. As one process removes them, another releases them into the ecosystem again.

Looking at carbon

The amount of carbon on Earth is fixed. Most carbon is found combined with other elements, for example, in fossil fuels and carbonate rocks. Carbon is also found dissolved in water in rivers, lakes and oceans. A small amount is in the air in carbon dioxide.

Producers use carbon dioxide to photosynthesise. The carbon is used to make carbohydrates, proteins, fats and DNA that form new biomass, which is eaten by consumers.

All organisms respire to release energy for cellular processes. They release waste carbon dioxide back into the environment, which is then used by plants.

1. How do organisms cycle carbon dioxide?

2. Why is most carbon dioxide on Earth not available for photosynthesis?

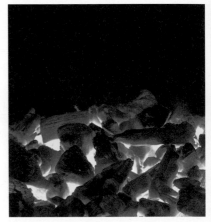

Figure 8.26 Burning fossil fuels releases carbon, as carbon dioxide, into the air.

Explaining the carbon cycle

The atmosphere contains about 0.04% carbon dioxide, which is enough for every plant to produce biomass (food), by photosynthesis. This process transfers energy from the Sun into chemical energy.

When animals eat plants, they absorb carbon from them. Carbon passes along food chains, even when organisms die and decay. Energy is transferred along the food chain and to the environment at each trophic level.

Carbon dioxide is returned to the atmosphere by:

- plants, animals and decomposers respiring:
    glucose + oxygen → carbon dioxide + water
- burning (combustion) of fossil fuels and wood:
    fossil fuel/wood + oxygen → carbon dioxide + water

The continual cycling of carbon is shown in Figure 8.27.

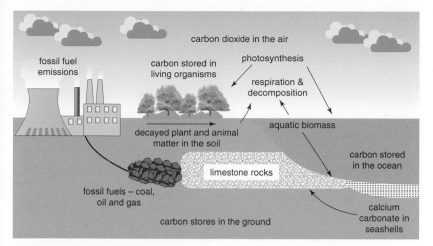

Figure 8.27 The carbon cycle

Burning fossil fuels and wood releases more carbon into the atmosphere. Scientists agree that levels of carbon dioxide in the atmosphere will continue to rise if current rates of fossil fuel burning continue. Increased levels of carbon dioxide in the atmosphere cause global warming.

3 **Name two processes that release carbon dioxide.**

4 **Use Figure 8.27 to describe the carbon cycle.**

Carbon stores

Shells of marine organisms contain carbonates. Corals and microscopic algae cover themselves with calcium carbonate. Shells of dead organisms fall to the sea floor. Over millions of years they are compressed to form limestone. Carbon dioxide reacts with rain to form carbonic acid. This acid rain weathers limestone and releases carbon dioxide.

Figure 8.28 What causes weathering of limestone statues?

Carbon dioxide can be absorbed by oceans and held in a **carbon sink**. During volcanic eruptions and forest fires, massive amounts of carbon dioxide are released into the atmosphere.

5 **Why is the carbon cycle important to all living organisms?**

6 **Explain the processes involved in the carbon cycle.**

> **REMEMBER!**
>
> The carbon cycle returns carbon from organisms to the air for plants to use in photosynthesis.

> **DID YOU KNOW?**
>
> Between 1000 and 100 000 million metric tonnes of carbon pass through the carbon cycle every year.

Learning about land use

Learning objectives:

- identify why land use has changed
- describe the effects of changing land use
- evaluate a change in land use.

KEY WORD

run-off

Scientists agree that human activity has changed environments and that we need to protect the Earth's biodiversity.

Human population growth

The world's population has increased rapidly, from 1 billion (1000 million) in 1880 to about 7 billion in 2012. People use increasing amounts of the Earth's resources, resulting in a decrease in the land available for other organisms.

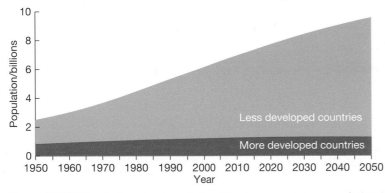

Figure 8.29 Why do less developed countries have a greater population increase?

Humans are using more land for:

- farming
- building
- quarrying
- dumping waste.

Sudden increases in the populations of animals and plants are usually controlled by predators, food availability, disease or toxic waste products. Humans have no predators, grow large amounts of food and have the ability to cure or prevent disease.

Figure 8.30 Intensive farming using fertilisers produces large crops.

1 How do humans change the use of land?

2 Why do farmers use fertilisers?

Using the land

As our population increases, biodiversity decreases:

- More land is needed for homes, shops, factories and roads. Building sites destroy habitats. Roads divide habitats, making it harder for organisms to find food and mates.
- New quarries are mined to provide stone, slate and metal ores for building materials. Habitats are destroyed.
- More farmland is needed and fertilisers are used. Many farms grow one crop over huge areas. This affects food availability for insect pollinators. There are fewer available nesting sites for birds.
- More waste is sent to landfill, and more sewage and industrial waste are produced. This can pollute the land.

Figure 8.31 An abandoned quarry

Human population is growing exponentially. This means that the increase in any year is greater than in the previous year because the birth rate is greater than the death rate.

3 Suggest the impact if human populations keep rising.

4 Describe the impact of two land-use changes.

Polluting water

Figure 8.32 Why are there no fish in this water?

If water contains a lot of fertilisers (caused by **run-off** from farmers' fields) or sewage, the nitrates and phosphates in the water increase and algal growth increases as a result. Algae cover the water surface and prevent light from reaching water plants. The plants and algae die. Bacteria respire as they break down dead plants and use up oxygen in the water. The other living organisms in the water die.

5 Explain the impact of fertiliser run-off.

6 Evaluate a change in land use.

7 Why do we need to maintain local and global biodiversity?

REMEMBER!

Humans reduce land availability for other organisms by building, farming, quarrying and dumping waste.

DID YOU KNOW?

When landfill sites are closed, the waste is left to degrade and stabilise. The land is re-used for parks, golf courses and even airports.

Changing the landscape

KEY WORDS

deforestation
peatlands

Learning objectives:

- identify the reasons for deforestation
- describe the impact of peat bog destruction and deforestation
- evaluate the destruction of peat bogs and forests.

Many species in tropical forests and _peatlands_ are struggling to survive as their habitat is destroyed.

Why are landscapes changing?

Huge areas of tropical forest are being destroyed. This **deforestation** is happening to:

- provide land for cattle and rice fields
- grow crops, for example, oil palm and sugar cane to make biofuels. Biofuel crops are sometimes grown at the expense of food crops.

Cleared forests are often used to grow a monoculture (one crop) over huge areas.

Figure 8.33 Peat cut to be used for fuel

Peat bogs form over thousands of years in marshy areas. Decomposers cannot completely break down plant material in acidic conditions with little oxygen, so peat forms. Peat stores carbon.

Peat is used as a fuel and as cheap compost by gardeners. Compost improves soil quality to increase food production.

1. Why are forests cut down?
2. What is peat and how is it used?

The impact of changing landscapes

Forests are often destroyed by burning. Mass destruction of trees has:

- increased the release of carbon dioxide into the atmosphere (due to burning and the respiration of microorganisms that are decaying the remaining plant material)
- reduced the rate that carbon dioxide is removed from the atmosphere (by photosynthesis)
- reduced biodiversity; some of the lost plants and animals may have been useful in the future
- increased methane in the atmosphere because cleared land is used to grow rice in swamp-like fields.

Figure 8.34 How will forest fires affect the atmosphere?

Insufficient trees are being replaced. Peat is being destroyed faster than it is being made. Peat and trees are both important carbon 'stores' that are being lost. The loss of peat bogs reduces the variety of different plants, animals and microorganisms that live there. Monocultures also reduce biodiversity.

3 **Describe and explain the impacts of deforestation.**

4 **How can woodland habitats be preserved?**

Balancing act

There is a massive conflict between:

- the need for deforestation to increase land available for food production
- the use of peat as cheap compost to increase food production
- the need to conserve forests and peatlands as habitats for biodiversity
- the need to reduce carbon dioxide emissions from using peat as a fuel and from burning forests.

5 **Evaluate the destruction of peatlands.**

> **REMEMBER!**
>
> Trees and plants in peatlands all use carbon dioxide to photosynthesise. Carbon is then stored in these plants.

Figure 8.35 Orangutans are losing their food sources.

> **DID YOU KNOW?**
>
> About 13 million hectares of forest have been cleared or lost through natural disasters. By 2030, there may only be 10% of our forests left.

Thinking about global warming

Learning objectives:

- recall what global warming is
- describe the causes of global warming
- explain how global warming impacts on biodiversity.

The future of the human species on Earth relies on us maintaining a good level of biodiversity, yet we are threatening it by our actions.

What is global warming?

The average global temperature of the Earth and its atmosphere is increasing. This is **global warming**. It is caused by increasing atmospheric levels of:

- carbon dioxide
- methane.

(a)

(b)

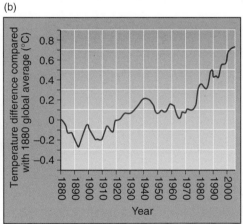

Figure 8.36 (a) CO_2 in the atmosphere 1000–2012; (b) temperature difference from 1880 global average temperature, 1880–2012. What do these graphs tell you?

These gases occur naturally in the atmosphere, but levels have increased over the last 150 years because:

- power plants burn fossil fuels
- petrol is used as fuel in vehicles
- rice crops and cattle farming are increasing
- deforestation and destruction of peatlands are increasing.

As the human population increases more pollution is produced from fossil fuels, particularly by relatively small populations in developed countries.

1 What is global warming?

2 What causes global warming?

Impact on ecosystems

Scientists think that global warming is changing the climate. The average world temperature rise is small (about 0.8°C since 1880), but some species such as coral reefs are sensitive to this.

3 **How do human actions affect global warming?**

4 **Explain how global warming might affect biodiversity.**

Case studies

The white lemuroid possum is the first mammal in Australia to have become almost extinct due to global warming. There are just four known adults left. The white possum's habitat spans cooler areas of high-altitude rainforest. Possums are vulnerable to increases in environmental temperature because they cannot maintain their body temperature.

Little terns are vulnerable to high tides and storms. These are happening more often because of global warming. Little terns migrate to the UK each spring and make their colonies just above the high tide line. Their nests are vulnerable to flooding by stormy seas.

Coastal mangrove forests grow in equatorial regions. Increasing numbers of storms and typhoons are undermining the fine sediment that the mangroves grow in. Seedlings cannot root and essential nutrients for the mangrove ecosystems are washed away.

Figure 8.37 Penguins are losing their habitats. Where else can they survive?

> **REMEMBER!**
>
> Learn three ways that global warming affects biodiversity.

> **DID YOU KNOW?**
>
> If sea levels rose by 1 m, half of the world's important coastal wetlands would be threatened.

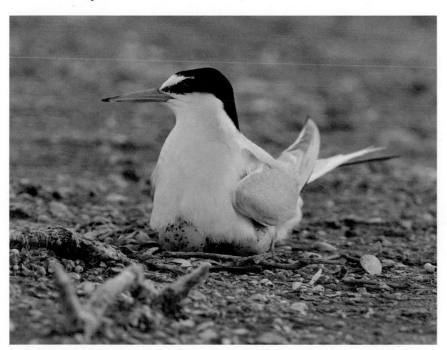

Figure 8.38 How does global warming affect little terns?

5 **Explain how global warming affects biodiversity.**

Looking at waste management

KEY WORD
....
sewage

Learning objectives:

- describe how waste production is linked to human population growth
- describe the impact of waste on ecosystems
- explain how waste impacts on biodiversity.

As our population keeps increasing, so our impact on the environment and biodiversity is also increasing.

Pollution

Human population growth and living standards are increasing, particularly in developed countries. We use more resources. As living standards increase, the demand for agriculture, manufacturing and industry increase, producing more waste.

Domestic and industrial waste must be handled correctly to avoid causing more pollution.

Waste substances include:

- **sewage**
- smoke and toxic gases
- herbicides, pesticides and fertilisers
- lead
- paper and cardboard
- plastic products.

Waste can kill plants and animals and reduce biodiversity.

Figure 8.39 Waste tips reduce biodiversity. They are home to decomposers and some birds.

1. Why is the amount of waste we produce increasing?

2. Name three types of waste produced by people.

Waste and ecosystems

Causes of pollution include:

- Fertilisers. These can enter waterways, causing rapid growth of algae, which blocks sunlight, so water plants die. Bacteria populations grow rapidly as they break down the dead material and use the oxygen in the water.
- Toxic chemicals from household and industrial waste. If taken to landfill sites, they can spread into soil and enter waterways. Pesticides and herbicides are also washed into waterways. Toxins build up in food chains, kill organisms and affect feeding relationships.
- Sewage. If untreated, chemicals and parasites can enter waterways. Microorganisms that decompose sewage use dissolved oxygen, causing aquatic organisms to die.
- Smoke and gases. Soot in smoke covers and damages trees; organisms may find breathing difficult.

3 **How do human actions affect water quality?**

4 **Suggest how soot damages trees.**

Acid rain

Acidic gases are produced when fossil fuels burn. They dissolve in water vapour to make acid (about pH 4). Acid rain:

- damages leaves and roots of plants
- washes mineral ions out of soil, causing mineral deficiencies in plants
- washes aluminium ions from soil into lakes, which affects gills in fish and they cannot survive
- acidifies waterways, so aquatic organisms cannot survive
- can travel in air; acid rain produced in the UK has affected trees and fjords in Norway.

Pollution reduces the available space for other organisms; some species cannot survive. We need to balance our development while sustaining the environment for future generations. Many countries (including the UK) have legislation that controls the use of toxic chemicals, use of landfill sites and treatment of sewage.

5 **Explain how dangerous levels of toxic chemicals can build up through trophic levels.**

REMEMBER!

Pollution reduces biodiversity. Learn how and where pollution is produced.

Figure 8.40 How does acid rain affect trees?

DID YOU KNOW?

The Mbeubeuss waste tip in Senegal is one of the world's largest waste tips, receiving 475 000 tonnes of rubbish a year. It covers about 175 hectares (around 266 football pitches).

Investigating pollution

KEY WORD

indicator species

Learning objectives:

- identify pollution levels using indicator species
- explain how indicator species measure pollution
- compare different methods of measuring pollution.

Scientists monitor environmental change to understand how it affects living organisms.

What is an indicator species?

Living organisms are sensitive to different abiotic conditions. If conditions change – for example, through pollution – the distribution of organisms can also change. Some organisms are used to measure environmental change. They are called **indicator species**.

Lichens grow on trees, roofs and rocks. They are rarely found growing in cities because they cannot survive in polluted air. The sampling of numbers and types of lichens informs scientists about pollution levels.

Lichens are sensitive to sulfur dioxide concentrations in the air.

Very few types and numbers of lichens grow near power stations. The further away they are, the greater the number and different species that are found.

Figure 8.41 The cleaner the air, the leafier the lichens that grow. (a) Leafy lichen; (b) crusty lichen.

1. How does pollution affect living organisms?
2. What is an indicator species?

More indicators

Pollution also affects the distribution and numbers of animals. Aquatic invertebrates are used as indicators of pollution and dissolved oxygen in water, as shown in the table.

- Sludgeworms can live in polluted water. This is because they are adapted to cope with the low oxygen levels in polluted water.
- Mayfly larvae can live in slightly polluted water. There is sufficient oxygen for their needs.
- Alderfly larvae cannot live in polluted water. They cannot survive when oxygen levels are low.

Figure 8.42 Power stations produce sulfur dioxide.

Animal	Sensitivity to pollution
stonefly larva	sensitive
water snipe fly larva	sensitive
alderfly larva	sensitive
mayfly larva	semi-sensitive
freshwater mussel	semi-sensitive
damselfly larva	semi-sensitive
bloodworm	tolerates pollution
rat-tailed maggot	tolerates pollution
sludgeworm	tolerates pollution

Pollution affects the distribution of aquatic invertebrates.

Water containing lots of different species is a healthy environment.

Pollution levels are also measured directly using:

- probes attached to computers to measure precise conditions, for example, pH, temperature, oxygen and carbon dioxide
- special tests to indicate levels of different chemicals, for example, nitrates.

3 **A water sample from a river contained sludgeworms but no stonefly larvae. Is the water polluted? Explain your answer.**

4 **Suggest two methods to measure the pH of a stream.**

Using indicator species

The animals in three different aquatic habitats near a town were sampled and identified. Unfortunately, the names of the habitats came off the sample jars. The samples were taken from a polluted pond, a stagnant pool near a water outlet and a fast-running stream.

Sample	Animals found
A	stonefly larva, mayfly larva, damselfly larva, alderfly larva, water snipe fly larva
B	rat-tailed maggot, sludgeworm, bloodworm
C	sludgeworm, damselfly larva, freshwater mussel

5 **Which sample came from which habitat?**

6 **Which sample contained the least dissolved oxygen? Explain your answer.**

7 **Suggest one advantage and one disadvantage of using chemical tests instead of indicator species to test for pollution.**

DID YOU KNOW?

Coral reefs are water quality indicators because they only tolerate narrow ranges of temperature, salinity and water clarity.

REMEMBER!

Pollution alters the numbers and distribution of plant and animal species.

Maintaining biodiversity

Learning objectives:

- describe some conservation measures
- describe the impact of breeding programmes
- explain how habitats are regenerated.

KEY WORDS

conservation
monocultures
regeneration
sustainable

Every species depends on others for food, shelter and pollination. Because of interdependence, if one species is removed the whole community is affected.

Protecting ecosystems

Programmes have been developed to reduce negative effects on ecosystems and biodiversity, which are caused by our actions. These measures include:

- Introducing breeding programmes for endangered species.
- The protection and **regeneration** (restoring) of rare habitats.
- Re-introducing field margins and hedgerows on farmland where **monocultures** are grown. Hedgerows are a habitat for many wild species.

Figure 8.43 Why are hedgerows being replanted?

- Reducing deforestation and carbon dioxide emissions. **Sustainable** strategies include replanting trees.
- Recycling resources instead of dumping waste in landfill. Many materials are recycled in the UK.
- Cloning plant species. Cloning can be done quickly and economically using stem cells found in the meristems. This protects plant species from extinction.

Figure 8.44 Why must we recycle waste?

1 **How are ecosystems and biodiversity protected?**

2 **How do hedgerows increase biodiversity?**

Conservation

Conservation programmes are introduced:

- because we have a moral responsibility to protect endangered species
- so more plant species may be identified for medicines
- to minimise damage to food chains and webs
- to protect future food supplies.

Captive breeding programmes are planned to ensure genetic diversity is maintained, such as for the Arabian oryx and for giant pandas. Successful programmes allow species to be reintroduced to the wild. The wild Arabian oryx became extinct in the wild in the 1970s, but a successful breeding programme means the animal has now been reclassified as 'vulnerable'.

Many endangered species, for example rhinos and tigers, are hunted and poached, despite legal protection. Seed banks store seeds carefully to protect plant species for the future.

Figure 8.45 Arabian oryx populations are growing.

3 Why are conservation programmes introduced?

4 How do breeding programmes help endangered species?

> **REMEMBER!**
>
> Learn the different programmes for protecting ecosystems and biodiversity.

Protecting rare habitats

There are many difficulties and issues associated with organising conservation programmes. Some of these include:

- ensuring long-term funding
- having qualified scientists who understand the issues
- animals and plants do not recognise boundaries
- many organisations and governments may be involved, working locally, nationally and internationally
- lack of 'policing' of protected areas.

Mangrove forests are rich ecosystems that prevent coastal erosion and reduce carbon emissions. They are declining rapidly due to land development, and their use as a fuel and building material. In Abu Dhabi, however, mangroves are increasing due to massive planting programmes over the last two decades. The local environment agency works with land developers and the public to maintain healthy, litter-free sustainable forests. The forests protect seagrass beds, which are the sole food of the endangered manatee.

Figure 8.46 Many species depend on sustainable mangrove forests.

5 What difficulties are involved in managing conservation programmes?

6 Explain how mangrove forests are protected and regenerated.

7 Explain why it is important to protect biodiversity.

> **DID YOU KNOW?**
>
> Siberian tigers are endangered because of deforestation, hunting and poaching.

MATHS SKILLS

Using graphs to show relationships

Learning objectives:

- to recognise direct proportionality in a graph
- to calculate reaction rates from linear graphs
- to use the gradient of a graph to calculate the rate.

It is sometimes useful to see how one variable relates to another, such as how much we exercise affects how fit we are. A graph is a good way of displaying the relationship.

Types of graphs

When we plot the results from investigations we sometimes get graphs in which the points are approximately in a straight line, so we can draw a straight line of best fit. Even if the line does not go through the origin (0,0), it has a strong correlation that approximates a **linear** relationship.

If this straight line passes through the origin (0,0), the relationship is **directly proportional**. This means that when one variable doubles in size, the other variable does too. The point where the line crosses the y-axis is called the **intercept**.

1. Where does the line intercept the y-axis in the top graph in Figure 8.47?

2. Where is the y-intercept for any line showing direct proportionality?

Using a graph to work out the rate at which something is happening

Sometimes when we use data to plot a graph, one variable is a measurement of time. This is common in biology as we are often interested in the **rate** at which something is happening.

Look at Figure 8.48, showing how puppies gain weight over the first couple of years. They all gain weight more quickly when they are young and the weight gain levels off when they become adults. The rate is shown by the **gradient**. The gradient is the steepness of the line. In this case, the steeper the gradient, the more weight the dogs are gaining each month. The graph also shows that the rate is greater for larger breeds. Knowing the gradient is useful.

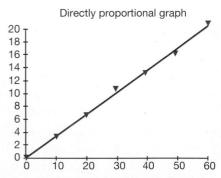

Figure 8.47 What is the difference between these two graphs?

Figure 8.48 Rate of growth of different dog breeds.

3 **a** How much weight will a German Shepherd puppy put on in the first 4 months?

    b On average, what would this be every month? (Your answer will be in kg/month – this is the rate.)

    c How much weight will the same dog add in the second 4 months?

    d What is the average rate during this period?

4 Why might dog breeders find a graph like this useful?

5 Why might people choosing a breed of dog find this graph useful?

Calculating gradients

Linear relationships, as we've seen, have straight lines. The gradient is constant. It means the rate of increase (or decrease) isn't changing over time.

The gradient is the change in the *y*-values divided by the change in the *x*-values.

For example, if we heat water, the longer we heat it, the hotter it gets, up to 100 °C.

In this experiment, from the end of the first minute to the end of the third minute the temperature went from 60 °C to 80 °C.

The change in *y*-values (the temperature) was 80 − 60 = 20 and the change in *x*-values (the time) was 3 − 1 = 2. The gradient of the graph can be calculated by dividing 20 by 2, which is 10, indicating that the rate at which the water is heated is 10 °C per minute i.e. for every minute on the graph, the temperature rises by 10 °C.

Figure 8.49 Graph showing how the temperature of water changes as it is heated.

6 Look at the graph from the end of the third minute to the end of the fifth minute.

    a What is the change in *y*-values?

    b What is the change in *x*-values?

    c What is the rate?

7 Why would this trend not continue after the fifth minute?

KEY INFORMATION

Straight-line graphs show a linear relationship. If the line goes through the origin, (0,0), it is also directly proportional.

Check your progress

You should be able to:

identify abiotic and biotic factors that affect ecosystems → explain the impact of introducing a new species or pathogen → explain how a gradual change in an abiotic factor can affect the distribution of species

describe how changes in the population of one organism can affect other organisms → explain how the size of a predator population will affect the numbers of prey and vice versa → explain why the cycles of predator and prey populations are out of phase with each other

construct food chains

describe how to use some sampling techniques → describe how to use a transect line → explain how to perform accurate sampling

recall that plants take in carbon as carbon dioxide → explain how carbon is recycled → interpret a diagram of the carbon cycle

recall causes of environmental change → describe the impact of environmental change → explain the impact of environmental change

Worked example

1 Some students investigated the average number of plant species growing in a habitat. They investigated different sized areas of the habitat. Look at the graph.

Describe what the graph shows.

The number of different plants found increases from 0 to 18

> Maximum number of plants found identified.
>
> More detailed responses include: as area sampled increases the number of species found increases; the ideal area to sample is 8 m².

2 Amy and Laura decide to investigate how the number and type of plant species growing in a salt marsh change with distance from the sea.

What equipment should they use to do this?

A quadrat

> A more detailed answer would include a measuring instrument, e.g. tape measure.

3 Describe how Laura and Amy should use this apparatus.

They make a straight line and place the quadrat every metre along it. Then count the different species and their numbers.

4 Why will the results of Amy's and Laura's investigation be an estimate of the population sizes?

They have only sampled the habitat

> Correct answer identified. A more detailed response would include that it is impossible to count every plant.

5 Laura and Amy repeat the process in two other locations. Explain why.

To improve the accuracy of their results

> This is a correct response.
>
> Overall, there is some good understanding of the topic shown but the answers need to be more detailed.

End of chapter questions

Getting started

1. What group of organisms break down dead organisms? — 1 Mark
2. What are quadrats used for? — 1 Mark
3. Why are indicator species used to investigate an ecosystem? — 1 Mark
4. Why can badgers be primary and secondary consumers? — 1 Mark
5. Why is good biodiversity important? — 2 Marks
6. Explain why bluebells grow before the trees in a wood are in leaf. — 1 Mark
7. Explain what an 'apex predator' is. — 1 Mark
8. Look at the data in the table to answer the questions.

Species	pH6.5	pH 6.0	pH5.5	pH5.0	pH4.5	pH 4.0
Trout	✓	✓	✓	✓		
Bass	✓	✓				
Perch	✓	✓	✓	✓	✓	
Frog	✓	✓	✓	✓	✓	✓
Clam	✓	✓				
Crayfish	✓	✓	✓			
Snail	✓	✓	✓			
Mayfly	✓	✓	✓			

   a Name two organisms that cannot live in water with a pH less than 6.0.

   b Which organism can live in water between pH 5.0 and 4.5? — 2 Marks

Going further

9. Why is it important to place quadrats in a random way rather than choose an area? — 1 Mark
10. Zoe has found sludge worms and bloodworms in the stream at the bottom of her garden. What does this tell her? — 1 Mark
11. Lemmings are adapted to live very cold conditions. Explain two adaptations of lemmings. — 2 Marks

12. Ken has lots of moss growing in his lawn. He wants to estimate what percentage of his lawn is moss. Describe how Ken could do this, making sure the data he collects is random. — 4 Marks

13 The graph shows human population growth and the number of extinctions over time.

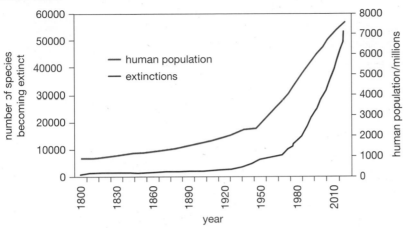

Describe what the graph shows.

`2 Marks`

More challenging

14 Give two functions of mangrove forests.

`2 Marks`

15 Explain how destruction of rainforests without replanting has helped increase the concentration of carbon dioxide in the atmosphere.

`2 Marks`

16 Alistair is going to investigate the population of dandelions in a field. Explain how he should do this.

`6 Marks`

Most demanding

17 Explain the difference between natural and artificial ecosystems.

`2 Marks`

18 Jessica is carrying out an investigation into how many dandelions plants there are in her school playing field. The field is 20 metres by 30 metres. She selects 9 spots at random and samples each spot with a 1 m² quadrat. Jessica's results are shown below.

Jessica calculates the mean number of dandelions to be 3.1.

a Calculate the median and mode values for the number of dandelions across the areas sampled.

b Use the data to estimate the number of dandelion plants in the playing field.

Sample number	Number of dandelion plants
1	5
2	4
3	2
4	4
5	3
6	1
7	3
8	2
9	4

`1 Mark`

`1 Mark`

19 Polar bears and killer whales live in the Arctic. They compete to feed on seals. Explain the types of competition that will occur and which will have the most impact on polar bears.

`6 marks`

`Total: 40 Marks`

Glossary

A

abiotic factor physical or non-living conditions that affect the distribution of a population in an ecosystem, such as light, temperature, soil pH

absorption the process by which soluble products of digestion move into the blood from the small intestine

abstinence method of contraception whereby the couple refrains from intercourse, particularly when an egg might be in the oviduct

accommodation ability of the eyes to change focus

acid rain rain water which is made more acidic by pollutant gases

active site the place on an enzyme where the substrate molecule binds

active transport in active transport, cells use energy to transport substances through cell membranes against a concentration gradient

adaptation features that organisms have to help them survive in their environment

ADH (antidiuretic hormone) a hormone released by the pituitary gland, which acts on the kidney in response to changes in the concentration of the blood plasma

adrenaline a hormone released quickly from the adrenal glands during a 'flight or fight' situation

adrenal medulla part of the adrenal gland that produces the hormone adrenaline

adult cell cloning a form of cloning where an embryo is produced from an adult body cell. The embryo is then implanted into a female animal or used for therapeutic reasons, (e.g. this process was used to created Dolly the sheep)

adult stem cells rare, unspecialised cells found in some tissues in adults that can differentiate only into the cell type where they are found, e.g. blood cells

aerobic respiration respiration that involves the use of oxygen

agar plate plastic dish, with a lid, containing a nutrient gel upon which bacteria are grown in a lab

alleles inherited characteristics are carried as pairs of alleles on pairs of chromosomes. Different forms of a gene are different alleles

alveolus (plural: alveoli) air sacs; the site of gaseous exchange in the lungs

amino acids small molecules from which proteins are built

amylase a digestive enzyme (carbohydrase) that breaks down starch

anaerobic respiration respiration without using oxygen

antibacterial chemicals chemicals produced by plants as a defence mechanism; the amount produced will increase if the plant is under attack

antibiotic e.g. penicillin; medicines that work inside the body to kill bacterial pathogens

antibody protein normally present in the body or produced in response to an antigen, which it neutralises, thus producing an immune response

antimicrobial resistance (AMR) an increasing problem in the twenty-first century whereby bacteria have evolved to develop resistance against antibiotics due to their overuse

antiretroviral drugs drugs used to treat HIV infections; they stop the virus entering the lymph nodes

antiseptic substance that prevents the growth of bacteria

antitoxins chemicals produced by white blood cells (lymphocytes) that neutralise toxins to make a safe chemical

antivirals drugs used to treat viral infections; they are specific to the virus but can only slow down viral development

aorta artery that carries oxygenated blood from the left ventricle to tissues around the body

apex predator carnivores with no predators, they are at the top of the food chain

aphids (greenfly) disease-causing small insects that reproduce rapidly; aphid infestation causes reduced growth, yellow leaves, wilting and death

archaea primitive bacteria that usually live in extreme conditions

artificial heart a temporary heart used to keep patients alive while they are waiting for a transplant

artificial pacemaker a device fitted under the skin that sends out electrical impulses to control the heartbeat

arteries blood vessels with thick elastic walls that carry oxygenated blood away from the heart under high pressure

aseptic technique measures taken to reduce contamination when preparing bacterial cultures, e.g. working with a flame

asexual reproduction reproduction involving only one parent

aspirin painkiller derived from willow bark

ATP molecule used to store energy in the body

atrium (plural: atria) the upper chambers of the heart that receive blood from the body or lungs

autoclave hot oven in which contaminated materials used in cell culture are sterilised

auxin a type of plant hormone produced at the tips of plant shoots and roots

B

bacteria single-celled microorganisms which can either be free-living organisms or parasites (they sometimes invade the body and cause disease)

bacterial growth curve bell-shaped curve that shows how bacteria in culture increase in number exponentially until a build-up of toxins in the culture causes them to die off

barrier methods of contraception; where a condom or diaphragm is used to prevent sperm reaching an egg

basal metabolic rate the level at which chemical reactions take place in the body at rest

behaviour animals adapt their movement and feeding patterns according to the conditions of their environment

Benedict's test a test for sugar in which Benedict's reagent turns orange-red in the presence of sugar

benign tumour slow-growing, harmless mass of cells that can usually be easily removed

bias when a data set is inaccurate or unrepresentative; it contains systematic errors

bile an alkaline substance made by the liver and stored in the gall bladder, which emulsifies fat to aid digestion

biotic factor factors caused by living organisms, such as food availability and competition between species

binary fission the process by which a bacterium divides and doubles its numbers, approximately every 20 minutes

binomial system the scientific way of naming an organism whereby each organism has a genus name and a species name; e.g. Homo sapiens

biodiversity range of different plant and animal species living in an ecosystem

biogas energy released when bacteria break down biomass, which can be used as a cheap fuel source

biomass the dry mass of organisms

Biuret reagent chemical indicator used to test for the presence of protein in a sample

blood sugar level the amount of glucose in the blood (controlled by the hormones, insulin and glucagon)

biological catalysts enzymes – molecules in the body that speed up chemical reactions

biotechnology using living organisms to make products to improve quality of life

body mass index (BMI) measure of someone's weight in relation to their height

breed new form of animal created with particular characteristics, created through selective breeding

bronchus (plural: bronchi) branches of the trachea – one going to each lung

C

calibrate the process of checking the accuracy a piece of equipment using standard data

camouflage a method of avoiding detection used by prey to avoid predators and by predators to surprise prey

capillaries small blood vessels that are one cell thick and permeable for diffusion of gases; join arteries to veins

capillary network tree of capillaries surrounding alveoli that are adapted for efficient gaseous exchange

carbohydrase enzyme that breaks down carbohydrates into simple sugars

carbohydrates one of the main groups of nutrients; e.g. glucose, starch

carbon cycle a natural cycle through which carbon moves by respiration, photosynthesis and combustion, in the form of carbon dioxide

carbon sink 'stores' of carbon dioxide in oceans or forests

carcinogen substance or virus that increases the risk of cancer, e.g. ionising radiation

carrier someone who is heterozygous for a disease-causing gene so that they do not have the condition but 'carry' the defective allele, which they could pass on to their children

causal mechanism where a direct link has been made between a risk factor and a disease; e.g. smoking and lung cancer

cell lines cells grown in a lab that are used to study a certain condition

cell membrane layer around a cell which helps to control substances entering and leaving the cell

cell cycle a series of three stages during which a cell divides

cellulose polymer of glucose; strengthening component of plant cell walls

central nervous system (CNS) collectively, the brain and spinal cord

cerebellum area at the base of the brain that coordinates muscular activity

cerebral cortex highly folded outer layer of the brain that controls consciousness, intelligence, memory and language

cervix the neck of the womb

Charles Darwin scientist who proposed the theory of evolution by natural selection

chlorophyll pigment found in plants which is used in photosynthesis (gives green plants their colour)

chloroplast a cell structure found in green plants that contains chlorophyll

chlorosis when a plant develops yellow leaves due to a lack of magnesium

chromosomes thread-like structures in the cell nucleus that contain DNA

cilia tiny hair-like structures found throughout the respiratory system that beat together to move mucus out of the lungs

classify to organise and present data in a logical order, e.g. in a table

clinical trial process during which a new drug is tested on patients and healthy individuals

clone in asexual reproduction, the offspring produced are identical to the parent (clones)

collision theory an explanation of enzyme action; enzymes cause more collisions between reactants thereby increasing the rate of reaction until reactants are used up

colony a spot containing millions of bacteria growing on an agar plate

combined contraceptive pill a hormonal method of contraception, taken orally, which contains synthetic forms of oestrogen and progesterone

communicable disease infectious condition caused by a virus, protist, bacteria or fungi; e.g. measles, HIV

community all the plants and animals living in an ecosystem, e.g. a garden

companion cells found next to phloem cells, companion cells control the activities of the phloem

compare to examine your data set next to a known set of results

competition when different species in an ecosystem compete for the same resources

complementary describes how each DNA strand in a double helix pairs with the opposite strand through base pairs (A-T and G-C)

complex diseases conditions that are caused by a combination of genetic and environmental factors

compost dead and decaying plant material

condom rubber sheath that covers the erect penis and prevents sperm reaching the egg; a barrier form of contraception

cones light-sensitive receptor cells in the retina that allow us to see in colour

conservation a way of protecting a species or environment

cooling the body loses heat through sweating

coordination centre region of the body that receives and processes information from receptors, e.g. brain, pancreas

cornea transparent region at the front of the eye through which light refracts when it enters the eye

coronary artery vessel that provides the heart muscle with oxygen and glucose for respiration

coronary heart disease a condition caused by build-up of fatty deposits in the coronary artery, leading to reduced blood flow and less oxygen and glucose reaching the heart tissue, which can cause a heart attack

correlation relationship between two sets of results

culture the growing of cells in a lab

culture medium the liquid (nutrient broth) or gel (agar) in which bacteria are grown in a lab

culture solutions liquids with known amounts of specific minerals in which plants are grown to investigate mineral deficiencies

cycle predator–prey relationships follow a cyclical pattern whereby the numbers of prey rise and fall over a period of years, and the numbers of predators follow the same pattern

cystic fibrosis disorder of cell membranes that is caused by a recessive allele

D

daughter cells cells produced during mitosis that are identical to the parent cell

deamination the removal of amino groups, as ammonia, from excess amino acids, in the liver

decomposer an organism that breaks down carbon in dead animals and plants

deforestation removal of large areas of trees to provide land for cattle or growing crops

dehydration result of the body losing too much water

demographic describes the structure of a population

denatured an enzyme is denatured if its shape changes so that the substrate cannot fit into the active site

depression a mental health condition

dialysis process by which the blood is filtered by a dialysis machine, in someone with kidney failure

diarrhoea a symptom of food poisoning, frequent passing of liquid stools

differentiation when cells gain certain features needed for their function; they become specialised

digitalis a heart drug extracted from foxgloves

directly proportional describes a relationship between two variables on a graph where the line of best fit goes through 0,0

disc-diffusion technique used to test effectiveness of antibiotics or disinfectants on plates of cultured bacteria using paper discs soaked in the test substance and measuring the size of clear area around the discs

disease resistance crop plants that are not affected by certain diseases and can therefore be cloned in large numbers for farmers

distribution how living organisms are dispersed/ spread out over an ecosystem

DNA (deoxyribonucleic acid) found as chromosomes in the nucleus – its sequence determines how our bodies are made, and gives each one of us a unique genetic code

DNA bases four chemicals that are found in DNA, they make up the base sequence and are given the letters A, T, G and C

domain the level of classification group above kingdom, first suggested by Carl Woese

dominant an allele that is expressed when one or two copies are present; represented by a capital letter

dominant hand the hand a person uses most often for single-handed tasks, e.g. writing

donor refers to the person or organism where donated cells or tissue come from

dormant describes seeds that have not germinated; they can be sprayed with the plant hormone gibberellins, which induces them to germinate

dose amount of a drug given to a patient

double-blind trial a drugs trial where neither doctors nor patients know whether the patient has received the test drug or the placebo

double circulatory system where the blood is pumped to the lungs then returned to the heart before being pumped round the body

double helix the shape of DNA – two strands of nucleotides that wind around each other like a twisted ladder

dredging the process of digging up sea beds; an example of environmental change induced by humans

dual bar chart bar graph on which two data sets are plotted at each point

E

Ebola a deadly virus that kills 50–90% of people infected

ecosystem the interaction of a community of living organisms with the non-living parts of their surroundings

effector muscle or gland that brings about a response to a stimulus

efficacy how effective a drug is at preventing or curing the disease

embryonic stem cells unspecialised cells found in the early embryo that can differentiate into almost any cell type in the body

embryo screening the process whereby a few cells are taken from an embryo produced by IVF are checked for any defective genes

embryo transplants form of cloning where cells are taken from a developing embryo from a pregnant animal, separated and grown in culture then implanted into host mothers

emulsify the process by which fats are broken into smaller droplets by bile

endocrine gland part of the body that releases chemical messengers, or hormones, directly into the bloodstream

endocrine system a control system in the body that communicates using chemical messengers, or hormones, to produce slow but long-lasting responses

endothermic reaction chemical reaction which takes in heat

environmental change a shift in the external conditions caused by human activity or a natural event

environmental variation differences between individuals that arise during development; e.g. wearing glasses

enzymes biological catalysts that increase the speed of a chemical reaction

epidemic an outbreak of a disease that spreads quickly to many people

epidermal tissues layers of cells that cover the top surface of a leaf; they let light penetrate

epiphyte rainforest plant that is adapted to grow above ground level (e.g. on trees)

estimate a guess based on prior knowledge

ethanol product of anaerobic respiration in plant and yeast cells; used in the manufacture of alcoholic drinks

ethene a plant hormone released as a gas that speeds up fruit ripening

ethical whether a process is considered to be right or wrong, based on moral considerations

eugenics refers to the notion of improving a population by selecting certain desirable characteristics

eukaryotic cells cells that contain a true nucleus in the cytoplasm; e.g. plant and animal cells

eutrophication when waterways become too rich with nutrients (from fertilisers), allowing algae to grow wildly and subsequently decay, resulting in the oxygen being used up

evaporation the process by which the body loses heat through sweating

evolution the gradual change in organisms over millions of years caused by random mutations and natural selection

evolutionary tree a diagram created by scientists that shows how animals are believed to have evolved from common ancestors

exchange surfaces specialised areas with large surface area to volume ratios for efficient diffusion

exothermic reaction chemical reaction in which heat is given out

extinction the elimination of all members of a species; there have been five mass extinctions over geological time

extracellular digestion referring to when food is broken down outside an organism, e.g. bacteria secrete enzymes to breakdown dead material

extremophile organisms that can survive very extreme environments, e.g. high temperature or high salt

F

factory farming a form of intensive farming where animals are reared in sheds or cages under controlled conditions

family tree a diagram used to show how a condition is passed down through a family

fermentation anaerobic respiration in yeast cells; produces ethanol and carbon dioxide

fertiliser chemical containing minerals (nitrates, phosphates, potassium and magnesium) put on soil to improve plant growth

fertility drug combination of hormones given to a woman with low FSH levels to stimulate egg production

field of view the area of a sample visible under a microscope

filtrate dissolved substances that cross into the kidney after the blood has been filtered

flaccid floppy

follicle the sac left once an egg is released in the ovary; it produces the hormone progesterone

food security when all people have access to a consistent supply of food to meet their needs

fossil the remains of organisms that lived millions of years ago

fossil record an incomplete account of organisms that lived millions of years ago

fraction (in genetics) the number of people affected by a recessive condition expressed as a fraction could be 1/4

FSH (follicle stimulating hormone) a reproductive hormone that causes eggs to mature in the ovaries

functional adaptation an adaptation involving how the body operates, e.g. camels don't sweat to avoid water loss

fungicide chemical used to kill fungi

G

gametes the male and female sex cells (sperm and eggs)

gel derived from silicone, the material that contact lenses are made from

gene section of DNA that contains the instructions for a particular characteristic

gene expression whether genes are switched on or off, which is regulated by non-coding DNA

generator large tanks full of rotting organic matter, used for biogas production

gene theory dogma developed in the twentieth century that brought together the work of many scientists on inheritance, DNA structure and the genetic code

gene therapy medical procedure where a virus is used to 'carry' a gene into the nucleus of a cell (this is a new treatment for genetic diseases)

genetic code a sequence of three DNA bases that codes for a single amino acid

genetic cross a way of working out the probability of the genotype of the offspring produced from the parents' genotype for a particular characteristic, e.g. using a Punnett square

genetic engineering transfer of specific genes from one organism to another

genetic marker gene a gene inserted into a modified organism alongside the required gene; the marker gene is often resistant to an antibiotic, so that when cultures of cells are treated with that antibiotic, cells that do not contain the marker gene will be killed

genetic variation the product of meiosis, mutations and sexual reproduction, which all lead to changes in our genome

genome the entire genetic material of an organism

genome editing an experimental method of detecting and correcting defective genes in an individual

genomics the science of studying the human genome to increase our understanding of human DNA

genotype the alleles present for a particular gene make up the organism's genotype

geotropism a plant's growth response to gravity (also called gravitropism)

gibberellins plant hormones that speed up seed germination

gills a gas exchange surface found in fish and tadpoles

global warming the increase in the Earth's temperature due to increases in carbon dioxide levels

glucagon hormone released by the pancreas that, along with insulin, controls blood glucose levels

glucose tolerance test a way of testing for diabetes by measuring how the body responds to glucose

GM crops varieties of crops that have had their genomes modified by the insertion of genes from a plant or other organism

goblet cells cells in the epithelium that produce mucus to trap dust particles

golden rice rice that has been genetically modified to contain β - carotene, which converts to vitamin A

gonorrhoea a sexually transmitted disease caused by bacteria, resulting in pain when urinating and a thick discharge from the vagina or penis

gradient the steepness of a line plotted on a graph

graticule piece of glass or plastic onto which a scale has been drawn, which is used with a microscope

Gregor Mendel Austrian monk who established the science of genetics through his work on pea plants

guard cells cells surrounding the stomata that open and close the pore to control the exchange of gases and water loss

H

habitat the place where an organism lives in an ecosystem; e.g. the worm's habitat is the soil

haemocytometer device used for counting the number of cells, e.g. under a microscope

haemodialysis filtering of the blood by a machine in patients with kidney failure; takes four hours, three times a week

haemoglobin chemical found in red blood cells which binds to oxygen to transport it around the body

health a state of compete mental and physical wellbeing

heterozygous a person who has two different alleles for a characteristic, e.g. someone with blond hair may also carry the allele for red hair

HIV (human immunodeficiency virus) virus transmitted through sexual contact that attacks the immune system

homeostasis the regulation of internal conditions, such as temperature, in the body

homozygous a person who has two alleles that are the same for a characteristic, e.g. a blue-eyed person will have two 'blue' alleles for eye colour

hormone chemical messenger that acts on target organs in the body

hybrid infertile organism created through interbreeding organisms from two different species

hybridoma cells cells made from combining tumour cells with lymphocytes, to give cells that can produce antibodies and divide (for the production of monoclonal antibodies)

hydrocarbon a compound composed of the elements hydrogen and carbon

hydroponics growing plants in mineral solutions without the need for soil

hyperopia long-sightedness; where people can see objects far away but not close up

hypothesis a scientific explanation formed based on prior knowledge that can be tested in an experiment

I

immune system the body's defence against pathogens

immunity when the body is protected from a pathogen as it has already encountered it and can therefore produce antibodies against it, rapidly

inbreeding breeding closely related animals

incubation period of time a culture of bacteria is left at a certain temperature in order for the bacteria to grow

indicator species organisms used to measure the level of pollution in water or the air

inoculating loop length of wire with a ring at the end used for transferring bacteria to an agar plate

insulin hormone made by the pancreas that controls the level of glucose in the blood

interbreeding organisms of the same species can interbreed to give fertile offspring

intercept the point where the line on a graph crosses the y-axis

interdependence plants need animals for carbon dioxide and seed dispersal; animals need plants for food and oxygen; i.e. they depend on each other for survival

interspecific competition competition between two different species of organism

intraspecific competition competition among organisms from the same species

invasive species a cause of extinction as a result of a new species of organism being introduced into a population, which may bring disease, be a predator or compete with native organisms

in-vitro fertilisation (IVF) a fertility treatment, whereby an egg is fertilised with sperm outside the body, in a laboratory

iodine an orange solution used to test for starch (turns blue-black when starch is present)

iris part of the eye that has sets of muscles that control the size of the pupil and regulate the light reaching the retina

IUD (intrauterine device) a device containing hormones that is placed in the uterus to prevent a fertilised egg from implanting; a hormonal method of contraception

IVF cycle the process of IVF from stimulation of the ovaries to implantation of an embryo; if unsuccessful, another cycle can be attempted after about two months

K

kingdom the level of classification above phylum and below domain of living organisms

L

lactic acid product of anaerobic respiration in muscles

larva immature but active form of an insect that's created from an egg and turns into a pupa

laser surgery a technique used to correct eye defects by changing the shape of the cornea

LH (luteinising hormone) a menstrual cycle hormone that stimulates an egg to be released from an ovary

lichen slow-growing plant that grows up trees

lignin substance found in some plant cell walls that gives them strength and rigidity

limiting factor factors such as light, temperature and carbon dioxide, which affect the rate of photosynthesis

lipases enzymes that digest fats into fatty acids and glycerol

lock and key theory to explain how enzymes work; the substrate is the 'key' and the active site is the 'lock'

lumen the central part of a vessel

lymphatic system network of vessels containing a colourless fluid into which fatty acids and glycerol are absorbed

lymphocytes white blood cells that produce antibodies and antitoxins to destroy pathogens

M

magnetic resonance imaging (MRI) scanning technique that uses strong magnetic fields to produce detailed images of the body; used to diagnose nervous system disorders

magnification the factor by which an object is enlarged by a microscope; calculated as: size of image/size of real object

malaria condition characterised by recurring fever, which is spread by mosquitoes and can be fatal

malignant tumour abnormal cancerous mass of cells that grows quickly and can spread to other parts of the body

mathematical model an independent method used to show that Mendelian genetics is consistent with evolution

median the middle number in a set of values when they are arranged in order from lowest to highest

medulla region at the base of the brain that controls unconscious activities, such as breathing

mean average value calculated by adding up all the values in a data set then dividing by the number of values

meiosis cell division that results in gametes being produced, with half the number of chromosomes as the parent cell

melanism darkening of appearance – a form of colour variation in animals, e.g. melanic moths

Mendelian inheritance name given to single-gene disorders, such as cystic fibrosis

menstrual cycle monthly cycle in females which is controlled by reproductive hormones

mental health a feeling of well-being, having a positive frame of mind

meristem regions at tips of roots and shoots where cell division takes place

metabolism the sum of all reactions in a cell or the body

micrograph image captured using a microscope

microorganisms tiny organisms that can only be viewed with a microscope – also known as microbes

migration patterns historical movements of humans across the world, which have been deduced through studying genomes

mimicry mechanical defence mechanism where a plant uses features to trick animals into not feeding or not laying eggs

mineral deficiency when a plant cannot get enough of an essential mineral from the soil

mineral ions substances found in the soil that are essential for a plant's survival; e.g. plants need magnesium ions to make chlorophyll

missing links evidence for evolution found as intermediate forms between different organisms, as they evolved

mitochondria structures in a cell where respiration takes place

mitosis cell division that results in genetically identical diploid cells

mixed population plants bred from two different varieties for their desirable traits

mode the most frequently occurring number in a set of values

monoclonal antibodies antibodies made from cells that are cloned from one cell that are specific to one binding site on an antigen. They are used in medicine to treat cancer, and in research

monocultures where only one crop is grown in an area

motor neurone nerve cell carrying information from the central nervous system to muscles

MRSA bacteria that are resistant to the antibiotic, methicillin

mulch compost or decaying leaves put around rose bushes in the spring to prevent rose black spot spores reaching the stems

mutation where the DNA within cells has been altered (this happens in cancer)

mycoprotein a protein-rich food made from microorganisms in fermentation vats

myelin sheath a fatty insulating layer that surrounds neurones and speeds up nerve transmission

myopia short-sightedness; when people can see objects at short distances but not far away

N

natural selection process by which advantageous characteristics that can be passed on in genes become more common in a population over many generations

negative feedback a regulatory process in the body whereby changes in the body can be reversed once they have happened

nervous system a control system in the body that uses electrical impulses to communicate rapidly and precisely

neurone a nerve cell that is specialised to transmit electrical signals

nitrates nutrients found in fertilisers and the soil that plants need for protein synthesis, and therefore growth

non-coding DNA sections of DNA that do not code for genes but turn genes on or off instead; they regulate gene expression

non-communicable disease conditions caused by environmental or genetic factors that are not spread among people; e.g. cancer, cardiovascular disease

non-invasive describes brain mapping techniques, such as MRI scans, that can be carried out without the need for surgery

nuclear transfer type of cloning that involves taking a nucleus from a body cell and placing it into an egg cell

nucleic acid group of complex molecules found in living organisms including DNA and various types of RNA

nucleotide a sugar and phosphate group with a chemical base (A, T, C, G) attached to the sugar

nutrient broth liquid used for growing bacteria

O

oestrogen the main female reproductive hormone produced by the ovaries

opiates a group of painkillers found in poppies

optic nerve nerve found at the back of the eye that carries impulses from the retina to the brain

optimum the conditions, in terms of temperature and pH, at which an enzyme works best

optimum dose the amount of a new drug needed to be effective, determined in a trial by starting at low doses

order a level of classification below class but above family; e.g. butterflies and moths are orders of the insect family

order of magnitude in microscopy, the difference between sizes of cells, calculated in factors of 10

organ group of tissues that carries out a specific function

organ system arrangement of organs in the body according to function; e.g. respiratory system

osmosis the diffusion of water molecules through a partially permeable membrane, from a dilute solution to a concentrated solution

out of phase refers to the cycle of a predator lagging behind that of its prey

ovulation release of an egg from the ovary

oxyhaemoglobin bright red substance formed when oxygen binds to haemoglobin in red blood cells; this is how oxygen is transported to tissues

P

pacemaker a group of cells in the right atrium that controls the heart rate

palaeontologists scientists who study fossils

palisade mesophyll tightly packed together cells found on the upper side of a leaf that carry out photosynthesis

pandemic when an outbreak of a disease becomes global

parasitism a relationship between two organisms where one benefits and the other is harmed, e.g. tapeworms in humans

partially permeable membrane a membrane that allows some small molecules to pass through but not larger molecules

pathogen harmful microorganism that invades the body and causes infectious disease

peatlands areas of peat bog formed in marshlands; peat is partially decomposed leaf matter that is used as fuel and cheap compost

peer review scientific findings are scrutinised by independent experts before they can be published

penicillin an antibiotic, isolated from Penicillum mould, which was discovered by Alexander Flemming

percentage a number or amount expressed per hundred

peripheral nervous system (PNS) network of nerves leading to and from the spinal cord

peristalsis the movement of food through the digestive system by muscle contraction

peritoneal dialysis a type of dialysis where fluid is pumped into the abdomen and waste products diffuse into it across a membrane in the body called the peritoneum

Petri dish plate, with a lid, used for growing bacteria in a lab

phagocyte a type of white blood cell that enters tissues and engulfs pathogens then ingests them

phagocytosis process by which a white blood cell (phagocyte) engulfs a pathogen

phenolphthalein indicator a pink solution (at pH 10) that turns colourless when fatty acids are added

phenotype the characteristic that is shown or expressed

phloem specialised transporting cells which form tubules in plants to carry sugars from leaves to other parts of the plant

phosphates nutrients found in soil and fertilisers that plants need for respiration and growth

photosynthesis process carried out by green plants where sunlight, carbon dioxide and water are used to produce glucose and oxygen

phototropism a plant's growth response to light

pituitary gland known as the 'master gland' as it controls other endocrine glands, such as the thyroid gland

placebo a treatment that does not contain a drug

placenta organ that forms during pregnancy that provides the foetus with oxygen and nutrients

plant cuttings in plant cloning, a leaf and stem are cut off a plant and then dipped in hormone powder to encourage rooting, a new plant then grows

plant organ system roots, stems and leaves, which collectively form a plant's transport system

plasma straw-coloured liquid part of blood

plasmid small ring of DNA found in prokaryotic cells

plasmolysis/plasmolysed the shrinking of a plant cell due to loss of water, the cell membrane pulls away from the cell wall

platelets cell fragments which help in blood clotting

polydactyl condition caused by a dominant allele in which the sufferer has extra fingers or toes

polymer a molecule, such as DNA, made up of repeating units

population the total number of one species in an ecosystem

potometer piece of equipment used to measure water uptake by plants

preclinical testing testing of a new drug in a lab using cells, tissues or live animals

prey animals that are eaten by a predator

primary consumer organism in a food chain that gets its energy from eating food (producers)

probability the likelihood of an event happening; e.g. there is a 1 in 4 chance of a couple who are both heterozygous for cystic fibrosis having a child with cystic fibrosis

producers organisms in a food chain that make food using sunlight

progesterone reproductive hormone that causes the lining of the uterus to be maintained

progestogen-only pill (or mini pill or POP) contraceptive pill that only contains progesterone (not oestrogen), which may be more suitable (than the combined pill) for women who are older or have high blood pressure

Prokaryota group of single-celled organisms including bacteria and Archaeans

prokaryotic cells single cells of bacteria and Archaeans with DNA found in a loop not enclosed in a nucleus

proportion (in genetics) the number of people affected by a condition expressed in relation to the total population

proteases digestive enzymes that break down proteins into amino acids

protist a type of single-celled organism, for example the pathogen that causes malaria

pruning snipping the tops off plant shoots in the spring, a treatment for rose black spot

pulmonary artery vessel that carries deoxygenated blood from the right ventricle to the lungs

pulmonary vein vessel that carries oxygenated blood from the lungs to the left atrium

Punnett square a grid used to determine possible outcomes of a genetic cross

pyramid of biomass table of dry weight of organisms at different trophic levels in an ecosystem, which forms a pyramid shape

Q

qualitative reagents chemicals used to test for the presence of a substance in a sample

R

radiometric dating method of determining the absolute age of rocks

range a measure of spread; the difference between the biggest and smallest values in a set

range bar line drawn on a graph to show the range of a set of values

rate the speed at which an event is occurring over time; can be calculated using the gradient on a graph

rate of photosynthesis is affected by temperature, light intensity, carbon dioxide concentration and amount of chlorophyll

ratio the relationship between two variables, expressed as 1:4, for example

reaction time the time it takes the body to respond to an event

receptors cells in the body that detect changes in the environment

recessive two copies of a recessive allele must be present for the characteristic to be expressed; represented by lowercase letters

red blood cells blood cells with a concave shape which are adapted to carry oxygen from the lungs to body cells

reflex action rapid automatic responses to a stimulus

reflex arc pathway taken by nerve impulses through the spinal cord during a reflex action

refraction the bending of light rays as they travel from one medium to another, e.g. as they enter the eye

regeneration restoration (of a habitat)

relay neurone neurone found in the spinal cord that transmits impulses from the sensory to the motor neurone

repeatability consistent data with a narrow range has a high repeatability; it is likely that the conclusions drawn from such a data set are valid

resolving power the ability of a microscope to distinguish between two points; the resolving power of electron microscopes is higher than that of light microscopes

respiration the process used by all organisms to release the energy they need from food

retina area at the back of the eye where light-sensitive receptor cells are found

ribosome structures in a cell where protein synthesis takes place

risk factor a lifestyle or genetic factor that increases the chance of developing a disease

rods light-sensitive receptor cells in the retina that allow us to see in dim light

root hair cells specialised cells in plant roots that are adapted for efficient uptake of water by osmosis and mineral ions by active transport

rose black spot fungal disease that affects plant growth; can be treated with fungicide or by destroying the leaves

run-off when fertilisers from a farmer's field are washed off into rivers or lakes (can lead to eutrophication)

rusts type of plant disease caused by fungi

S

Salmonella a type of bacteria that causes food poisoning

sampling techniques methods used to choose a small, representative number of individuals from a large population

scale bar a line drawn on a micrograph used to measure the actual size of the object

scanning electron microscope (SEM) works by bouncing electrons off the surface of a specimen that has had an ultrathin coating of a heavy metal, usually gold, applied. Used to view surface shape of cells or small organisms

sclera tough outer layer of the eye

secondary consumer organism in a food chain that gets its energy from eating primary consumers

secondary sex characteristics features that develop during puberty, as a result of sex hormones being released, such as a deep voice and hair growth in boys, and breast development in girls

secondary tumour abnormal growth of cells that forms from a malignant tumour elsewhere in the body

secrete to produce a substance; e.g. decomposers secrete enzymes to help break down food

selective breeding process of breeding organisms with the desired characteristics (also known as artificial selection)

selective reabsorption in the kidney, useful substances, such as glucose and amino acids, are absorbed back into the blood after filtration

selective weedkiller preparations of synthetic plant hormones that only kill weeds with broad leaves, for example, and leave grasses and crops unharmed

self-supporting ecosystem all ecosystems can support themselves; i.e. everything organisms need for growth and survival is present

sensory neurone nerve cell carrying information from receptors to central nervous system

sewage waste water and excrement, a form of pollution

sex chromosomes a pair of chromosomes that determines gender; XX in females, XY in males

sex determination whether a fertilised egg develops into a male (XY) or female (XX) depends on the 23rd pair of chromosomes

sexual reproduction form of reproduction involving two parents, which introduces variation

sexually transmitted disease (STD) disease spread through sexual contact; e.g. HIV

sieve plates the end walls of phloem cells that contain many small pores

species basic category of biological classification, composed of individuals that resemble one another, can breed among themselves, but cannot breed with members of another species

specialised when cells or tissues become adapted to carry out their specific function

speciation formation of a new species over a long period of time, through separation of a population

spermicide a cream that is toxic to sperm; it is used alongside other contraceptive techniques, e.g. condoms

sphere shape that has the smallest surface area compared with its volume

spiracles tiny holes along the side of an insect's body used in gas exchange

spongy mesophyll layer of cells found in the middle of a leaf with an irregular shape and large air spaces between them for diffusion of gases

spores small seed-like particles released by a fungus to help it spread

stacked bar chart bar graph where two data sets are stacked on top of each other for each group/bar

standard form way of writing very large or small numbers using powers of ten; e.g. $1.0 \times 10-3$

starch a complex carbohydrate found in animals and plants

statins drugs that stop the liver producing so much cholesterol

stem cells unspecialised body cells (found in bone marrow) that can develop into other, specialised, cells that the body needs, e.g. blood cells

stents a treatment for heart disease; a catheter with a balloon attached is inserted to open up a narrowed coronary artery

sterilise the process of removing contaminated material (e.g. from an agar plate)

stomata (singular stoma) small holes in the surface of leaves which allow gases in and out of leaves

structural adaptation a physical adaption to a body part of an animal, e.g. elephants have larger ears to maximise heat loss

surface area to volume ratio the relationship between the surface area of an organism or structure and its volume; SA:V ratios are large in single-celled organisms for efficient diffusion

suspensory ligaments ligaments in the eye that are attached to the ciliary muscle and hold the lens in place

sustainable long-lasting; something that can be maintained for future generations

sustainable fisheries measures to improve fish stocks, which were declining due to over-fishing, to include controls on net size and fishing quotas

synapse the gap between two neurones

systematic error mistakes made during data collection that give false outcomes

T

target organ the site where a hormone has its effect

testosterone male sex hormone produced by the testes that stimulates sperm production

therapeutic cloning the process of creating stem cells with the same genes as the patient, through nuclear transfer

thermoregulatory centre a region in the brain that detects changes in body temperature

three-domain system developed by Carl Woese, a classification system where organisms are divided into Archaea, Bacteria and Eukaryota (animals, fungi and plants)

thyroid gland gland at the base of the neck that makes the hormone thyroxine

thyroxine hormone produced by the thyroid gland that increases the body's metabolism

tissue group of cells that work together, with a particular function

tissue culture process that uses small sections of tissue to clone plants

tobacco mosaic virus (TMV) pathogen that causes mosaic pattern of discolouration on leaves and affects growth of plant

trachea (lungs) windpipe, through which air travels to the lungs

trachea (insects) small tubes in insects containing water, through which gases diffuse into body cells

transect line across an area to sample organisms

translocation the movement of sugars through a plant

transmission electron microscope (TEM) uses an electron beam to view thin sections of cells at high resolution

transpiration the movement of water up through a plant and its loss from the leaves

trend a pattern in a data set

trophic level feeding positions in a food chain

tropism the response of a plant by growing towards or away from a stimulus

tundra regions in the Arctic where few plants grow as the subsoil is permanently frozen

turgid plant cells which are full of water with their walls bowed out and pushing against neighbouring cells

type 1 diabetes a condition where the pancreas cannot produce enough, or any, insulin

type 2 diabetes a condition where the body cells no longer respond to insulin produced by the pancreas

U

umbilical cord joins the foetus to the mother during pregnancy and is a source of stem cells

uncertainty a measure of the range about the mean, calculated by the range divided by two

urea waste products formed by breakdown of excess proteins, excreted in urine

V

vaccination injection of a small quantity of inactive pathogen to protect us from developing the disease caused by the pathogen

vaccine preparation of an inactive or dead form of a pathogen given by injection or nasal spray

valid refers to results that are accurate, representative and repeatable

valves flaps of tissue that prevent the backflow of blood in the heart and in veins

variation the differences between individuals brought about by both genetic and environmental influences

vascular bundle (veins) group of xylem and phloem cells that transport water and glucose around the plant

vasoconstriction in cold conditions, the diameter of small blood vessels near the surface of the body decreases, which reduces blood flow

vasodilation in warm conditions, the diameter of small blood vessels near the surface of the body increases, which increases blood flow

vector a carrier, usually a plasmid, used to transfer a gene into an organism to be genetically modified; also, mosquitoes are vectors – they spread malaria but don't cause it themselves

veins blood vessels with thin walls and valves to prevent backflow, that carry blood at low pressure back to the heart

vena cava vein that carries deoxygenated blood from the body to the right atrium

ventilate the movement of air into and out of the lungs

ventricles the lower chambers of the heart that pump blood around the body (left) or back to the lungs (right)

W

Wallace (Alfred Russel) scientist that proposed the theory of evolution through natural selection, independently from Darwin

warning colouration bright colours or patterns found on animals, used to deter predators

X

X-chromosomes sex chromosome present in males (XY) and females (XX)

xylem cells specialised for transporting water through a plant; xylem cells have thick walls, no cytoplasm and are dead, their end walls break down and they form a continuous tube

Y

Y-chromosomes sex chromosome found only in males

yield the amount (of crop) produced

Z

zones of inhibition areas of no bacterial growth on an agar plate around an antibiotic disc

zygote a fertilised egg cell

Index